Research, Evaluation and Audit

Key steps in demonstrating your value

Edited by
Maria J. Grant, Barbara Sen and **Hannah Spring**

facet publishing

Published by Facet Publishing,
7 Ridgmount Street, London WC1E 7AE
www.facetpublishing.co.uk

Facet Publishing is wholly owned by CILIP: the Chartered Institute of Library
and Information Professionals.

British Library Cataloguing in Publication Data
A catalogue record for this book is available from the British Library.

ISBN 978-1-85604-741-8

First published 2013

Text printed on FSC accredited material.

Typeset from editors' files by Flagholme Publishing Services in 10/14 pt Palatino
Linotype and Frutiger.
Printed and made in Great Britain by CPI Group (UK) Ltd, Croydon, CR0 4YY.

Contents

About the Editors

Maria J. Grant BA (Hons) MSc (Econ) PG Cert (Ed)
Research Fellow (Information), School of Nursing, Midwifery and Social Work, University of Salford, UK

Maria has an academic background in information science and is a qualified librarian with over 25 years' experience working in health information. She has published a typology of reviews and associated methodologies and has contributed to the searching, appraisal and synthesis of evidence into literature and systematic reviews on a wide range of topics. These have included reflective practice in the library and information sector and an investigation of current and future roles of library and information services in facilitating the uptake of e-health services in the management of personal health.

Maria is Editor-in-Chief of the ISI-listed *Health Information and Libraries Journal* and has a particular interest in the role of published information, both its production and its application in practice. In 2006 she was instrumental in the establishment of a cross-university writers' group to facilitate life-long learning around writing theory and practice. The group resulted in a measurable increase in the quality, quantity and diversity of the output of group members and in 2011 Maria established, and still leads, a similar group at a local level.

Barbara Sen BA MA MCLIP
Lecturer, Information School, University of Sheffield, UK

For a number of years Barbara was Programme Co-ordinator for the MA Librarianship programme. She currently holds two roles: Deputy Co-ordinator for Health Informatics and Director of Postgraduate Recruitment. She teaches mainly on the MA Librarianship and Health Informatics programmes. Her teaching interests focus on the management of library and information services and self-management. She has a keen interest in personal and professional development.

Barbara's research interests are: the strategic management of library and information services, reflection and reflective practice, information literacy, health information, and Situational Analysis as an analytical approach in qualitative research. She is involved in a number of research projects currently: one on market orientation and UK public libraries, another investigating the roles and skills of health information professionals funded by EAHIL, and a JISC-funded project, RDMRose, on Research Data Management (RDM), the priority being to up-skill academic liaison librarians in the support of RDM.

Before coming into academia she worked for eight years as an information practitioner in the health sector, firstly for the Health and Safety Executive, and latterly in the UK National Health Service (NHS).

Hannah Spring BA (Hons) PGCE PhD MCLIP
Senior Lecturer, York St John University, UK

Hannah is Senior Lecturer in Research and Evidence-Based Practice within the Faculty of Health and Life Sciences at York St John University in the UK. Before working at York St John Hannah held a variety of posts in government and NHS settings. By background she is a clinical information specialist and is particularly experienced in working with health professionals in the primary and secondary healthcare, and academic sectors.

As well as her ten years' teaching experience, Hannah has worked in a variety of independent consultancy roles, including working with Nottingham University as an independent reviewer and content provider for the Intute Health and Life Sciences database, and as a consultant information specialist for general practitioners. Currently, Hannah is Feature Editor for 'Learning and Teaching in Action' a regular feature of the *Health Information and Libraries Journal,* and a member of the editorial advisory board.

Hannah's specialist interest areas include systematic reviews and associated research methodologies, clinical librarianship in primary care and the allied health professions, the impact of internet and web 2.0 technologies on learning and information behaviour, information literacy and health, evidence-based health practice and research development in health LIS professions. Hannah has published widely in these areas and has recently completed a PhD investigating research engagement in health librarianship.

Contributors

Elizabeth Buchanan BA (Hons) MLIS (Information Science) PhD (Philosophy)
Director, Center for Applied Ethics, University of Wisconsin-Stout, USA

Sarah Coulbeck (née Newbutt) BA (Hons) MA
Leeds Grammar School, UK

Andrew Cox BA MA MSc MA MEd PhD
Lecturer, Information School, University of Sheffield, UK

Jenny Craven BA (Hons), MA (Information and Library Management), MCLIP
Information Specialist, National Institute for Health and Clinical Excellence, UK

Stuart Ferguson MA (Hons) PG Dip MPhil PhD
Assistant Professor in Information Studies, University of Canberra, Australia

Robert Gent BA, DMS
Former Deputy Director, Cultural and Community Services, Derbyshire Libraries, UK

Maria J. Grant BA (Hons) MSc (Econ) PG Cert (Ed)
Research Fellow (Information), School of Nursing, Midwifery and Social Work, University of Salford, UK

Jillian R. Griffiths BA (Hons), MPhil (Information Science)
Lecturer, Manchester Metropolitan University, UK

Emma Hadfield BA (Hons) MA MCLIP
Learning Resources Manager, Thomas Rotherham College, UK

Clare McCluskey BA (Hons) MSc PG Cert MCLIP FHEA
Academic Support Librarian, York St John University, UK

Michelle Maden MA (Hons) MA PG Cert (Ed)
Clinical Information Specialist, Edgehill University, UK

Alison J. Pickard BA (Hons) PG Dip PhD
Lecturer, Northumbria University, UK

Miggie Pickton BA MSc PhD MCLIP
Academic Librarian, Northampton University, UK

Barbara Sen BA MA MCLIP
Lecturer, Information School, University of Sheffield, UK

Jane Shelling BAppSc AFALIA(CP)
Manager, National Drugs Sector Information Service, Australia

Hannah Spring PGCE BA (Hons) PGCE PhD MCLIP
Senior Lecturer, York St John University, UK

Christine Urquhart BSc MSc PGCE PhD
Senior Lecturer, University of Wales – Aberystwyth

Graham Walton BSc (Hons) MA MBA PhD MCLIP
Service Development Manager, Loughborough University, UK

Foreword

Hazel Hall

I was delighted when the editors of *Research, Evaluation and Audit: key steps in demonstrating your value* invited me to write the foreword to this new work. This volume of contributions has been designed to meet the needs of practitioners eager to conduct research to inform their own practice and to develop the library and information science (LIS) evidence base. As such, it addresses an ongoing concern of the LIS community: the research–practice gap. In your hands is an artefact of the efforts of some key actors within the LIS research and practitioner community to close the gap by sharing their knowledge and expertise so that others can undertake their own research projects.

Although the research–practice gap has been evident for some time, since 2009 renewed investment in the UK LIS research infrastructure, alongside a number of smaller parallel initiatives, has drawn greater attention to it. The most significant of these initiatives derived from a base of informal discussions about the state of UK LIS research in 2006. [1] Five key stakeholders – the British Library, the Chartered Institute of Library and Information Professionals (CILIP), JISC, the Museums Libraries and Archives Council (MLA) and the Research Information Network (RIN) took action in 2009 by making a three-year investment to facilitate a co-ordinated and strategic approach to LIS research across the UK. Known as the Library and Information Science Research Coalition, from the start this project focused on five key goals. [2] Amongst these were two that relate directly to the content of *Research, Evaluation and Audit* (1) to promote LIS practitioner research and the translation of research outcomes into practice; and (2) to promote the development of research capacity in LIS.

In the final year of its implementation in 2011–12 the Coalition's main aim was articulated as 'supporting practising librarians and information scientists, both in how they can access and exploit available research in their work, and in their own development as practitioner researchers'.[3] The Coalition was keen to encourage research-led practice so that librarians and information scientists would be able to:

- exploit existing LIS research for improved decision-making in services delivery
- enhance the value of prior work by capitalising on the significant investment in earlier studies through reuse
- demonstrate the value and impact of library and information services to individuals, citizens/society and specialist user groups, and thus secure future investment in services delivery
- derive job satisfaction through intellectual stimulation, enjoyment of learning, career progression, leadership development, and pride in enhanced work practice that engagement in research brings.

Again you will find that this book addresses key elements of these themes.

The Coalition also supported projects that focused on specific goals to support LIS research in the UK, notably to develop a formal UK-wide network of LIS researchers (the AHRC-funded *Developing Research Excellence and Methods project* – DREaM),[4] and to determine the factors that increase or hinder the impact of research project outcomes on practice (*Research in Librarianship Impact Evaluation Study* – RiLIES).[5] A second RiLIES project led to the production of a series of outputs[6] to support the use and execution of research by librarians and information scientists. The authors of this handbook also recognize the importance of networks and the links between research and practice.

Around the same period as the LIS Research Coalition's implementation others turned their attention to the question of research in the UK library and information science practitioner community. For example, in redrafting its *Professional Knowledge and Skills Base* (PKSB),[7] CILIP brought research to the fore as one of the eight top-level domains of professional expertise. Meanwhile, members of the Health Information and Libraries for Evaluation and Research network (HEALER)[8] worked on the development of a research toolkit.[9] The successful bid by Alison Brettle and Maria Grant to host the *Sixth Evidence Based Library and Information Practice (EBLIP6) Conference*[10] in the UK at Salford University in June 2011 encouraged further debate as to the role of library and information science practitioners as researchers.

This book's content draws on the knowledge of expert practitioner researchers from a range of LIS sectors, many of whom have been involved in the initiatives mentioned above. For example, one of the co-editors was instrumental in the successful delivery of *EBLIP6*, and four of the contributors helped develop the *HEALER* research toolkit on which the handbook is based. A third of the authors were actively involved in the work of the LIS Research Coalition through, for example: participation at Coalition-organized events as programme committee members, speakers and delegates; membership of the DREaM project network and the DREaM project cadre;[11] and helping to organize and taking part in RiLIES project events such as focus groups[12] and briefing sessions.[13] Added to this, the list of authors include individuals who have won prizes for their research work, including a member of the North West Clinical Librarian Systematic Review and Evaluation Group, the winner of the LIS Research Coalition sponsored *Practitioner Researcher Excellence Award* in 2012. The full pedigree of the editors and contributors demonstrates the authority of this new work.

Research, Evaluation and Audit: key steps in demonstrating your value is thus a timely, practical and valuable addition to the research methods literature. It has long been recognized that librarians and information scientists are highly skilled in supporting the research efforts of others, but rarely are they perceived as active researchers themselves. Equally a good range of research methods texts is available to those involved in academic research in library and information science (LIS), yet – to date – budding practitioner researchers have lacked a handbook that can take them through the stages of getting started with research, executing projects, disseminating findings, and translating the evidence gathered into practice. This book meets this need at the right level with appropriate direction on the need to reflect and apply learning to the case studies presented in the text.

A key argument in the final chapter of *Research, Evaluation and Audit: key steps in demonstrating your value* is that findings of practitioner research projects should have impact in practice, for example in prompting a change of policy or an improvement in services delivery. I am confident that in appealing directly to its intended audience, and serving as a valuable tool for LIS practitioner researchers, the book itself will have its own impact in promoting practitioner research, translating this research into practice and developing research capacity within the LIS practitioner community.

Dr Hazel Hall
Professor of Social Informatics, Edinburgh Napier University
Executive Secretary, Library and Information
Science Research Coalition, 2009–2012
http://hazelhall.org

References

1 http://lisresearch.org/history/.
2 Hall, H. (2010) 5 goals of the Library and Information Science Research Coalition. Invited paper presented at CILIP NW branch AGM and Members' Day 2010, Bolton, UK, 3 March 2010. Slides available at: www.slideshare.net/LISResearch/5-goals-lis-research-coalition-3317734.
3 http://lisresearch.org/about-lis-research/.
4 http://lisresearch.org/dream-project/.
5 http://lisresearch.org/rilies-project/.
6 http://lisresearch.org/?s=rilies2.
7 www.cilip.org.uk/cilip/jobs-and-careers/professional-knowledge-and-skills-base. Documents/Your%20Professional%20Knowledge%20and%20Skills%20Base.pdf.
8 www.libraryservices.nhs.uk/healer/.
9 http://researchflowchart.pbworks.com/w/page/6839792/Welcome-and-Acknowledgements.
10 www.eblip6.salford.ac.uk/.
11 http://lisresearch.org/dream-project/dream-workshops/dream-workshop-cadre/.
12 For example, http://lisresearch.org/2011/07/04/links-between-research-and-practice-the-health-and-medical-librarians-perspectives/.
13 For example, http://lisresearch.org/2012/07/17/lis-research-resources-briefing-workshop-evaluation/.

Preface

Maria J. Grant

This handbook has been written specifically to meet the needs of library and information science (LIS) practitioners interested in doing research to inform their own practice and the wider library and information evidence base. Whether you are a complete novice or have limited experience of undertaking evaluations, audits or 'research', this handbook is about you and, rather than supporting the research activities of others, it seeks to support your development and explains how evidence-based library and information practice is relevant to you. It is based on the ten steps of the HEALER research toolkit and is divided into three sections, guiding those new to research through the key phases of a planning, doing and disseminating research.

In Part 1 the handbook introduces the concept of research and provides strategies for novice researchers to build their confidence as they seek to define their research question, write their research plan and consider the ethical implications of their research.

In Part 2 you get down to the nitty-gritty of research, covering familiar topics such as reviewing literature as well as being introduced to the range of qualitative and quantitative methods available. It provides a pain-free overview to data analysis techniques and explores the range of easy-to-use tools available to assist you along the way.

In Part 3 you consider how best to maximize the impact of your research in terms of writing the project up for internal and external audiences, implementing your findings into practice and the potential for the wider dissemination of your work.

Each chapter is structured to begin with a comprehensive introduction to a discrete topic area complemented with case studies drawn from a broad range of LIS contexts to illustrate the issues raised and provide lessons transferable to your own context. There are also opportunities to reflect on what you have learnt, with the intention of enabling you to apply your learning practically within your own setting.

The authors are LIS practitioners and researchers from a diverse range of sectors and geographical locations, including business, finance, national information services, public libraries, research bodies, sixth-form colleges and universities from areas including Australia, the UK and the USA. They have been individually chosen to contribute to this handbook to ensure that it achieves the best possible blend of technical knowledge within genuine LIS settings; real knowledge which will resonate with your own experiences and be applicable in your own setting.

With an emphasis on practicality, this handbook will meet the needs of any LIS worker looking to develop a good grounding in the realities of planning, undertaking and disseminating research.

Part 1

Getting started

What are research, evaluation and audit?

Barbara Sen, Maria J. Grant and Hannah Spring

'I don't do research. I don't have the time. I am too busy with the day-to-day running of the library. I do evaluations of my service to ensure that it meets the needs of my users, and that the journal providers give good value for money. But that's not research is it?'

'I'm a practitioner not a researcher.'

'I run a service, so have nothing to research.'

The existence of a workable definition of research is an important one, as a common barrier for becoming involved in research is a lack of understanding or misunderstanding of what research is.

Research is identified by French, Reynolds and Swain (2001) as the simple process of systematic enquiry and of finding out. Across the board, professional disciplines from industry, business, science and law to the arts and humanities, the definitions of research are essentially the same. For instance, in relation to business studies, Saunders et al. (2003) identify research as the undertaking of processes in a systematic way in order to find things out about business and management. Cameron and Price (2009, 4) define research as 'any systematic attempt at collecting and interpreting data and evidence in order to inform thinking, decisions and/or actions in relation to an issue of interest to an organization and/or its stakeholders'. Elsewhere, the UK Department of Health (2005) defines research as 'the attempt to derive generalisable new knowledge by addressing clearly defined questions with systematic and rigorous methods'.

Why is research important?

Research can demonstrate the relevance, value, impact and effectiveness of the day-to-day business of library and information provision. As the above definitions imply, research provides us with the means of finding answers to questions. Supplementing your professional knowledge and experience, Rycroft-Malone et al. (2004) highlight 'local' data (gathered through audit) and customer experience and preferences (gathered through evaluation) as activities that you may use to investigate your day-to-day practice – activities which can count as research.

The output from research, evaluation and audit are all appropriate in the information and library sector and can be carried out by people who would consider themselves to be either practitioners or academic researchers. The skills and methods required for research, evaluation and audit are very much the same and will ultimately provide evidence on which you can ensure your activities are evidence-based (see Figure 1.1). All require a basic understanding of the various research methods and the ability to assess which are applicable to the problems under scrutiny. So, if the skills required are largely the same, why does the terminology matter? The answer is, it only matters if the terms used are barriers to you getting involved.

At this point it is worth noting that ethical requirements vary from sector to sector and country to country. However, being ethically aware is good

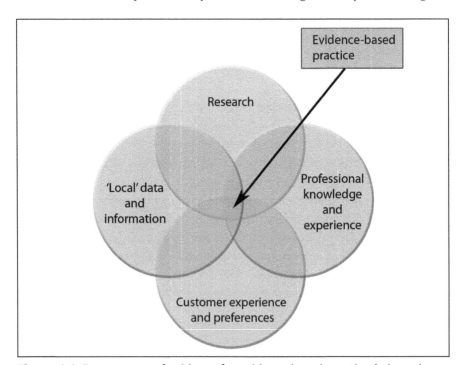

Figure 1.1 *Four sources of evidence for evidence-based practice (adapted from Rycroft-Malone et al., 2004, 87, Figure 1)*

practice for any researcher and this will be considered in more detail in Chapter 5.

Research, evaluation or audit?

The key similarity between research, evaluation and audit is that all begin with a question. They all expect to inform practice and require data collection using appropriate methods to reach their conclusions. However, there are some key differences to note.

Evaluation has its focus on service effectiveness. Seen as a form of applied research, i.e. it has its application in the workplace, evaluation is practical in nature and seeks:

> to produce information about the implementation, operation and ultimate effectiveness of policies and programmes designed to bring about change.
>
> Clarke and Dawson, 1999, 35

As well as providing practical information about service development, evaluations also require judgements to be made about the value of what is being evaluated. Patton distinguishes evaluation from research when he states that:

> Research is aimed at truth. Evaluation is aimed at action.
>
> Patton, 1986, 14

An audit can be understood in two ways. First, that audit is a review of a process, service, department or organization, carried out to learn more about an issue or issues being studied to enable improvements to be made. Secondly an audit can be the use of a predetermined (audit) tool as a checklist to see if a process or service, or intervention is meeting the required standards. Table 1.1 will help you to quickly determine which approach is most appropriate in answering your question.

The case studies that follow give illustrations of three published projects: a research project; an evaluation project; and an audit project. Whilst some people think that only research is worth publishing and sharing, in reality the results of an evaluation or audit of your library or information service can provide valuable evidence in informing the direction to other service developments. Other people can learn from the results of your work. The following case studies demonstrate this most effectively.

Table 1.1 *Extract from table: Differentiating clinical audit, service evaluation, research and usual practice/surveillance work in public health (National Research Ethics Services, 2009)*		
Research	**Evaluation**	**Audit**
The attempt to derive generalizable new knowledge including studies that aim to generate hypotheses as well as studies that aim to test them.	Designed and conducted solely to define or judge current service or any other service.	Designed and conducted to produce information to inform delivery of best service.
Quantitative – designed to test a hypothesis. Qualitative research – identifies/explores themes. Follows established methodology.	Designed to answer: 'What standard does this service achieve?'	Designed to answer: 'Does this service reach a predetermined standard?'
Addresses clearly defined questions, aims and objectives.	Measures current service without reference to a standard.	Measures against a standard.
Usually involves collecting data that are additional to routine care.	Usually involves analysis of existing data but may include administration of interview, questionnaire, or focus groups.	Usually involves analysis of existing data but may include the administration of a simple interview or questionnaire.
Normally requires Research Ethics Committee review. Some studies using only secondary data may not.	Does not normally require Research Ethics Committee review.	Does not require Research Ethics Committee review.

Case studies

Case study 1.1 An example of a project that reports on a research project

Cooper, J. and Urquhart, C. (2005) The Information Needs and Information-Seeking Behaviours of Home-Care Workers and Clients Receiving Home Care, *Health Information and Libraries Journal*, **22 (2)**, 107–16.

Aims and objectives: Discusses findings from doctoral research on the information behaviour of home-care workers and their clients. The paper focuses on the findings, which have implications for health library and information services.

Sample and methods: The qualitative research methods included participant observation in the homes of clients (n = 7), over a period of 18 months, in a city in the UK, complemented by in-depth interviews of home-care staff (n = 47).

Results: Home-care staff perceived requests for information on a variety of topics as an indivisible part of their caring role. Clients asked for more information than they had in the past, and home-care workers were expected to respond to a wide variety of enquiries about health, welfare, leisure and domestic concerns. Clients trusted their advice as much as they might have trusted members of the family. Home-care workers from an agency used a variety of resources at the agency office to help them, such as leaflets on welfare benefits, and health conditions. Few had used NHS Direct, and library use (by a third of the home-care workers) was generally associated with course work or training. Some family members and home-care staff used self-help groups, but the research found that family members were sometimes reticent to ask advice on sensitive issues in self-help groups. Home-care workers learnt from each other and shared experience.

Conclusions: Libraries and information services need to target provision of formal information carefully, as it is advice and counsel that is required in the home-care setting. ▪

This case illustrates a piece of research carried out by a postgraduate student studying for a PhD. It follows established qualitative research methods, 'participant observation' and 'in-depth interviews' (see Chapter 7). It deals with home-care staff and their clients and required observing people in their homes and work environments. This is potentially a sensitive situation. The researcher would have to be aware of the participants' rights, would preferably have to have had some initial training prior to carrying out the study, and would have to have applied for ethics approval to carry out a research project of this nature (see Chapter 5). With qualitative data the samples are often quite small, but a lot of rich data can be gathered (see Chapter 7). The personal safety of the researcher must also be considered when going into people's homes, and plans must be in place to support the researcher in this situation. These plans might include making others aware of when and where the research is being carried out, and having emergency contact procedure in place.

Case study 1.2 An example of a project that reports on an evaluation of a
service.

Moysa, S. (2004) Evaluation of Customer Service Behaviour at the Reference Desk in an Academic Library, *Feliciter*, **50** (2), 60–3.

Background: This case study describes the development, use and impact of a customer service staff evaluation instrument at the reference desk of a large academic library, the Science and Technology Library at the University of Alberta in Canada. It shows how in the past, the Reference Coordinator evaluated an individual's reference performance from information gleaned while working alongside the staff member at the desk, from direct interaction with the individual's supervisor, and through input received informally.

Approach: In order to establish more objective and standardized tools, two reference librarians in the SciTech Library were charged with the following mandate: 'Evaluate the behavioural skills of the Reference staff as they appear to the library patron.' Only behavioural aspects, not content, would be identified and evaluated. The goal was to develop a type of instrument, in the form of a checklist, for use in future staff evaluations. A literature review was conducted to identify desirable customer service behaviour and methods of assessing customer service behaviour. They also conferred with colleagues and current documentation. From this a preliminary list of desired customer service behaviours was developed and was sent to all reference staff in the Science and Technology Library for their review and comment. Three major areas of behaviour were identified: *Approachability*, *Interest*, and *Positive Attitudes*. All identified traits were grouped into one of these three categories to form a scale for evaluating the frequency with which desired customer service behaviours were observed was developed. Staff behavior could be scored against this scale; *Almost always*, *Occasionally*, *Almost never*. The list was presented to the reference staff, in one of their regular monthly meetings, for further review and discussion.

The evaluation process: The evaluation process involved two steps: self-assessment, and observation by an evaluator. This self-assessment was to be strictly confidential, with no sharing of information. Following the self-assessment, the two librarians used the same evaluation sheets to observe and evaluate each staff member. While staff were made aware that this evaluation would occur, they were not told when. Two evaluations were done, at separate times, for each staff member. Results were then shared with the individual, on a voluntary basis, and discussions took place about what had been learned. An analysis of traits exhibited by group members, both positive and negative, was made, and a report was written to provide recommendations for future activities and goals. The reference staff have been part of the process from the beginning of the pilot to the current integrated model. At the outset of each evaluation period, the Reference Coordinator reminds all staff that the assessment will be taking place. The Coordinator then randomly selects reference shifts to observe. The observing is not intrusive; if possible, it is done while the staff member is not particularly aware that it is taking place. Once the observing has taken place, each staff member meets with the Coordinator to discuss the results. This is now a regular, expected part of each staff member's review, and forms part of the assessment in the annual appraisal.

Outcomes: The process is being modified slightly to allow staff to provide their own evaluation, as they did at the beginning of the pilot project. This project has been successful in identifying appropriate customer service behaviours to the reference staff, and in having these specific observable behaviours linked to their performance appraisals and expectations. A more consistent evaluation process has been developed, and the unit has generally achieved a greater consistency of service. The process will continue to be reviewed, modified and changed as reference services change and grow. The process is considered to be a useful addition to the performance appraisal system. ■

This study has clearly been carried out to evaluate an aspect of the service delivery. This study is classed as evaluation, not research, yet it shares many processes with more formal research projects, e.g. exploring the evidence through a thorough review of the literature (see Chapter 6) that informed the development of the scale. Measurement scales such as these are often used in research projects. Other issues are evident, such as the importance of confidentiality (of the individual's performance – see Chapter 5), reliability (using two assessors and self-evaluation – see Chapters 7, 8 and 9), and objectivity (having a standardized scale, so that all staff are assessed against the same criteria – see Chapter 7). The results illustrate how application of the new evaluation tool has benefited the service with the changes bringing improvements.

Case study 1.3 An example of a project that reports on an audit of a service

Chapman, A. and Massey, O. (2002) A Catalogue Quality Audit Tool, *Library Management*, **23** (6/7), 314–24.

Abstract: The current need for performance measurement and quality targets for services to users requires suitable performance indicators for libraries to use. This paper looks at the self-assessment audit tool for catalogue quality developed by UKOLN in collaboration with Essex libraries. For the tool a checklist of errors was drawn up, which can then be used to assess the quality of records within a catalogue using a sample of library stock. The tool can be used to assess the quality of catalogue records for monographs and non-book materials (but not serials), for complete collections or parts of collections and for records created at different periods. This paper describes the tool and the process of making the assessment and reports on the results of the pilot study carried out at the University of Bath library in 2000.

This study developed a 'checklist' or audit tool to assess the quality of the library catalogue. The tool provided a predetermined checklist to assess the quality of the catalogue (see Table 1.1). This audit will not have required ethics approval (see Chapter 5). The results have been published in the literature, as they will be useful to other practitioners. With this type of paper it is common to include the tool used so that others can benefit from replicating the audit or adapting the tool for their own use.

Ten practical steps

Having identified the purpose of your project and determined whether you need to adopt a research, evaluation or audit approach, it's time to get down to the practicalities of how to plan and execute it. Figure 1.2 guides you through the ten steps of a project, from turning your idea into a research question, designing your study, writing and funding your proposal, collecting, analysing and interpreting data through to reporting and disseminating your findings.

Each of these discrete areas is covered in the coming chapters and will guide you through the research process. Although not all projects will need to incorporate all ten steps, it is important to be aware of each step and to know when they are relevant to your own project.

Summary

This chapter has provided an overview of the research process within the library and information sector. It has introduced the concepts of research, evaluation and audit and highlighted the decisive factor in selecting the approach to adopt in your project.

The HEALER research toolkit demonstrates the ten steps in undertaking a research project and will guide the structure of the rest of this book. Not all ten steps will be applicable within all projects.

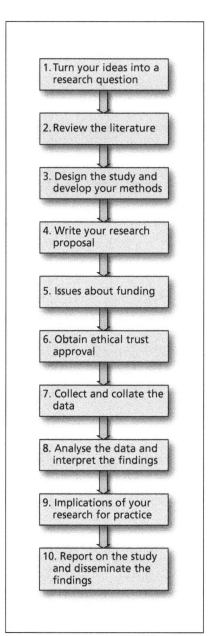

The case studies given in this chapter illustrate the value of research, evaluation and audit in contributing to the evidence base for library and information services. All these differing types of 'research' are worthy of dissemination through library and information networks, conferences and the published literature.

Points for reflection

- Think about an aspect of your work that could be explored or developed through research-based activities, then identify a question that reflects the area you have chosen to investigate. Referring to Table 1.1, consider whether your question is research, evaluation or audit.
- Bearing in mind the research toolkit in Figure 1.2, do you have the skills and resources to carry out the project successfully?
- If not, do you need to read more? Engage in further training? Discuss the project with others? Where can you look for good sources of material that will help? What training might you need? Who might be able to help?

Figure 1.2 *HEALER Research Toolkit*
Modified from the RDInfo research toolkit for supporting researchers in health and social care (National Institute for Health Research), the HEALER research toolkit (HEALER, 2010a) has been specifically designed for use across library and information sectors. HEALER is a UK-based network aimed at ensuring a co-ordinated approach to increasing the production of good quality research, primarily within the health information management sector (HEALER 2010b.)

References

Cameron, P. and Price, D. (2009) *Business Research Methods: a practical approach*, CIPD, London.

Chapman, A. and Massey, O. (2002) A Catalogue Quality Audit Tool, *Library Management*, **23** (6/7), 314–24.

Clarke, A. and Dawson, R. (1999) *Evaluation Research: an introduction to principles, methods and practice*, Sage Publications, London.

Cooper, J. and Urquhart, C. (2005) The Information Needs and Information-seeking Behaviours of Home-care Workers and Clients Receiving Home Care, *Health Information and Libraries Journal*, **22** (2), 107–16.

Department of Health (2005) *Research Governance Framework for Health and Social Care*, 2nd edn, www.dh.gov.uk/en/Publicationsandstatistics/Publications/PublicationsPolicyAnd Guidance/DH_4108962.

French, S., Reynolds, F. and Swain, J. (2001) *Practical Research: a guide for therapists*, 2nd edn, Butterworth-Heinemann, Oxford.

HEALER (2010a) *HEALER research toolkit*, http://researchflowchart.pbworks.com/w/page/6839792/Welcome-and-Acknowledgements.

HEALER (2010b) *Health Information and Libraries for Evaluation and Research (HEALER)*, www.libraryservices.nhs.uk/healer.

Moysa, S. (2004) Evaluation of Customer Service Behaviour at the Reference Desk in an Academic Library, *Feliciter*, **50** (2), 60–3.

National Institute for Health Research, *Your Research Project: how & where to start?* www.rdinfo.org.uk/flowchart/Flowchart.html.

National Research Ethics Services (2009) *Defining Research*, National Patient Safety Agency, London, www.nres.npsa.nhs.uk/EasySiteWeb/getresource.axd?AssetID=355&type= Full&servicetype=Attachment.

Patton, M. Q. (1986) *Utilization-focused Education*, 2nd edn, Sage, Newbury Park, CA.

Rycroft-Malone, J., Seers, K., Titchen, A., Harvey, G., Kitson, A. and McCormack, B. (2004) What Counts as Evidence in Evidence-based Practice?, *Nursing and Health Care Management and Policy*, **47** (1), 81–90.

Saunders, M., Lewis, P. and Thornhill, A. (2003) *Research Methods for Business Students*, 3rd edn, Prentice Hall, London.

Recommended further reading

DePoy, E. and Gitlin, L. N. (1998) *Introduction to Research: understanding and applying multiple strategies*, 2nd edn, Mosby, London.

Pickard, A. J. (2013) *Research Methods in Information*, 2nd edn, Facet Publishing, London.

2

Building confidence

Hannah Spring and Clare McCluskey

'Audit? I really don't feel confident about how to start!'

'I feel very unsure about what skills I need to carry out an evaluation in my workplace.'

'I would love to be research-active but don't feel I have enough understanding of how to go about it.'

In a stretched global economic environment, evidence-based practice has a key role to play in demonstrating the value, impact and importance of library and information services. Evidence-based practice provides library and information science (LIS) practitioners with a platform from which to support both decision-making and their accountability within the organization, and research, evaluation and audit are often the fundamental elements that underpin it. Using research to inform practice is therefore a key component of evidence-based practice (Crumley and Koufogiannakis, 2002), and the benefits of research in informing LIS practice have been highlighted elsewhere in the literature (Clapton, 2010; Hall, 2010). For these reasons, it is becoming increasingly important for information practitioners to carry out research within the workplace (Hallam and Partridge, 2006).

This chapter aims to provide a useful starting point to help you begin building confidence in doing research, evaluation or audit. A collection of ideas, examples, and supportive, practical solutions will be offered to help you begin your first steps into practical LIS research. This chapter begins by discussing some of the common barriers to engaging in research, evaluation or audit by LIS practitioners and is followed by a section covering ideas and techniques for collaboration. Further sections include advice on guiding and mentoring, using research diaries and getting involved with research networks. It is hoped that the approaches to building confidence offered in this chapter will provide you with the resolve you need to begin getting involved in these types of activities and/or to begin your own project.

Barriers to engagement in research, evaluation or audit

As highlighted in Chapter 1, the term 'research' is often associated with empirical research carried out by academics, and this can often make it seem inaccessible and intimidating to those in LIS practice (Feather, 2009; Lawal, 2009). Furthermore, research funded by larger funding bodies may be relevant, but not always applicable at a local level. This issue is often referred to as the 'research–practice gap'. The gap between LIS practitioners and researchers highlighted here is one area that can prevent active engagement in research by practitioners. However, there are a number of other barriers to research engagement frequently cited in the LIS literature. Studies carried out seeking to review aspects of engagement in LIS research have identified some of the problems associated with research activity amongst practitioners. These problems include resourcing issues such as financial and time constraints, fragmented funding sources, lack of strategic direction, lack of support, cultural issues, and low skills and confidence levels in carrying out research (Hall, 2010; Klobas and Clyde, 2010; Koufogiannakis and Crumley, 2006; McNicol and Nankivell, 2003; Powell, Baker and Mika, 2002; Petty, 2007).

It is commonly understood that many information practitioners feel daunted by the idea of carrying out research, and lack the confidence needed to become involved in research activities. Although there is a common misconception that research is difficult, intimidating or only for the academics, the good news is that many LIS practitioners are in fact research-active without realizing it (Hall, 2010). Small projects that involve collecting and analysing data and reporting the findings, for instance to evaluate a particular aspect of a library and information service, are research, audit or evaluation projects in their own right. Although such projects are usually carried out and reported at a local level, they can often provide value to a wider audience than just their own organization (Clapton, 2010). LIS practitioners are often unaware of the wider value their work might have, and so relevant aspects of such projects are often not disseminated externally; this is clearly a missed opportunity for those who do this sort of activity in their workplace. Whilst lack of confidence is a common barrier to becoming research-active, there are some simple and easy approaches to dealing with this. The following sections will discuss some of these approaches, which are outlined specifically to help improve your confidence levels and make engaging with research, evaluation or audit more accessible than you might originally have thought.

Collaborating in research

If starting a research project on your own, however small, seems too overwhelming, an excellent way of gaining confidence and a skill is by collaborating with others. Many organizations will have someone who is already researching and they are usually very happy to have someone to help them out! For those who work in academic institutions, accessing relevant people is likely to be reasonably easy. For those who work in other sectors, advice on how to find others from who you can learn from and work with in research, evaluation or audit are given in the following sections. Alternatively, working with other new researchers can be equally rewarding, as you can support and guide each other through the process. For instance, researchers such as McNiff and Whitehead (2009, 173) advocate collaboration with 'critical friends' as a key way of ensuring you gain critical feedback on projects.

If you work in higher education, look out for opportunities such as Teaching Fellow projects. Teaching fellowships are available to apply for in many countries and usually aim to further pedagogic research and share and promote best practice via networks. These can be good introductions to research, on a small scale, and often provide the opportunities to work with others. They also give you access to people who have knowledge of how to navigate procedures such as gaining ethics approval, if your research requires it, or identifying ways of disseminating the outcomes of the project. Often these networks have their own online publications, which will allow you to publish your work so that it can be used and evaluated by others, but without having to think about conference or journal submissions.

Lumsden, McBryde-Wilding and Rose (2010), through the use of a collaborative approach, were able to produce some very valuable research on information skills for Level 1 undergraduate students at university. This research shows the lack of awareness of library services by this group of students and the ways in which they have tried to remedy this in a higher-education institution. This is an issue that is grappled with, not just in higher education, but also with library services encountering new users across the sectors. It is also the sort of issue librarians try to deal with by implementing new procedures or initiatives, but how many actually take a research approach and then publish it for others to learn from (even if it is within one's own organization)? By working with a more experienced researcher, this project has gained momentum and is benefiting the work of many librarians in many different disciplines and sectors.

Evidence of effective collaboration in the health sector is another example from which we can learn. Bradley et al. (2010) show how research carried out between health librarians and administrative staff led to new evidence-based medicine initiatives for medical practitioners. Likewise, Harwell et al. (2008) document a collaborative project that led to new training on online databases, and many other examples exist (Joint, 2005; Childs and Dobbins, 2003).

All of this advice, of course, relies on your identifying someone to collaborate with. This is likely to be easier in the higher education and health sectors. If you are a specialist librarian, perhaps working alone, it may seem as if these opportunities will not present themselves. In cases such as these, the Research Networks section in this chapter will help you. Other options are also worth trying. For those who use Twitter, a brief mention of some ideas you have may well lead to interested parties getting in touch. For information practitioners, social networking is an ideal platform to kick-start collaboration. Giustini and Wright (2009, 11) have investigated this method and they highlight a key attribute of 'ability to follow people outside your social network and with whom you normally do not come into contact'. This is useful in any environment, but lone workers could find a wealth of contacts.

Guiding and mentoring

Anyone who has gone through practitioner accreditation or revalidation will be familiar with mentors and the support they can offer, and others will have encountered it in work, perhaps in a new role, as highlighted by Level and Mach (2004). In the UK, Yorkshire Accord provides a good example of a scheme which encourages people from across differing workplaces to come together, 'to provide individuals with personal and practitioner development, support and challenge by offering the opportunity to work on a one-to-one basis with an individual from a different organization in a mentoring relationship' (York St John University, 2012). In other parts of the world good examples of practice in using mentorship for LIS research also exist (Fuller, 2000; Jacobs and Berg, 2013).

Outside the library world, mentoring is now used in many environments to support and encourage the sharing and building of knowledge. Looking into other sectors, it can be seen that it is a valuable tool in encouraging research. Johnson, Rose and Schlosser (2007, 64) highlight the traditional role of the PhD supervisor in aiding research. Those then going into the workplace from academia can then continue the practice (Dougherty, Turban and Haggard 2007, 139), often occurring naturally rather than as a result of formal schemes.

Mentoring takes on many forms and could easily be part of a collaborative network or a research group, both of which are specifically covered in this chapter. In essence a mentor should 'pass on their knowledge to help the mentee learn what's required' and 'exploit their connections to help advance their protégé's career' (Anon., 2010). If you can locate someone connected to research, evaluation or audit in your work or social network who is willing to offer these options, a mentoring relationship to develop your research skills and opportunities could be very fruitful.

Case study 2.1 Using research diaries

> Possibly the best way of monitoring how you are developing the capacity for self-reflection is by keeping a learning journal.
>
> McNiff, J. and Whitehead, J. (2009) *You and Your Action Research Project,*
> Routledge, 145.

This section is a case study of one higher education librarian's use of a research diary during her first attempt at carrying out research since her dissertation at library school.

Research diaries are an excellent way of pinpointing where research, evaluation or audit can be carried out and can also form part of the evidence in an action research project, as recommended by McNiff and Whitehead above. For example, here is an early extract from the diary in question:

> A fairly typical thing happened today. Had a one-to-one tutorial with a 3rd year student. He said he had never used journals before and didn't have a clue about searching, accessing or using them. He was so enthusiastic about his research project and it was awful to think how much he may have been held back up until now just from a lack of input about information skills. It only took an hour for him to acquire the skills he needed to get his project off the ground and find the background reading for the particular area of interest. He said he wished he could have had a workshop as part of the research module back in November, when he was getting started with it. I wish he could have had regular input throughout his course so that

many more of his assignments had been informed by good journal articles. I wish the whole cohort had had this. Another tale of being told to use journal articles with no back-up about the info searching process. I asked him to feed back to his tutors. It can only help.

Reflective journal, January 2010

Followed by another entry a little later:

I saw ten 2nd year students from the same programme in the last week of term. They had been booked as three separate one-to-ones, but two of these students wanted to bring friends with them. One ended up as a one-to-seven! All of the students had been told that they had to use more journal articles if they wanted to get good marks in their assignments. Not one of them even knew what a journal article was, never mind how to access them. I've had no embedded sessions on this programme and it really shows. After just an hour with these students, they said they felt much more confident about literature searching and said they wished they had had this input earlier. The irony is that they were offered elective drop-in sessions last term, but no one showed up. A clear case of not knowing what they don't know! If only I could get embedded sessions off the ground . . .

Reflective journal, March 2010

These diary entries triggered an idea for a research project on promoting information literacy partnerships between faculty and the library for this programme. The research was not on a large scale. It consisted of gathering literature showing the effectiveness of embedding information literacy in academic programmes, followed by running staff development sessions on the findings from this review. The diary was then useful in helping to understand whether these staff development sessions had had a positive effect:

One of the tutors came to the first session and said she could identify with a lot of the issues we were highlighting. We started discussing how I could help improve her students' use of appropriate resources and agreed that I should go into her second year modules next year to give them help at the point they are given their assignments.

Reflective diary, March 2010

From this, a pilot project could begin to be used to gather more evidence, via focus groups and questionnaires, to take to management in the faculty with a view to expanding the provision. It is something librarians in this sector tackle on a regular basis, but by using the research diary, the process was documented, evaluative procedures could be put in place and findings presented – a research project.

Some choose to keep diaries private, whilst others decide to blog about their experiences. Several librarians are using blogs to great effect to get feedback on their work. For example, look at Aussie Librarian Blogs or the work of Jo Alcock, Ned Potter and Laura Woods (see the end of the chapter for URLs). ▨

Research groups and networks

Sound research rarely happens in isolation.

Pierce, 2005

Networks are most often founded on the collaborative hypothesis that by working together we can be more effective than working alone.

Care Services Improvement Partnership, 2006

As previously highlighted, there are many benefits to collaborating in research, evaluation or audit and a further form of collaboration is through the use of networks. The usefulness of research networks to increase research capacity is well documented, and we can learn a lot about good practice in using networks, particularly if we look to the healthcare professions. In healthcare research, networks of individuals and/or organizations are a widely used mechanism for building research capacity. The use of networks and partnerships as an effective approach to research engagement is also recognized by some LIS practitioners. In the UK, for instance, in the most recent review of NHS libraries a key recommendation was that 'research to measure the impact of the application of best available evidence in decision making should continue to be pursued vigorously and routinely by health librarians, in partnership with researchers' (Hill, 2008). More broadly, this is also recognized by Hall (2010), who suggests that one way for LIS practitioners to build confidence in research, evaluation and audit activities is to seek partners and collaborators. Using networks is one method of finding these research allies.

LIS practitioners are noted both anecdotally and in the literature (Wildridge et al., 2004) as having good networking skills and there are many excellent networks in existence that can be accessed for the purposes of research support. Research networks can provide support and also signpost you to other sources of support. They work by giving you access to a community of like-minded individuals and/or organizations and can provide a wealth of knowledge, expertise and advice based on the real experiences of others. Indeed, it is noted that networks can provide 'a better sense of belonging, ownership and understanding' (Care Services Improvement Partnership, 2006).

If you are keen to begin learning or to develop your existing research skills before you embark on a live research, evaluation or audit project, being part of a research network can provide a supportive environment in which to do this. Networks can provide you with details of learning opportunities such as workshops or training courses, for instance, or put you in touch with other people interested in collaborating in research.

A good starting point for finding LIS-related research support near you is to use your practitioner body (e.g. the American Library Association (USA); Australian Library and Information Association (Australia); CILIP: the Chartered Institute of Library and Information Professionals (UK)). These organizations often have subsidiary groups and networks specializing in specific areas of practice or interest. Such groups can provide useful support, research skills workshops and networking opportunities for those interested in LIS-related research. They can also provide information about LIS research opportunities, networking opportunities, promote LIS practitioner research, the development of research capacity in LIS and the translation of outcomes into practice.

More broadly, look at organizations such as the Research Information Network (RIN) in the UK. This provides a particularly good example of research support for information professionals, and works to develop and support research in a number of ways. It specifically includes the provision of guidance to all institutions, funders, researchers, information practitioners and anyone else who has a role in research information. Its website contains a very useful section developed directly for library and information practitioners, containing links to a variety of research-related resources including funding, useful organizations, publishing, social networking, blogs and others. General resources for researchers are also available from this site. It is useful to remember that resources provided not specifically for LIS practitioners can be equally useful, particularly where funding sources and research methods are concerned, so remember to think outside of the box! Resources such as those accommodated by the organizations above provide some excellent starting points for support by being part of a research specific network.

Virtual networks are now commonplace and are a useful, convenient resource to help develop your research skills and increase your research opportunities. Being a member of a web-based discussion forum will, for instance, offer you an environment in which to ask questions, keep up to date with research-related communities of practice, or be alerted to events, training opportunities and research grants on offer. Wikis are also increasingly being used as forums for the purposes of sharing information, for instance about current research, evaluation or audit projects, and providing support for those doing research or wishing to develop their skills. As mentioned in the collaboration section earlier, Twitter is another useful resource for accessing virtual networks in your area of interest. Look online and you will probably be surprised at what is available.

Case study 2.2 provides an example of how virtual networks can be used to support both your own personal research and also the communities of practice they serve. It can be surprising how much people can learn from each other, and perhaps the example below will encourage you to join the virtual community for the purposes of research, evaluation or audit.

Case study 2.2 Does anyone know? Using a virtual research community

You have learned of a research grant that has been made available to bid for, to complete a systematic review of the impact of information skills training in undergraduate students. In order to write up your research proposal and funding bid, you need to provide a breakdown of costs necessary to carry out the study. Although you have experience of conducting systematic reviews, this is the first time you have ever had to cost one out and you are unsure about how to approach it. You post a message out to an e-mailed based LIS research discussion group to ask if any other members have experience of costing out a systematic review. You also send a post to the Twitter feed of an LIS research network you have become aware of. You receive a number of very helpful responses, and these enable you to cost out your systematic review. After you have done this, you put together a digest of the responses you received and post it back to the list for everyone in the virtual community to benefit from.

The benefits of this approach are as follows:

- Both you and the virtual community members can benefit from the knowledge and experience of each other, and can share in and benefit from the production of new knowledge. Supportive environments such as this are an excellent means of building research confidence. It is also, in itself, a form of evidence-based practice.
- Through using existing groups you have learned a new research-related skill

that would have been difficult to acquire without the virtual research communities you accessed. ▪

If you are interested in going one step further and setting up your own network, then consider starting small. Perhaps begin with a small local network or group of colleagues who are interested in learning about, or working together on research activities in a supportive environment. A good example of how this sort of network or group is used is the journal club, a forum for practitioners to meet, discuss and appraise published research papers that are relevant to their area of practice. The benefits of journal clubs has been reported in the literature by Grant (2003), who points out their value in developing research skills for the purposes of evidence-based practice. The scope of these groups can of course be extended beyond the critical appraisal of journal articles, to other aspects of the research process. Why not use your group meetings to consider different aspects of the research, evaluation or audit process, for instance different research methodologies, publishing or to discuss ideas for potential research studies? Case study 2.3 provides a scenario in which the activities described above could be used productively in a work-based research project. This should help contextualize how the advice provided in this chapter can be used in a real-life research situation, and hopefully inspire you in getting research active in your own organization.

Case study 2.3 Strength in numbers! Using a research group

You work in a local public library and recently ran some 'silver surfers' courses, a series of free beginners' internet training sessions aimed at older people in the local community. Although you gave out some basic evaluation forms for the participants to complete at the end of the training sessions, you are keen to know more about the impact of these sessions and although you have no idea where to begin, have decided to conduct an evaluation of it. You are aware that some other local libraries in your district have been running the same courses as part of a public libraries initiative supported by the local authority and decide to see if any of the other libraries would be interested in working together on an evaluative research study. You arrange a group meeting with a representative from each of the local public libraries that ran the silver surfers course and are interested in collaborating to discuss a small research project.

The benefits of this approach are as follows:

- Carrying out a collaborative research project pools resources and means one person does not have to be responsible for all the work. Aspects of the project and write-up can be shared out amongst the group members and this will be a substantial saving in terms of time, and makes doing the study considerably less daunting.
- Group members can benefit from the knowledge, expertise and support of each other, and can share in the learning process, thereby helping to build research confidence.
- The research study will be a stronger study if all the libraries in the group are included, as you will be covering a larger geographical area than one individual library. The study will enable you to assess the impact of your silver surfers course on a wider scale, but the results for each individual library can easily be separated to support any organizational evaluations and to demonstrate evidence-based practice locally to each organization.

If you are feeling really brave and want to set up your own local network, some excellent guidance can be found in a tool developed by the Care Services Improvement Partnership (2006). This is a checklist-style tool designed to be used in the development of networks and can easily be used by LIS practitioners looking to use or develop their own network.

As previously mentioned, one thing LIS practitioners are good at is networking, so capitalize on something the profession already does well, and make it work for you in developing your confidence to become a researcher in a supportive environment with other like-minded practitioners.

Summary

This chapter has considered some of the common barriers that sometimes affect the confidence of LIS practitioners to get involved in research, evaluation or audit and provided some practical solutions in how to overcome them. In particular, it has shown how LIS practitioners can use things that they are already good at, such as collaborating and networking, to help them engage in research. Other activities covered, such as guiding and mentoring, and the use of reflective practice in research have also been presented, all of which are intended to inspire you with the confidence you need to get that research project off the ground.

In order to get the best out of this chapter, some points for reflection are provided below. Take some time to consider these – they will help to both focus and stimulate your thoughts and ideas around activities you can do today to help increase your confidence to become a researcher. Remember, have confidence in your abilities as a researcher! Research does not have to be a daunting or difficult process, particularly for a group of practitioners who naturally possess the skills and qualities that lend themselves perfectly to the processes and activities involved with research.

Points for reflection

Having read this chapter, consider and reflect on the following points:

- What new activities will you do to develop your confidence in doing research?
- What things about your current practice will you change?
- Who will you contact?

References

Anon. (2010) Mentors and Minorities: how to create a united workplace. *Development and Learning in Organizations*, **24** (2), 28–30.

Bradley, D., Rana, G., Lypson, M. and Hamstra, S. (2010) A Centralized Practice-based Learning and Improvement Curriculum for Residents and Fellows: a collaboration of health sciences librarians and graduate medical education administration, *Journal of the Medical Library Association*, **98** (2), 175–8.

Care Services Improvement Partnership (2006) *Designing Networks for Collaborative Advantage: practice-based evidence on how to set up networks to improve partnership working and achieve positive outcomes*, www.developbromley.com/public/ ResearchandDevelopment/Tools/CollabNetworks.pdf.

Childs, S. and Dobbins, S. (2003) The Research-Practice Spiral, *Vine*, **33** (2), 51–64.

Clapton, J. (2010) Library and Information Science Practitioners Writing for Publication: motivations, barriers and supports, *Library and Information Research*, **34** (106), 7–21.

Crumley, E. and Koufogiannakis, D. (2002) Developing Evidence-based Librarianship: practical steps for implementation, *Health Information and Libraries Journal*, **19** (2), 61–70.

Dougherty, T., Turban, D. and Haggard, D. (2007) Naturally Occurring Mentoring Relationships Involving Workplace Employees. In Allen, T. and Eby, L, (eds), *The Blackwell Handbook of Mentoring: a multiple perspectives approach*, Blackwell, Oxford, 139–58.

Feather, J. (2009) LIS Research in the United Kingdom: reflections and prospects, *Journal of Librarianship and Information Science*, **41** (3), 173–81.

Fuller, S. (2000) Enabling, Empowering, Inspiring: research and mentorship through the years, *Bulletin of the Medical Library Association*, **88** (1), 1–10.

Giustini, D. and Wright, M-D. (2009) Twitter: an introduction to microblogging for health librarians, *JCHLA/JABSC*, 30, 11–17.

Grant, M. J. (2003) Journal Clubs for Continued Practitioner Development, *Health Information and Libraries Journal*, **20** (1), 72–8.

Hall, H. (2010) Promoting the Priorities of Practitioner Research Engagement, *Journal of Librarianship and Information Science*, **42** (2), 83–8.

Hallam, G. and Partridge, H. (2006) Evidence Based Library and Information Practice: whose responsibility is it anyway? *Evidence Based Library and Information Practice*, **1** (3), 88–94.

Harwell, T., Gesink, D., Ander, J. and Helgerson, S. (2008) Increasing State Public Health Practitioners' Proficiency in Using PubMed, *Journal of the Medical Library Association*, **96** (2), 134–7.

Hill, P. (2008) *Report of a National Review of NHS Library Services in England: from knowledge to health in the 21st century*, Institute of Health and Society, Newcastle, Newcastle University.

Jacobs, H. and Berg, S. (2013) By Librarians, for Librarians: building a strengths-based institute to develop librarians' research culture in Canadian academic libraries, *The Journal of Academic Librarianship*, **39** (1), 227–31.

Johnson, B., Rose, G. and Schlosser, L. (2007) Student-faculty Mentoring: theoretical and methodological issues. In Allen, T. and Eby, L. (eds), *The Blackwell Handbook of Mentoring: a multiple perspectives approach*, Blackwell, Oxford, 49–70.

Joint, N. (2005) Promoting Practitioner-Researcher Collaboration in Library and Information Sciences, *Library Review*, **54** (5), 289–94.

Klobas, J. and Clyde L. (2010) Beliefs, Attitudes and Perceptions About Research and Practice in a Professional Field, *Library and Information Science Research*, **32** (4), 237–45.

Koufogiannakis, D. and Crumley, E. (2006) Research in Librarianship: issues to consider, *Library Hi Tech*, **24** (3), 324–40.

Lawal, I. (2009) *Library and Information Science Research in the 21st Century: a guide for practising librarians and students*, Chandos Publishing, Oxford.

Level, A. and Mach, M. (2004) Peer Mentoring: one institution's approach to mentoring academic librarians, *Library Management*, **26** (6/7), 301–10.

Lumsden, E., McBryde-Wilding, H. and Rose, H. (2010) Collaborative Practice in Enhancing the First Year Student Experience in Higher Education, *Enhancing the Learner Experience in Higher Education*, **2** (1), 12–24.

McNicol, S. and Nankivell, C. (2003) *The LIS Research Landscape: a review and prognosis,* CILIP: the Chartered Institute of Library and Information Professionals, London.

McNiff, J. and Whitehead, J. (2009) *You and Your Action Research Project,* Routledge, London.

Petty, H. (2007) Barriers to Evidence Based Library and Information Practice, *Feliciter,* **53** (1), 30–2.

Pierce, L. (2005) Rehabilitation Nurses Working as Collaborative Research Teams, *Rehabilitation Nursing,* **30** (4), 132–9.

Powell, R., Baker, L. and Mika, J. (2002) Library and Information Science Practitioners and Research, *Library and Information Science Research,* **24** (1), 49–72.

Wildridge, V., Childs, S., Cawthra, L. and Madge, B. (2004) How to Create Successful Partnerships: a review of the literature, *Health Information and Libraries Journal,* **21** (S1), 3–19.

York St John University (2012) *Yorkshire Accord Mentoring Scheme,* www.yorksj.ac.uk/docs/Yorkshire%20Accord%20Additional%20Information%20 for%Line%20Managers%202012.doc.

Yorkshire Accord Coaching and Mentoring Scheme (2012) www.yorkshireaccord.co.uk.

Blogs cited

Aussie Librarian Blogs, http://asearchinglibrarian.wordpress.com/2011/08/10/aussie-librarian-blogs-worth-following.

Jo Alcock, www.joeyanne.co.uk.

Ned Potter, http://thewikiman.org/blog.

Laura Woods, http://woodsiegirl.wordpress.com.

Recommended further reading

Alred, G. and Garvey, B. (2010) *Mentoring Pocketbook,* 3rd edn, Management Pocketbooks, Hampshire.

Booth A. (2001) Turning Research Priorities into Answerable Questions, *Health Information and Libraries Journal,* **18** (2), 130–2.

Booth, A. and Brice, A. (2004) *Evidence-based Practice for Information Practitioners: a handbook,* Facet Publishing, London.

Brice, A. and Booth, A. (2005) Practical Issues in Creating an Evidence Base for Library and Information Practice, *Library and Information Research,* **30** (94), 52–60.

Genoni, P., Haddow G. and Richie, A. (2004) Why Don't Librarians Use Research?

In Booth, A. and Brice, A. (eds), *Evidence-based Practice for Information Practitioners: a handbook*, Facet Publishing, London.

McNicol, S. (2004) Practitioner Research in Libraries: a cross-sectoral comparison, *Library and Information Research*, **28** (88), 34–41.

Sivak, A. (2007) Activating Research in the Library Community, *Feliciter*, **53** (1), 8–11.

3

Asking the right question

Sarah Coulbeck and Emma Hadfield

'Where do project ideas come from?'

'What makes a good research question?'

'Should I work in collaboration with other researchers?'

Most researchers would acknowledge that knowing how to begin can be the hardest part. However, Fourie (2012) urges every library and information science (LIS) practitioner to play their part in contributing to the evidence base that so directly informs decision-making, while Lerdal (2006) suggests that we can positively affect the future of our profession by building up a bank of professional knowledge which can be applied to our daily practice.

There is no defined place to begin the process of generating your research question, which can instead be viewed as an iterative and cyclical process (Beck and Manuel, 2008) or, as Blaxter, Hughes and Tight (2006) refer to the research process, a research spiral. Both approaches indicate that research is a never-ending process that can be entered at almost any point, and so finding a research idea that interests you is a good first step and, as Beck and Manuel suggest, can be a key determinant in the later success of a project. This chapter provides guidance through those first essential stages of generating ideas and formulating research questions.

What makes a good research question?

The key to a strong piece of research is a question that is answerable, well built and focused (Lerdal, 2006). Your question will be the foundation on which the search strategy, methodology (see Chapters 7 and 8), literature review (see Chapter 6) and ultimately the conclusion is built upon. Research questions should be clearly defined (Bryman, 2008) and answerable. This may sound simple and obvious but compare the approach of formulating a research statement versus a research question. Your research statement might be 'Young people's impressions of librarianship as a career'. However, changing it to pose it as a question will help ensure that it is tightly and accurately defined (Boden, Kenway and Epstein, 2005, 30), for example, 'What impressions do young people have of librarianship as a career?'

Identifying the desired outcome of the project arising out of your research question will shape the formulation of your question. There are typically three main types of questions: prediction, intervention and exploration questions (Eldredge, 2002, as cited in Booth, 2006). Prediction questions begin with a hypothesis that can be supported or otherwise, for example, 'Do young people who regularly use the library get higher grades in their subjects?' Intervention questions draw comparisons in order to measure success, for example 'Does the ability to renew online versus renewing in person reduce the number of user fines?' Exploration questions don't come with a predetermined expectation but aim to investigate an area in detail and often 'seek to answer the question "why?"' (Booth, 2006, 360): for example, 'Why do some users prefer e-books to printed books?'

Alongside this, even at this early stage in the process, consideration should be given to appropriate methods of data collection for the topic, as this will influence the wording of the question. If the choice is to obtain qualitative data that will result in a more wordy answer, for example via interviews, the question should begin with words such as 'why', 'how' or 'what'. Alternatively if a quantitative approach is considered that will result in statistical data that are measurable, the question should begin with words such as 'how many', 'how often' or 'where'. The exact same research idea when worded differently will lead to the use of different methodologies and ultimately different results, for example, 'What innovative activities are being used in school libraries?' could be researched qualitatively with the use of descriptive case studies of the activities to be found, whereas the question, 'Can innovation activity in schools libraries be measured?' would require a quantitative approach with the use of measurement scales. It is a good exercise to ascertain which data collection methods to use by looking at the way the question is worded, then looking at appropriate methods (see Chapters 7 and 8, respectively, for qualitative and quantitative approaches).

Having the question set in stone at this early stage is not essential;

however, understanding the direction of your project is, as this will lead to the development of the research idea.

Developing a research idea

Research opportunities are all around, particularly within the workplace. The key to identifying these opportunities is being a reflective practitioner. This involves an ongoing process of thinking about the strengths of the service and your role within it, and areas that could be improved. Traditionally PESTLE (Political, Economic, Social, Technological, Legal and Environmental factors) and SWOT (strengths, weaknesses, opportunities, threats) analyses are used to identify improvements to a service and these can also lead to a research idea.

Evidence-based information practice is an essential part of drawing research ideas directly from the workplace. Booth and Brice (2004, 13) state that evidence-based librarianship is a practice that is founded 'on up-to-date, valid and reliable research'. Therefore by identifying an issue within the workplace you can develop a question to carry out research that will ultimately lead to the improvement of the service (see Chapter 13). Case study 3.1 demonstrates how evidence-based librarianship can generate a research idea.

Case study 3.1 Developing an idea for an audit: workplace need

---

Bridget, a senior-school librarian, wanted to develop an information skills programme for the Year 7 students. Through this workplace need, she realized this presented a research opportunity, because she would need to find out current student knowledge in order that her programme would meet the students' needs.

An audit of the students' skills at the beginning of the year informed the development of the information skills programme; for example, only 37% of students knew that the non-fiction books were arranged numerically by classification number. This resulted in an additional information skills lesson being created with a focus on using the library classification system to locate books. Realizing the benefits of conducting this audit, she conducted a further audit of students' learning at the end of the programme, which highlighted what students had achieved through the tailored lessons. The same question about how non-fiction is organized now generated a positive response of 84% knowing that non-fiction books were arranged numerically, showing a distinct improvement.

Although only a small-scale research idea, it completely fulfilled its purpose of informing in-house practices. ■

Points for reflection

- A research idea doesn't have to be on a large scale as long as it has a purpose. A variety of workplace needs are valid and important.
- What is useful to you may also be useful to others working in similar situations. On completion of a small-scale idea, think about what you have gained from the process and consider expanding this and sharing your research with others (see Chapter 11).

Another place to identify research opportunities is through conferences. Attendance at conferences, as well as being essential for continued professional development, can also produce research ideas. Different lectures and workshops can stimulate interest in reflecting on an area in a particular service or drawing comparisons with other sectors/countries (Fourie, 2012). Many conference providers now run numerous social media activities (see Chapter 10) parallel to the live conference, meaning that actual attendance isn't always necessary to benefit from the wealth of content that can aid in the generation of research ideas.

Alongside this, there are numerous library-related conferences. Calls for papers can be inspirational when developing a research idea through looking at the various themes and offer a good opportunity to conduct research with a clear goal to aim for.

Case study 3.2 outlines how a research idea can be generated through an invitation to contribute to the wider profession.

Case study 3.2 Developing a research idea: invitation to contribute

Jeremy is a library manager working in the further education sector. He is also on the committee of a professional librarianship special interest group. As part of the special interest group he was invited to contribute to a forthcoming conference on information literacy.

Although Jeremy was not provided with a formal research question, his interest and involvement in the group provided him with the opportunity to explore a research area that he hadn't previously considered. The broad conference theme allowed him to tailor the project to meet his research interest while addressing a topic of concern for his organization, that of developing the academic skills of final-year project students. A research plan was developed to ensure that the project was feasible in the time available. ▪

Points for reflection

- Networking can lead to research ideas and opportunities, so attend conferences and/or join committees/groups related to the profession where possible.
- Don't shy away from invitations to conduct research, even if you haven't considered an area before; if it sparks an initial interest, it is worth pursuing.

Research ideas can come at any time and can have the annoying habit of only being half remembered when you have the time to think about them in more detail. A solution to this is to keep a pen and pad (or notes feature on a phone) with you to jot down your ideas as they arise, to revisit at a more convenient time. Beck and Manuel (2008) suggest that the more widely you participate in professional activities, the more likely you are to have ideas for research topics. Examples include reading the professional literature, engaging with social media, electronic discussion groups, blogs and informal conversations with other library professionals (see Chapter 10).

It is important to highlight that a research idea does not necessarily have to be original. Although originality is, of course, beneficial to the profession, replicating research can provide a good introduction to carrying out research, because the approach has already been tried and tested and your work findings will help confirm, consolidate or bring into question the findings of previous studies (Blaxter, Hughes and Tight, 2006).

The importance of literature in helping formulate the question

A basic review of current literature (see Chapter 6), using simple keywords originated from initial ideas, can help to help you formulate your ideas more fully (Boden, Kenway and Epstein, 2005, 13). For example, a professional publication may have an article about the percentage of children who are read to by their parents at home. Librarians who work in public or school libraries may wonder if this situation is true in their borough and therefore the literature plants a seed that can grow into a potential research question, such that some research is conducted to find out.

Alternatively, you may already have a topic of interest, but be uncertain how to develop it into a piece of research. The literature review can outline matters already researched and current issues surrounding the topic, identifying gaps in the literature to add or contribute to. Later, through a discussion of your project findings, updating the literature review could demonstrate that something has changed (Beck and Manuel, 2008).

As ideas progress, the literature review enables a more precise formulation of the research question (Pickard, 2007). As the question grows and begins to take shape the literature review helps to confirm the feasibility and achievement of the aims.

Things to consider

When generating a research idea and the subsequent research question, it is imperative that a number of elements are given careful consideration, as they will dictate how the research will progress. Before developing a research question, ensure that the requisite tools are in place to succeed in effectively answering the question.

Resources

Access to adequate resources, e.g. bibliographic databases, are a key element in developing your research idea and subsequent question, though these may not always be available in every workplace. Thankfully, professional bodies generally provide access to specific resources to their members and local university libraries often offer an external borrower scheme, allowing users to access their collections and borrow their books. Depending on licensing agreements, it may also be possible to access online sources along with an interlibrary loan facility. The collections of national and public libraries are also worth considering.

Scope

The scope of a research question can be heavily dependent on available time, finances and participants (if applicable).

Time

The feasibility of your chosen topic and subsequent research question or questions is important, and research often comes with a deadline, whether it is a conference, publisher or internal workplace deadline. In order to produce good-quality research, consider exactly what is achievable within the timeframe (Blaxter, Hughes and Tight, 2006). Research novices may find it advantageous to consider a smaller-scale project, with a question that is not too involved. As experience and confidence grows, larger-scale research projects will develop.

Finance

The focus of the question may be dependent on what funding is available. Depending on your research question, it may be possible to incorporate your project into your day-to-day practice but, most often, projects will incur some costs. It may be that your project involves a certain amount of travel, perhaps to conduct interviews, meet research partners (see below) or visit libraries. Ideas and questions need to be developed in line with the finances available. There may also be dissemination costs, for example presenting your project findings at a conference. Professional bodies and regional associations often offer sponsorship or grants to undertake research and attend conferences. Workplaces may also be able to offer part or full contribution, particularly when the research can advocate the institution. Alternatively, you may wish to consider funding the project yourself, either directly through funding to travel, etc., or by conducting the work in your own time (see Chapter 4).

Participants

At the point of developing the question you should consider whether the research would involve contributions from other people, whether it is in the form of interviews, surveys or focus groups, and the ethical issues that may arise from this (see Chapter 5). The availability and willingness of participants can be the difference between a successful research question and one that never progresses.

Research partners

As previously identified in Chapter 2, research doesn't have to be a solitary pursuit. Ideas and questions can be developed as a team of two or more LIS practitioners. People to collaborate with might include colleagues within the workplace or within the wider profession. Working in partnership with others has a number of pros and cons.

Pros

- Two heads are often better than one in bringing ideas to the table. The more knowledge that can be drawn from at the outset the stronger the question that can be formulated without having to rely heavily on the literature alone.
- Input from different sectors can produce a research question that is likely to have a wider appeal. Different sectors will look at issues from different angles, ensuring a holistic research topic.
- Technology provides easier ways of working together and discussing ideas without being in the same room, through facilities such e-mail, videoconference, online chat and, of course, the telephone.

Cons

- Three (four, five, six) can be a crowd. Whilst working with more people has its benefits, consider the logistics of bigger teams. Meeting face-to-face can be problematic, dependent on people's locations, and other communication methods have to be sought.
- Different people have different circumstances and commitments. All parties need to be able to contribute the same time and effort; otherwise, a situation could arise whereby one person is doing more work. This could lead to feelings of resentment that will reduce motivation.
- Different methods and styles of working can be a positive with the right balance of strengths. However, there can be clashes, for example, when two or more members possess similar styles such as leadership. If this arises at the outset a question may never even get off the ground.

Case study 3.3 shows that researching with others can be a positive working experience and help to develop a question.

Case study 3.3 Research partners

Emma works as a library manager within a sixth-form college. On seeing a call for papers for a conference related to information literacy transitions through the educational sectors, she realized she could contribute to this if she had input from other sectors. She therefore e-mailed two contacts: Sarah, who worked in a school library, and Pete, who worked in a university library. These contacts had been made during previous studies and so there was an awareness of each other's personal and work circumstances and working styles and methods, which meant they were confident this would be a productive working partnership.

As a team they had an initial conference call in which they brainstormed ideas around the conference theme and developed a set of desired outcomes. These were clearly linked to workplace needs in order that each member of the team would be able to use the research to inform future practices.

Following this meeting it was agreed to split the initial literature review along with undertaking some individual reflection. A face-to-face meeting then took place to focus the ideas based on individual findings. A Gantt chart was created to identify the amount of time required to meet the conference deadline. Individual availability and time commitments helped to inform which methodology and type of question was most feasible. Combining all of these factors resulted in the formulation of a research question that would encompass their combined knowledge and experience in line with the conference requirements.

The result of this partnership generated a worthwhile piece of research that appealed to a wider professional network and ultimately created a much stronger conference submission.

Points for reflection

- If you have a research idea, but feel it is too big to tackle alone, consider working collaboratively with others to develop a research question. The experience can be extremely valuable, as you have more ideas, can share the workload and can often cover a topic in far greater detail.
- Network and make contacts as often as you can, as you never know when these people could become your future research partners. Never forget your initial network gained during your studies – many of these will be in the same profession as you and can be invaluable when considering a research area.

Focusing the idea and developing the research question

Bringing together the initial ideas and the results of your literature review will enable you to focus your research idea and inform the development of your research question (Boden, Kenway and Epstein, 2005).

There are a number of key methods that can assist with focusing an idea, including visual techniques and communication.

Visual techniques

Being able to see everything all in one place will help to focus on current knowledge and future needs. Concept maps, often referred to as mind maps, can be a useful tool when visually organizing ideas, key words and gaps in knowledge; these are often much better than linear notes (Buzan, 1993). A concept map encourages the use of key words, rather than writing in sentences and phrases, which will prove useful for forthcoming literature searching (see Chapters 6 and 10). Using this method clearly identifies the areas that generate the most interest, that are more achievable and that are clearly linked to the intended outcome, ultimately developing a strong, focused question.

Communication

Alongside the use of a visual focusing activity, it is extremely beneficial to discuss ideas with others. Discussions through professional networks, which can be in the form of contacts made at events or previous studies, workplace colleagues or members of relevant mailing lists, require articulating ideas clearly, thus helping to focus and refine.

The question

As the research progresses and new information is discovered, there may be a need to revise the original research question and project focus (Blaxter, Hughes and Tight, 2006). This is a natural part of the cyclical nature of the research process and it can be positive. As discussed previously, refer back to the proposed methodology and question types to ensure the purpose, focus and scope of the original idea is maintained.

Aims and objectives

Once the question has been finalized you should produce a set of aims and objectives to provide you with a sense of direction for your project (Moore, 2006). The aims of the research are the broad statement of intent and the objectives are how to achieve this (Gravells, 2011). As with the research question, the wording of aims and objectives is important. Aims should state the overall purpose of the research, often drawing wording directly from the question. Objectives can be treated like a to-do list of measurable outcomes; therefore they often begin with a verb to show they are something you can do (Pickard, 2007). The wording used in the aims and objectives will provide further areas to pursue during a search strategy.

Case study 3.4 outlines an example of aims and objectives. Note that it is standard practice to have more objectives than aims.

Case study 3.4 Example aims and objectives

Research question

To what extent have women progressed and made an impact on organizational structures and management styles in UK academic libraries?

Aims
- to discover to what extent women in academic libraries have had an impact on organizational structures and management styles
- to suggest future targets for women in the profession.

Objectives
- to identify and interview women currently holding senior management positions in UK academic libraries
- to analyse management theory and identify any changes
- to obtain and analyse statistical evidence identifying changes in the number of women in senior roles in UK academic libraries
- to identify key themes within both the literature and the interview data.

Summary

This chapter has introduced the importance of developing an idea into a well defined question and demonstrated that this is a cyclical process. It has introduced the need for an initial literature review to progress ideas or spark interest and provided a list of issues to consider when embarking on a question, including access to resources, feasibility and scope and considering the benefits of working in collaboration with others. It has discussed how to focus an idea through visual techniques and communication with others, in order to refine a carefully worded and answerable research question that draws from workplace evidence and informs future practices. It has outlined how to formulate aims and objectives and the importance of appropriate wording in these. The development of key words at each stage has been highlighted to contribute towards a successful search strategy.

Points for reflection

- Within your place of work, think about areas that could be improved, or strategies you could implement, if you had appropriate and relevant evidence of what was required. Write down your thoughts and do a basic literature search to see if it might develop into a research idea of your own.
- Read current and relevant professional literature and identify areas that relate to your workplace or personal interests. Think about what you could add or contribute to this area.
- Look at how other researchers have framed their research question by exploring work published in the academic literature.
- When you have an idea, reflect on that idea, spend time drafting possible research questions, thinking about their feasibility, and redrafting them until you have refined your ideas.

References

Beck, S. and Manuel, K. (2008) *Practical Research Methods for Librarians and Information Professionals*, Neal-Schuman Publishers, New York.

Blaxter, L., Hughes, C. and Tight, M. (2006) *How to Research*, 3rd edn, Open University Press, Buckingham.

Boden, R., Kenway, J. and Epstein, D. (2005) *Getting Started on Research*, Sage Publications, London.

Booth, A. (2006) Clear and Present Questions: formulating questions for evidence based practice, *Library Hi Tech*, **24** (3), 355–68.

Booth, A., and Brice, A. (2004) *Evidence-based Practice for Information Professionals: a handbook*, Facet Publishing, London.

Bryman, A. (2008) *Social Research Methods*, 3rd edn, Oxford University Press, Oxford.

Buzan, T. (1993) *The Mind Map Book*, BBC Books, London.

Eldredge, J. (2002) Cited in Booth, A. (2006) Clear and Present Questions: formulating questions for evidence based practice, *Library Hi Tech*, **24** (3), 359.

Fourie, I. (2012) Content Analysis as a Means of Exploring Research Opportunities from a Conference Programme, *Health Information and Libraries Journal*, **29**, 197–213.

Gravells, A. (2011) *Preparing to Teach in the Lifelong Learning Sector*, 4th edn, Learning Matters , Exeter.

Lerdal, S. (2006) Evidence-Based Librarianship: opportunity for law librarians?, *Law Library Journal*, **98** (1), 33–60.

Moore, N. (2006) *How to do Research: a practical guide to designing and managing research projects*, Facet Publishing, London.

Pickard, A. J. (2007) *Research Methods in Information*, Facet Publishing, London.

Recommended further reading

Bell, J. (2010) *Doing your Research Project*, 5th edn, Open University Press, Maidenhead.

Dawson, C. (2009) *Introduction to Research Methods: a practical guide for anyone undertaking a research project*, 4th edn, How to Books, Oxford.

Gorman, G. E, and Clayton, P. (2005) *Qualitative Research for the Information Professional: a practical handbook*, Facet Publishing, London.

Grix, J. (2004) *The Foundations of Research*, Palgrave Macmillan, Basingstoke.

JISC (2012) *Pestle and Swot Analyses*, www.jiscinfonet.ac.uk/tools/pestle-swot.

Kourogiannakis, D. and Crumley, E. (2006) Research in Librarianship: issues to consider, *Library Hi Tech*, **24** (3), 324–40.

Roberts, B. (2007) *Getting the Most Out of the Research Experience: what every researcher needs to know*, Sage Publications, London.

Wilkinson, D. (2000) *The Researcher's Toolkit: the complete guide to practitioner research*, Routledge Falmer, London.

4

Writing your project plan

Miggie Pickton

'How do I convince my employers to give me time to do my project?'

'I can see the need for producing a plan but what do I need to put in it?'

'I have a great idea for improving my service but how do I gather the evidence to show that it is needed?'

As you start to read this chapter you are likely to be at the stage when you wish to translate your research question, aims and objectives into a full-scale project. You probably have some idea of what you would like to do, how you intend to do it and when. You may also be wondering whose support you need for it to happen.

This chapter will demonstrate how a project plan or proposal can be just what you need to organize your project and convince prospective supporters of its value. It will show you how a plan is valuable for any research, evaluation or audit project, whether large or small, funded or not. It will describe the various purposes of a research plan and emphasize the importance of the audience to how you construct and write the plan.

Each of the different elements of the plan will be considered in turn, from choosing a title to evaluating the project. You will see that not all elements are necessary for every project, but you will learn how to choose those that are right for yours.

The chapter will wrap up with some further things to think about once you have completed your plan.

A plan or a proposal?

It could be said that the main purpose of a proposal is to persuade somebody else to support a piece of work, whilst the primary function of a plan is to guide you through the project. In practice there is a high degree of overlap between the two. In fact, they are essentially the same thing, but written for different audiences. In this chapter we will cover elements of both plans and proposals, noting the differences as they arise. We use the term 'plan' throughout, but all of the points raised would also apply to a research proposal.

Why write a project plan?

Your project plan is exactly that – a plan. It outlines your aims and objectives; your justification for doing the work; how and when you intend to do it; the resources you will need; and what you expect to produce as a result of having completed the work. The process of planning requires you to focus your thoughts, to decide not only what you may wish to do, but also what is realistic, given the constraints of your work and life.

Importantly, the plan is the blueprint for your project. A well articulated plan can be referred to again and again, keeping you on track throughout the project and even occasionally reminding you of why you wanted to do the research in the first place.

Note that although I am occasionally using the term 'research plan', I might equally substitute 'evaluation plan' or 'audit' plan. In each case there is a need for clarity, order and a considered approach. Successful execution of any type of project relies on careful planning.

Writing for an audience

You will almost certainly need somebody's support in order to carry out your research. Your line manager, a potential funder, a course supervisor or your colleagues may each need persuading of the value of your project (see Chapter 13).

In making the case to your line manager you might stress the contribution that the project will make to the service and reassure them that the time spent on the project is justifiable; colleagues, on the other hand, might be motivated by the chance to inform practice, raise a personal profile, enhance a CV, perhaps even get published.

Any potential funder will expect you to respond to its needs, as outlined in the call for funding. They will want to know that the research area is worthy of funding, that you are capable of doing the work and that you will deliver it on time and within budget. They will also expect you to demonstrate some expertise in the area, either through your past experience or through the understanding that you show in your literature review.

If you are doing your research project as part of a course of study, such as a Master's degree or a Postgraduate Certificate in Education, there will probably be specific guidelines to follow. In your planning you will need to convince your supervisor that the project you propose is viable in the timescale and that you have the skills to undertake it.

Elements of your project plan

The 15 main elements of a research plan are listed below. Not all will be essential to every project and you may choose to present some elements in a different order. The content of each section will of course depend on the research question (see Chapter 3), the purpose of the plan and its audience. If you are creating the plan in response to a call for funding then elements of the plan such as section headings, word limits, layout, font sizes and so forth may all be specified for you and it is important that you are aware of and conform to the funder's exact requirements.

1. Title

The title of your project should be clear, accurate, concise and unambiguous. It should be indicative of both content and purpose. Your title will appear in a wide range of places, for example on reports, in presentations, on publicity materials and in the eventual dissemination of the results (see Chapter 12), so if possible try to make it short and memorable. This should not however be at the expense of clarity. You will want your project outputs to be found when people search using relevant key words, so make sure you use appropriate terminology.

An example of a clear and unambiguous title comes from Hannah Rose and Gillian Siddall, winners of the 2011 Library and Information Research Group (LIRG) Research Award:

> An investigation into the use of reading lists as a pedagogical tool to support the development of information skills amongst Foundation Degree students.
>
> Rose and Siddall, 2011, 1

An abridged version of Rose and Siddall's research proposal will be used as an example in a number of the sections below.

2. Abstract or summary

The abstract is a synopsis of the proposed project. It is important because it will be one of the first things that your audience will read. From it they will gain an overall impression of the project and of your ability to conduct it.

The abstract should be a succinct overview, never more than one page long. It should include the rationale for the work, its main objectives and the methods to be used for achieving these. If you are submitting your plan as part of an application for funding, you might also include a brief statement of why you or your organization is particularly suited to carry out the work.

It is often easier to write the abstract after you have written the rest of the research plan. By that stage you will be clearer in your mind about exactly what you hope to achieve and how best you might 'sell' the project to potential supporters.

3. Background, context or rationale

This is where you contextualize your research, evaluation or audit. You should set the scene here, referring briefly to relevant literature, policy, theory or practice, and explain how your proposed project will contribute to these. This is the section where you should describe why you wish to conduct the project, and why it is relevant, important and timely (Eve, 2008, 20). Not only does this section offer justification for the proposed work, it also demonstrates to the reader that you are aware of current developments in your field.

4. Aims and objectives

There should be a clear connection between the research question (see Chapter 3) and the aims and objectives.

The aim of a research project is usually a fairly general, high-level statement of what it is that you wish to explore, while the objectives are more specific or focused questions that will address different aspects of the aim.

Case study 4.1 Example of aims and objectives from Rose and Siddall, 2011, 2–3

The aim of Rose and Siddall's project was:

> To investigate the use of reading lists as a pedagogical tool to support the development of information skills of Foundation Degree students in Health and Education.

And their objectives were:

- to understand how level four foundation degree students use and respond to academic reading lists
- to assess academic staff perceptions of the use and value of reading lists
- to investigate whether the use of annotated reading lists can support the development of FD students' information skills.

In a project management context it is often stated that objectives should be 'SMART' i.e. specific, measurable, achievable, relevant (or realistic) and time-bound. These qualities are certainly desirable when setting research objectives, but in practice it may be difficult to frame them in this way. Much research is exploratory in nature and prone to throwing up new and interesting lines of enquiry. The findings of one part of a research project may fundamentally alter the direction of another part. Sometimes the research method itself will mitigate against the creation of SMART objectives. For example, an action research project requires the researcher to plan, take action, evaluate the results of that action and feed that knowledge into the next cycle of planning, action and evaluation. This cyclical approach does not lend itself to the setting of a specific and measurable objective.

For an audit or service evaluation, however, you may well be able to construct some SMART objectives. The existence of a predefined dataset and some standard criteria against which to assess those data should provide sufficient clarity to generate some SMART objectives.

5. Hypothesis (where appropriate)

For a more 'scientific' or experimental approach, you may choose to generate and test a hypothesis. A hypothesis is a statement of anticipated behaviour, and it is usually expressed in a 'null' form, for example:

> There is no relationship between the daily rate for library fines and the number of books returned late to the library.

You would then attempt to demonstrate that the null hypothesis is false, or specifically, that the likelihood of the null hypothesis being true is so low that it can be safely rejected.

Hypothesis testing usually involves a quantitative approach (see Chapter 8) and some statistical analysis, and so it is not suitable for all types of research, particularly qualitative studies (see Chapter 7). However, if you do intend to construct and test a hypothesis then you should include it in your plan.

6. Literature review

Do not take too narrow a view of 'literature'. In this context literature may comprise not only scholarly papers but also national, local or organizational policy documents, in-house reports and a range of other project-relevant documentation.

Pickard describes the purpose of the literature review as twofold, 'to acquaint you with current thinking in your subject area, and to find out about methods and research processes used by other researchers investigating this topic' (Pickard, 2013, 51 – see Chapter 6). Having completed the literature review you should be familiar with the key issues and theories from your subject area and be able to identify any gaps (McCaig and Dahlberg, 2010, 73). Unless you are undertaking a replication study, you will also have established that your proposed area of research has not already have been covered by another researcher.

The extent of your written review at this stage will depend on the audience for your plan or proposal and the nature of your project. The breadth and depth that you demonstrate, how much seminal or recent research you include, the number of significant themes and theories that you identify and the way you organize and synthesize the literature will all differ from one plan to another. Don't forget that the literature review at the planning stage is indicative rather than comprehensive and a more extensive review may follow when the project has received approval (see Chapter 6).

7. Research design and methods

In many respects, this section will be the heart of your research plan. Its purpose is to describe how you will answer the research question and achieve the project's aims and objectives. You should justify the decisions you have made with respect to the options available and the needs of the project. It should cover the following:

- **The overall approach to the research**. Sometimes referred to as the research methodology, this is the overarching framework within which your project rests. Your choice of approach will determine your theoretical perspective and all the assumptions that go with it. You might, like Rose and Siddall (2011), choose to take a 'mixed methods' approach, combining both qualitative and quantitative techniques (see Chapters 7 and 8 for more information about these).

- **Choice of research method, technique and tools**. Here you should describe the methods, techniques and if appropriate, tools that you intend to use to collect and analyse the data. Suitable methods might include desk research, surveys, interviews, case studies, observations and so forth. Corresponding data collection techniques are questionnaires, interview schedules and observation checklists. You should also list here the tools you intend to use for data collection and analysis (see Chapters 9 and 10). The information you give about how you will collect and analyse data must be sufficiently detailed for the reader to be convinced that the research objectives can be met.
- **Scope and boundaries**. This is where you set the limits to your research project. It is important to state both what you will do and what you will not do. Being realistic at the start will mean that there is less chance of expectations being unfulfilled later. A plan that is too ambitious and difficult to achieve is more likely to fail (Dawson, 2009, 64) and therefore less likely to receive support in the first place.
- **Sampling**. If appropriate, you should describe your sampling plan, the number of participants or observations you will make, and whether you will be able to generalize from your sample group to the full population (see Chapter 8).
- **Research data management**. Many funders, especially those responsible for distributing public monies, now expect researchers to re-use existing datasets if possible and, correspondingly, to make their own data openly available. This places far greater responsibility on researchers to be systematic in the management of their data. A data management plan, outlining how you intend to collect, process, store, document and provide access to your data, would be a useful addition to your research plan. For a prospective funder it would indicate a commitment to good research practice; to your research team it will be a useful practical guide.

8. Ethical issues

If you plan to involve either people or animals in your research then you will almost certainly need to seek ethical approval for your work. Even if you don't, you should be aware of any potential ethical issues and know the steps that you will take to overcome these (see Chapter 5).

For the purposes of the research plan you should show an awareness of any relevant organizational, professional or legal guidelines. You should describe the main ethical issues likely to arise from your project and indicate how you intend to handle these, e.g. by observing anonymity and confidentiality.

You should indicate whether ethical approval has already been sought or obtained, and if not, this must be built into the project timetable.

9. Project timetable

Having described how you intend to complete your research project, you now need to pin it down to a realistic and achievable timescale. If you are applying for external funding then the funding period may be predetermined and it will be incumbent upon you to fit within this. Even if you are running a modest in-house project there may well be constraints on the timing of your project, for example limiting your research to when key service users are available or when service changes are implemented.

To determine the overall time span of your project you need to work out how long each part of the project is likely to take, whether any activity depends on the completion of another and whether tasks can be done concurrently. So, for example, it may be possible to transcribe earlier interviews in between conducting the later interviews (so that the two activities are concurrent or parallel) but data analysis cannot be started until data collection is complete (thus these tasks are sequential). With this information you will be able to calculate the minimum time you need to complete your project. A task list that demonstrates this is shown in Table 4.1.

As mentioned above, if your research method relies on emergent theory, such as in the case of action research or grounded theory (O'Leary, 2010, 101), then it may be difficult to define the task list. You should still, however, try to give yourself time limits for the different iterations of your research, or else you risk losing control of the timeline and failing to complete the project.

It can be helpful to present the project timeline in diagrammatic form, for example using a Gantt chart (see Figure 4.1).

A Gantt chart shows each activity in the project as a time-bounded line or bar, enabling you to see at a glance which tasks should be done when in order to complete the project on schedule. It can be helpful at this stage to identify milestones, or particularly important completion points. For example, in order that potential interviewees are still available you may need to ensure that the design of your final interview schedule is completed by a specific date.

Table 4.1 *Simplified task list for a short research project*

	Task	Earliest start date (week)	Duration (weeks)	Parallel or sequential	Dependent upon
A	Literature review	1	12	Parallel	–
B	Develop interview schedule	2	2	Sequential	–
C	Conduct pilot interviews	4	1	Sequential	B
D	Finalize interview schedule	5	1	Sequential	C
E	Select participants	4	2	Parallel	–
F	Conduct interviews	6	3	Sequential	D, E
G	Transcribe interviews	7	4	Parallel	F
H	Analyse transcriptions	11	2	Sequential	G
I	Write up research	13	4	Parallel	A, H

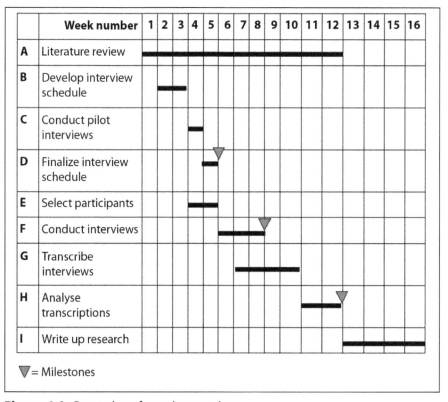

Figure 4.1 *Gantt chart for a short project*

The Gantt chart will enable you to identify the shortest completion time for your project (the 'critical path'), help you to monitor your progress and prompt you to take action when the timetable slips.

You might choose to build in some contingency time for your project: for example, to allow for ethical approval or data collection taking longer than planned or for consideration of new information thrown up by data analysis (Wilkinson, 2000, 21). These and other factors may be the subject of your risk assessment (see below).

10. Deliverables, outputs and outcomes

Your project deliverables represent your commitment to yourself and others. They mark the end point of your research and articulate its impact on your institution, academia and society.

A list of project deliverables enables your audience to judge whether your project will supply what they need and may be crucial to gaining support for the work. However, do not promise more than you are able to deliver (Annersten and Wredling, 2006, 102).

Deliverables fall into two broad categories: outputs and outcomes. Examples of outputs from the short project described above might include '50 library users interviewed' or 'one conference paper'. Outputs typically are discrete entities that are tangible and measurable. Outcomes, on the other hand, are the results or consequences of the project and may be harder to pin down. Sometimes outcomes are unintended or unexpected. Outcomes arising from the short project might include 'greater staff awareness of users' attitudes towards the library', or 'improvements in services for library users'. The outcomes best describe the difference that the project will make.

Rose and Siddall (2011) were able to identify both outputs and outcomes. For example, one planned output was new reading lists for level four foundation degree students in health and education that would scaffold the development of their skills and confidence in accessing, retrieving and using information. An anticipated outcome was a change in tutors' perceptions of reading lists following their involvement in the study.

Depending on the nature of your research project, you might wish to include a dissemination plan here. This will describe how you intend to disseminate the findings of your work and is particularly important if the intended audience for your work lies beyond your own organization. Chapter 12 makes a number of suggestions about disseminating your research.

11. Risk assessment

Every project contains an element of risk. Timescales, project management, resources availability, technology, the research environment – any of these may be subject to an unplanned occurrence and therefore to risk.

When planning a research project, therefore, researchers must ask themselves a number of questions:

- What risks might prevent a successful outcome to the project?
- What is the probability of each risk occurring?
- What would be the impact on the project if a risk occurred?
- How will a risk be managed?

Options for managing risks include accepting the consequences of the risk; transferring the risk (e.g. to an insurer); reducing it (e.g. by taking regular back-ups of your data); or avoiding it.

A table of risks is a useful tool. In this, each risk is outlined and a score is given for its likelihood and severity. By multiplying the two scores you can gauge how important each potential risk is to your project and therefore plan appropriate mitigating action. An example of a risk table is given in Table 4.2.

Table 4.2 *Risk management in a project*

Risk	Probability (P) 1 = low 5 = high	Severity (S) 1 = low 5 = high	Risk score (P x S)	Mitigation
Data are lost due to computer failure	3	5	15	Ensure data are backed up securely at the end of each day. Keep copies of data on multiple (secure) storage devices.
Project is not completed on time	3	3	9	Build in extra time at key stages of the project. Monitor progress against the project Gantt chart. Seek additional resources if slippage threatens final completion date.
Project costs exceed budget	1	5	5	Build in contingency funds. Monitor costs throughout project. Consider making savings in non-essential activities.
Recording device fails during interview	2	2	4	Test device beforehand. Use two recording devices for each interview. Take notes.

It is strongly recommended that having drawn up your risk table you then seek a second opinion from a colleague. Another person may identify some risks that you have missed or suggest alternative mitigating action.

12. Resources and costs

The resources required for a project can range from one researcher with a PC to a multinational research team and a wide range of expensive equipment.

If you intend to involve other researchers, you should consider which staff you will need (based on their skill set, experience and availability), when you will need them and for how long. For larger projects, a research team will ideally comprise individuals with a blend of skills and experience, but for smaller projects it may be necessary to bring in consultants or work with partners to have access to the skills you need. The budget therefore could include any or all of the following:

- staff costs (sometimes included as 'direct' costs, e.g. salaries or hourly wages)
- overhead costs (or 'indirect' costs, including staff benefits, facilities and administrative costs – these are often calculated as a percentage of direct costs)
- consultancy or professional fees (e.g. for transcription, training, leading focus groups)
- equipment (including purchase and hire of specialist equipment)
- hardware and software (e.g. for data analysis)
- materials (e.g. printing costs and other consumables)
- travel and expenses (e.g. to attend project meetings, interview participants, present at conferences, visit other libraries)
- publication costs (e.g. to self publish a project report or to cover 'author pays' charges to a commercial publisher)
- marketing and promotion costs (e.g. to attract participants, provide incentives to encourage participation, disseminate findings)
- training.

If several organizations are collaborating on a research project then the budget should clearly allocate costs to those responsible for the work. A funder will often choose to give funding to the lead institution and let them reallocate funds to the rest of the project partners through a form of partnership or subcontracting agreement (Anderson and Garg, 2001, 411).

It is becoming increasingly common for funders to expect organizations to make a contribution to the cost of a research project (this is often referred to as 'matched funding'). If your funder requires this then you should state the proportion of funding that you are bringing to the project.

Even if your project is a small, in-house piece of research, producing a budget will show your line manager that you are aware of the financial and resource implications of spending time on this work. It may also help your case to show that a relatively small investment may result in a significant outcome for the organization.

13. Project evaluation

One way of evaluating the success of a project is to define formal success criteria. These may be expressed in terms of the research aims and objectives, the research process, or the achievement of deliverables. So, for example, Rose and Siddall (2011) might have defined the following success criteria:

- Academic staff are actively engaged in debate over pedagogic value of reading lists.
- Foundation Degree students have greater confidence in accessing information.
- Project deadlines are met.

Corresponding measures of success for these could be the number of staff interviewed, the range and quality of suggestions for improving reading lists, the uptake of annotated reading lists, the effect on student assignment grades and the number of project milestones reached on time.

The project plan should indicate how, when and by whom the success of the project will be measured. The evaluation process may be formative (i.e. ongoing throughout the project with the purpose of informing the research process) or summative (i.e. taking place at the end of the project and assessing project outcomes).

A reflective approach to evaluation (asking questions such as 'What went well?', 'What could have been done differently?' or 'What can others learn from the project?') might lead into a discussion of areas for future investigation and may spark an idea for your next research project, audit or evaluation.

14. References

Any documents, websites, or other resources referred to in the proposal must be correctly referenced. If your prospective funder, course tutor or employer has a preferred referencing style then follow that, otherwise choose an appropriate style with which you feel comfortable and be consistent in following it.

15. Appendices

Never use an appendix to circumvent the page limit to your main research proposal (Rawl, in Groves et al., 2011, 8); at best the appendix will be ignored and at worst it may result in the proposal being rejected out of hand. However, if permitted, an appendix may be used for supplementary information, for example a copy of a questionnaire or an interview schedule, or for other supporting documentation.

Further considerations

Irrespective of its content, there are a few things you can do to make sure your research plan is as effective as possible:

- Keep your language straightforward and direct. Try to be concise and to the point. Short sentences are good. Avoid waffling.
- Develop your ideas clearly and logically. This will help the reader understand not only what you wish to do, but why.
- Use 'signposts' such as headings and linking sentences between sections to emphasize the flow through the plan.
- Make sure your facts are accurate and that you have covered all necessary points.
- Emphasize key points, not details.
- Check for typographical errors and spelling mistakes – do not rely on your computer's spell-checker, since it cannot distinguish between words with different meanings (such as 'there' and 'their').
- Avoid jargon. Assume your audience are non-expert and may not be familiar with your subject matter.
- Avoid the use of too many acronyms, but where unavoidable, write them in full the first time you use them.
- Avoid repetition.
- Make use of figures and illustrations. A picture can sometimes convey

more information than a lengthy block of text.

- Pay attention to the presentation of your plan. A clear and tidy plan suggests a clear and tidy approach to work. A messy plan will not only be more difficult for the reader to follow; it may also be taken to indicate sloppiness and lack of rigour in research.

(Based on O'Leary (2010), 67)

Evaluating your project plan

Having followed all the steps listed above, you are sure to have produced the perfect research plan. Or have you? The research planning tick sheet in Figure 4.2 at the end of this chapter may help you here. It is always worth re-reading your plan, at the very least, to check for continuity, typographical errors and spelling mistakes.

If possible, ask a colleague to take a look at your research plan. A fresh set of eyes may well spot inconsistencies or notice important omissions. Do not be afraid to receive constructive criticism; remember its purpose is to improve your research plan and the likelihood of a successful outcome to your project.

Finally, take time to reflect on the overall plan. Ultimately, will the planned project meet its aims and objectives and answer the research question?

Summary

In this chapter we have considered why it is important to have a research plan and how the plan must be adjusted to meet the needs of different audiences. Each element of the plan has been considered in some detail, although it has been recognized that not every element is essential for every research project.

Points for reflection

Consider a possible project that you would like to undertake:

- Do you need to develop a *plan* or a *proposal*? How will this affect how you write this document?
- Produce a list of activities for your planned project. Which tasks are dependent on others? Create a Gantt chart showing the timeline for your project.

Evaluate a plan/proposal of your own using the research planning tick sheet (Figure 4.2 below). Ideally you should be able to answer yes to every question posed. If not, consider how you might strengthen that section of your plan/proposal.

Can you answer 'Yes' to the following questions?			
1 2 3	Title	Is the title clear and unambiguous? Does it accurately reflect the content? Is it concise?	Y/N Y/N Y/N
4 5 6 7	Abstract or summary	Is the abstract a succinct overview? Does it state the purpose of the project and the method(s) to be used? Will it 'sell' the project to the reader? Is it less than one page long?	Y/N Y/N Y/N Y/N
8 9 10	Background, context or rationale	Have you demonstrated your awareness of relevant literature, policy, theory or practice? Have you explained how your project will contribute to literature, policy, theory or practice? Will the reader be convinced that your project is relevant, important and timely?	Y/N Y/N Y/N
11 12 13 14	Aim and objectives	Do the aim and objectives support your research question? Does the aim comprise a high level statement about what you wish to explore? Are the objectives specific and focused? If possible, are your objectives SMART?	Y/N Y/N Y/N Y/N
15 16 17	Hypothesis	If you are testing a hypothesis: Have you stated both the research and the null hypotheses? Are you confident that you will be able to conduct the necessary statistical analysis to test the hypothesis?	 Y/N Y/N
18 19 20 21 22	Literature review	Have you examined a range of relevant literature (e.g. scholarly, policy, in-house)? Have you demonstrated that you are aware of key themes, theories, methods and issues relevant to your project? Have you presented an appropriate selection of literature? Have you identified any gaps in the literature that your project might fill? Is your literature review well structured and clearly written (e.g. starting with a broad overview and then narrowing down to your topic)?	Y/N Y/N Y/N Y/N Y/N
23 24 25 26 27	Research design and methods	Are your research design and methods consistent with the aim and objectives of your research? Have you described and justified your methodology and choice of method? Have you defined the scope and boundaries of your project? Have you stated how many participants will be involved and how you plan to select these? Have you included a data management plan?	Y/N Y/N Y/N Y/N Y/N

Figure 4.2 *Research planning tick sheet*

28	Ethical issues	Have you described the main ethical issues in your project and explained how you will deal with these?	Y/N
29		Have you demonstrated your awareness of any organizational or professional ethical guidelines?	Y/N
30		Have you either obtained ethical approval or allowed time for this in your project plan?	Y/N
31	Project timetable	Do you know how long your project will take?	Y/N
32		Are you sure you are not being over-ambitious?	Y/N
33		Have you made allowance for any constraints on time (e.g. availability of resources or participants)?	Y/N
34		Have you included a Gantt chart?	Y/N
35		Have you identified key milestones?	Y/N
36		Have you allowed for contingency time in your project?	Y/N
37	Deliverables	Have you listed all deliverables – including both outputs and outcomes?	Y/N
38		Have you considered your stakeholders' requirements when specifying your deliverables?	Y/N
39		Have you included a dissemination plan?	Y/N
40	Risk assessment	Are you aware of all the risks to the successful outcome of your project?	Y/N
41		Have you estimated the likelihood and impact of each risk occurring?	Y/N
42		Have you stated how you will manage each known risk?	Y/N
43		Have you sought a second opinion on your risk assessment?	Y/N
44	Resources and costs	Does your research team comprise individuals with an appropriate range of skills and expertise?	Y/N
45		Have you agreed (in writing) an appropriate division of costs between all project partners?	Y/N
46		Have you estimated both direct and indirect staff costs?	Y/N
47			Y/N
48		Have you included consultancy and professional fees?	Y/N
49		Have you included the cost of additional equipment, hardware and software?	Y/N
50		Have you included the cost of consumables, incentives, project promotion and publication?	Y/N
51		Have you estimated the full cost of travel and related expenses for yourself and your research team?	Y/N
		Have you included the cost of any necessary training?	Y/N
52	Project evaluation	Have you defined success criteria for your project?	Y/N
53		Do you have clear measures for evaluating your project against the success criteria?	Y/N
54		Have you stated who will be responsible for project evaluation?	Y/N
55	References	Are all documents, websites and other resources fully and accurately cited and referenced?	Y/N
56		Have you followed your funder's or institution's preferred referencing style?	Y/N
57	Appendices	Are appendices permitted?	Y/N
58		Are all your appendices necessary?	Y/N
59		Is it clear why you have included each appendix?	Y/N

Figure 4.2 *Continued*

60	Presentation	Is your writing style clear, concise and to the point?	Y/N
61		Does your plan have a logical flow?	Y/N
62		Have you used appropriate headings and other signposts to help the reader?	Y/N
63		Have you avoided acronyms and jargon?	Y/N
64		Have you checked for typographical and spelling errors?	Y/N
65		Are figures and illustrations used appropriately and referred to in the text?	Y/N
66		Does your plan look tidy and well ordered?	Y/N
67		Have you removed all non-essential text?	Y/N
68		Are you within any externally imposed page or word limits?	Y/N
69	Other	Have you written your plan with the appropriate audience(s) in mind?	Y/N
70		If responding to a call for projects, have you read the guidelines carefully and fulfilled all the requirements of the call?	Y/N
71		If responding to a call for projects, have you made it as easy as possible for the reviewer to assess your proposal?	Y/N
72		Have you asked a critical friend to read your research plan and give feedback?	Y/N
73		Will the reader be convinced that you have the skills, knowledge and experience to successfully complete the project?	Y/N

Figure 4.2 *Continued*

References

Anderson, G. L. and Garg, D. P. (2001) Suggestions for Skilful Proposal Writing, *Journal of Intelligent Material Systems and Material Structures*, **12**, 409–14.

Annersten, M. and Wredling, R. (2006) How to Write a Research Proposal, *European Diabetes Nursing*, **3** (2), 102–5.

Dawson, C. (2009) *Introduction to Research Methods: a practical guide for anyone undertaking a research project*, 4th edn, How To Books, Oxford.

Eve, J. (2008) Writing a Research Proposal: planning and communicating your research ideas effectively, *Library and Information Research*, **32** (102), 18–28.

Groves, P. S., Rawl, S. M., Wurzbach, M. E., Fahrenwald, N., Cohen, M. Z., McCarthy Beckett, D. O., Zerwic, J., Given, B., Algase, D. L., Alexander, G. L. and Conn, V. (2011) Secrets of Successful Short Grant Applications, *Western Journal of Nursing Research*, **34** (1), 6–23.

LIRGweb, *LIRG Research Award*, http://sites.google.com/site/lirgweb/home/awards/lirg-research-award.

McCaig, C. and Dahlberg, L. (2010) Writing a Research Proposal or Brief. In Dahlberg, L. and McCaig, C. (eds), *Practical Research and Evaluation: a start-to-finish guide for practitioners*, Sage Publications, London, 59–75.

O'Leary, Z. (2010) *The Essential Guide to Doing Your Research Project*, 2nd edn, Sage Publications, London.

Pickard, A. J. (2013) *Research Methods in Information*, 2nd edn, Facet Publishing, London.

Rose, H. and Siddall, G. (2011) *Research Proposal: LIRG research award*, unpublished.

Wilkinson, D. (2000) Planning the Research. In Wilkinson, D. (ed.), *The Researcher's Toolkit: the complete guide to practitioner research*, Routledge Falmer, London, 15–23.

Recommended further reading

For general advice on writing research plans and proposals

Dawson, C. (2009) *Introduction to Research Methods: a practical guide for anyone undertaking a research project*, 4th edn, Oxford, How To Books.

Pickard, A. J. (2013) *Research Methods in Information,* 2nd edn, Facet Publishing, London.

Research Councils UK. *RCUK Common Principles on Data Policy,* www.rcuk.ac.uk/research/Pages/DataPolicy.aspx.

For the research funder's viewpoint:

Anderson, G. L. and Garg, D. P. (2001) Suggestions for Skilful Proposal Writing, *Journal of Intelligent Material Systems and Material Structures*, **12**, 409–14.

Booth, A. (2000) Research, *Health Libraries Review*, **17** (3), 173–5.

Grove, L. K. (2004) Writing Winning Proposals for Research Funds, *Technical Communication*, **51** (1), 25–35.

Groves, P. S., Rawl, S. M., Wurzbach, M. E., Fahrenwald, N., Cohen, M. Z., McCarthy Beckett, D. O., Zerwic, J., Given, B., Algase, D. L., Alexander, G. L. and Conn, V. (2011) Secrets of Successful Short Grant Applications, *Western Journal of Nursing Research*, **34** (1), 6–23.

Project management

In addition to standard texts on the subject, a number of websites offer tools and advice to support project management, for example:

Mind Tools, www.mindtools.com.
Business Balls, www.businessballs.com.
Bizhelp24, www.bizhelp24.com.

5

Ethics and best practice

Elizabeth Buchanan and Stuart Ferguson

'I'm only doing a local project.'

'What kinds of ethics are there?'

'Ethics only apply to health projects, right?'

Ethical practice in research is about doing what is possible, while protecting the stakeholders involved in the process (see Chapter 13). Accepted practice prevents researchers from engaging in data collection before receiving ethical approval but the process by which this approval is obtained will vary, depending on your local circumstances. Your own organization may invest responsibility for ethics review in a specific individual, such as a senior or research and development manager, while universities and research centres have formal ethics panels. Some organizations may operate a system of 'gatekeepers', with formal ethics boards only handling 'high-risk' applications and referrals from 'lower' gatekeepers such as departmental ethics committees or individual delegates, e.g. research students' supervisors.

Even if your proposal doesn't need to go through a local ethical approval process, it is important that it reaches a comparable standard. There must be a clear idea of research purpose (see Chapters 3 and 4), a body of relevant research to draw from (what we know already – see Chapter 6), specified research methods to be used (see Chapters 7 and 8), appropriate research processes and techniques, and a sound prediction of the foreseeable risks and benefits.

Throughout this chapter, we will call attention to the many and various ethical challenges that may face you as a researcher.

Why are ethics important?

Actual physical and psychological harms to research participants have been well documented over the years, and are of course to be avoided, but less horrific instances of unethical research are often overlooked. Ethical misconduct can take many forms, ranging from plagiarism, fabrication or falsification of data, misrepresentation of findings, to collaborator disputes and errors of judgment.

Ethics are about what is 'right' or 'wrong' in a given condition, and they are about behaviours and conduct. Robust ethical research practices make for sound, valid and reliable research. Your disciplinary or professional peers must trust your research and, as a researcher, you are responsible for the ethics of your actions and decisions.

Risks/harms and benefits

Harm, in and of itself, to participants can be defined as not only physical, bodily harms, but also informational or reputational harms. Research regulations are in place to guide the research process in most countries and are informed by universal principles of beneficence, respect for persons, justice, and research merit and integrity.

Beneficence

This refers to the idea that we maximize benefits while minimizing the risk of harm (Lawal, 2009). It is important therefore that you consider the outcomes and are able to articulate the potential benefits of your project to the reviewers of your proposal and, if applicable, to the participants in your project. Have you considered the welfare of the participants? Is any risk to participants acceptably low?

Respect

Does your research respect your participants' right to anonymity and confidentiality? If there are risks, how are they managed? These risks might relate not only to your study participants but your own personal safety as a researcher.

Justice

Related to beneficence, are there are any benefits to participants in your project and, if so, are they distributed fairly among them? Is there an unfair burden for specific individuals or groups? Is the recruitment process fair? Is there potential for any participants to be exploited? Is there an existing relationship between the researcher and any of the participants and, if so, are there any issues of power or dependency?

Research merit and integrity

Merit may not immediately seem like an ethical issue, but if the proposed project simply revisits old research, what is the justification for asking participants to replicate the study? In relation to research integrity, are there any potential conflicts of interest (see Case study 5.1.)? Will there be an opportunity for participants to review their contribution to the research before it is published? Will the research findings be disseminated in ways that allow for public scrutiny?

Case study 5.1 Researcher objectivity

Edmondson, R. (2011) *National Film and Sound Archive: the quest for identity: factors shaping the uneven development of a cultural institution* (PhD thesis), University of Canberra,
www.canberra.edu.au/researchrepository/items/b433f19b-0f56-351a-c914-5aa319fb1300/1/.

Background:
This study traces the evolution of the National Film and Sound Archive of Australia (NFSA) from 1935, as an entity within the then Commonwealth National Library, to 2008, when it finally gained independent statutory status. It examines the Archive's critical transition points: emergence within the National Library; demerger from the Library in 1984 to become a distinct institution within a government portfolio; 'repositioning' and 'rebranding' as ScreenSound Australia in 1999; merger with the Australian Film Commission in 2003; demerger and gaining of statutory status in 2008.

Research questions:
What were the historical factors that made the emergence of the NFSA so erratic and protracted? What were the effects and risks and how were they dealt with? What were the broader consequences? What lessons may be learned?

Research design:

The project is a historical study with an interpretivist perspective. It draws on a range of written and audio-visual qualitative evidence: published documents such as annual reports; contemporary publications such as media articles (the institution as others see it); the unpublished record, such as correspondence; personal recollections, such as oral histories; and existing literature. In addition, new oral history interviews were recorded as part of the project, in an effort to capture recollections and mature reflections of players in the events before these are lost. The chapter in which the interviews were analysed was sent, in draft, to each interviewee and feedback was incorporated into the final text of the chapter or, if appropriate, elsewhere in the thesis. ▥

Issues of objectivity and subjectivity were a key consideration in this case study given the researcher's former role as Director of the NFSA. Early in the project, the researcher recorded some reflections on his role in the NFSA's story and, on the project's completion, he reviewed the journey, revisited his original assumptions and reflected on how the journey had affected his interpretation of events. The researcher also concluded that the objectivity of interviewees could be maximized if a knowledgeable third party conducted interviews. This decision was based on the belief that the interviewees would be less constrained in their comments and afforded greater freedom to comment on the role of the former Director as well as others within the NFSA.

The universal principles of beneficence, respect for persons, justice, and research merit and integrity are at the core of ethical research and exemplified by the following areas.

Participant selection and consent

Depending on the research regulatory framework of a given country, before data can be gathered from individuals, you will be required to obtain informed consent from potential participants. For consent to be informed you must give participants enough information to make a decision (for instance, have the potential benefits and risks been explained to them), the participants must be capable of giving consent (see Case study 5.2 below) and have free choice (which can be a problem if you are perceived to have some authority over your participants, as seen in Case study 5.1). If there is a pre-existing relationship that could affect the research, participation and/or consent, then how will it be managed? It is critical that you know what research regulations apply in your specific setting to determine if and under what conditions consent is required, if documentation of consent is required, or under what conditions consent can be waived.

Case study 5.2 Participant consent

Nielsen B. and Borlund P. (2011) Information Literacy Learning and the Public Library: a study of Danish high school students, *Journal of Librarianship and Information Science*, **43** (2), 106–19.

Aims and objectives:

This is a study of high school students' perceptions of the public library's role in learning. It seeks to identify how they perceive learning and user education in the public library, how they perceive information literacy and their own use of information and which competencies they wish public librarians to have.

Research design:

The present study is based on a phenomenographic research approach in which data collection has as its aim to collect information about how people understand or perceive certain phenomena rather than making statements about what these phenomena are. A semi-structured interview guide was designed for data collection.

The sample used in a phenomenographic study is purposive instead of randomly chosen. In this case high school students were recruited as test participants in collaboration with the teachers. This was done to ensure that as many viewpointsias possible were adequately represented within this group. As a result the study's participants are eight girls and four boys from the age 15 to 20 and studying at the first to third levels.

Interviews were transcribed word-by-word and analysed to resolve the various ways in which the high school students perceived the topics. The analysis consists of a number of consecutive readings of the interviews until a limited number of 'categories of description' can be resolved. The categories of descriptions are constructs that build on statements from one or more high school students. ▨

In this case study, the main ethical issues revolve around participant consent. Legal compliance will vary from country to country but, generally speaking, in the case of the younger students, parental consent would normally be required. The older students would be considered capable of giving consent for themselves and their signed consent would therefore be a requirement. It is likely, however, that the researchers would give a consent form to the younger students, as well as to their parents, on the principle that students in their mid-teens are considered more autonomous and capable of giving consent than, for instance, primary school students.

Since participant selection is purposive, that is, participants are selected based on the contribution they can make to your research question (see Chapter 7), it would need both to *be* fair and to be *seen* to be fair. It would also need to be clear to parents and students that there would be no consequences should the students decline to take part. In any communication with students and parents, researchers need to assure them that students are free to withdraw from the interviews, should they change their minds about participating, again without penalty. This latter point is slightly problematic in a school, in that students may feel an unequal power relationship with teachers (although, in this case, this is mitigated by the fact that the researchers themselves are external to the school).

The processes used to identify potential participants are important (see Chapter 7). If it is considered necessary to 'screen' or assess the suitability of potential participants then will this be a transparent process? Would it disadvantage a potential participant in any way if it became known by others that he/she had been recruited to, participated in or was excluded from the project? If participants are to be free to withdraw from the study, even after giving consent (which is ethically desirable), are there any consequences of which they should be made aware, before giving consent?

As a researcher you should only approach individuals to participate in your study once ethical approval is obtained. You are possibly already familiar with the systems in your own organization but if your project is due to take place in another organization, the first step in recruiting participants would be to contact the relevant 'gatekeeper' in the organization, such as a senior manager. Typically, the gatekeeper will assist in selection by putting you in contact with specific individuals, teams and/or sections. You may identify other potential participants in the course of the project, in which case you should liaise with the gatekeeper of the host organization to ensure that all ethical considerations regarding the inclusion of additional participants are respected (see below). Depending on the research, it may be necessary to seek ethical approval from the host organization in addition to gaining participant consent.

Anonymity and confidentiality

Anonymity and confidentiality are closely related but not synonymous (see Table 5.1). When undertaking a project, measures are needed to ensure that participant confidentiality is respected and their identities are disguised as much as possible. In Case Study 5.1 above, interviewees were each assigned a random code letter and the complete list of interviewees was known only to the researcher, his supervisors and the interviewer. Confidentiality should also be observed when writing up and disseminating your project findings. It is not, however, possible to always assure confidentiality. For instance, in an organization or a small research population, it may be relatively easy for an informed reader to identify key players. Researchers must minimize the risks to those individuals and ensure that they understand the potential risks of participating.

Table 5.1 *What is the difference between confidentiality and anonymity? (Virginia Polytechnic Institute and State University, 2013)*	
Confidentiality	Anonymity
Maintaining confidentiality of information collected from research participants means that only the investigator(s) or individuals of the research team can identify the responses of individual subjects; however, the researchers must make every effort to prevent anyone outside the project from connecting individual subjects with their responses.	Providing anonymity of information collected from research participants means that either the project does not collect identifying information of individual subjects (e.g. name, address, e-mail address), or the project cannot link individual responses with participants' identities. A study should not collect identifying information of research participants unless it is essential to the study protocol.

Anonymity is a different matter. Clearly participants are not anonymous to you, the researcher, and in some forms of research the identities of participants may be obviously known to other participants e.g. in the case of focus groups where members of a specific group can identify the others present. Thus, expectations of and terms to protect confidentiality need to be spelled out to participants in advance.

The extent to which it is possible to anonymize data has been debated in the literature, with some suggesting that:

> The utility and privacy of data are linked, and so long as data is useful, even in the slightest, then it is also potentially reidentifiable. Ohm, 2010

When seeking ethical approval the emphasis is therefore on who will have access to the information, and how the information will be shared, stored, and deleted.

Storage of data

Over the past few years, organizations have been coming to terms with the fact that research data need to be stored in a systematic way, ideally in well organized data repositories. Practice varies considerably, with some institutions leaving it to individual researchers or supervisors, in the case of research students, to store the data. However, many institutions have developed institutional repositories that showcase research outputs such as publications, and some have now turned their attention to research repositories that store the research data (Digital Curation Centre, 2013).

Organizations increasingly have policies pertaining to the retention or deletion of data for a predefined period and, as with the repositories, metadata are required that specify who has access to the data, how long they are to be retained and what is to happen to them at the end of the retention period. Disposal could mean destruction but, with the agreement of researchers and participants, it could mean retention in an archive, quite possibly in another institution. One of the drivers behind repository development is the notion that much research is publicly funded and some research data may be re-usable by other researchers.

Data needs to be stored securely, in such a way that those with the authority to do so can access them, but no one else. It is notable that the Office for Human Research Protections in the United States reports that theft of devices, e.g. laptops and tablets, are the breaches of data security most commonly reported by researchers, investigators and ethics boards. With this in mind, you need to make arrangements for electronic data to be stored and password protected, preferably on a network server. Where physical objects, such as paper-based transcripts, are retained, they need to be securely locked away. In all cases, your policy on data storage should be clearly stated in your project plan (see Chapter 4) and in communications with your prospective participants.

Informed consent and participant information sheets

When research involves people, it is good research practice to produce well designed consent forms and participant information sheets. These help to protect all parties – participants, researchers and participating institutions – and ensure that they are well informed. Providing participant information sheets in advance means that potential participants or those signing consent forms on behalf of participants (such as the parents in Case study 5.2) have a clear idea of what is involved and are all receiving the same information.

Information commonly provided includes – but is not necessarily limited to – the following:

- title of the research project
- names and contact details of the researchers
- purpose of the research
- the conduct or methodology of the research
- what participation will involve (including time commitment)
- confidentiality and security of research data
- details of the body/bodies providing ethics clearance
- a contact for queries and concerns
- other details where necessary, such as a counsellor who can help.

It is also strongly recommended that you:

- **Use plain English** – as in any such document, speak to your audience! Typically, ethics boards ask researchers to write in a manner that an 11-year-old can understand. An easy way for reviewers of research to approach the evaluation of research is to read the informed consent sheet first. This would be the subject or participant's first exposure to the research, and so it should be clear, readable, and succinct.
- **Keep it brief** (one sheet, if possible) – don't expect participants to read an essay!

A consent form could be expected to contain the following information:

- title of the research project
- a consent statement
- an indication, where appropriate, of the parts of the project to which the signatory consents
- space for participant's name, the name of the signatory (if not the participant), an appropriate signature and date
- space in which the participant may insert an address in the event of wishing to have something forwarded, such as an interview transcript or final research report.

Keep the consent form, like the participant information sheet, concise and to the point. The consent statement would normally include an acknowledge-ment that the signatory had read and understood the information about the research, has had any queries answered to his/her satisfaction and agrees to participation in the project. Significantly, the signatory may agree to only partial participation. For example, participants may agree to be interviewed but not to being observed (Cooper and Urquhart, 2005). Similarly, some may agree to being interviewed but not to being digitally recorded. Consent forms should not request personal details such as age, gender, and so on.

You may also find that you need to design more than one consent form, particularly in cases in which there are different categories of participant.

Publishing research

In seeking to extend the knowledge base, the publication of your project findings, being open to public scrutiny and contributing to further research, should be considered an ethical imperative. It may also be that public money has funded your project and therefore the wider community has a right to access to the findings. Chapters 11 and 12 discuss issues around writing up and disseminating your project findings in more detail. From an ethical perspective, acknowledging the origins of your data (in the case of both secondary sources and the research itself) and the ownership of research findings are key considerations.

Legislation

As a researcher, you need to be aware of both your ethical and legal responsibilities and rights. Certainly some of the ethical requirements at a national level are enshrined in legislation: for example, discrimination in research is not permissible, ethically or legally. Second, some legislation overrides ethical considerations, e.g. someone going into a children's library or school library may be required to complete police or background checks in some countries. There is a degree of overlap between the legal requirements across the European Union, with strong data protection regimes, which strengthen the need for strict attention to confidentiality and data security.

Summary

Research is a process; it is iterative and cumulative. Ethical issues can arise at any given point in the process. It is a researcher's responsibility to be equipped to prepare for and manage ethical challenges, and embrace ethical possibilities. When we engage in research, we are taking the public trust into our hands, minds and laboratories. It is a privilege to be a researcher, and we must not betray the public trust with unethical research.

Points for reflection

- Think of some research about which you read recently or which was reported in a conference you attended. Can you think of ways in which participants could potentially receive 'harm'? If so, how would you minimize the risk?
- If you have recently or are currently developing a project proposal, what ethical considerations have you incorporated into your project? Having read this chapter what, if anything, would you change in your proposal?
- What sources would you turn to in order to ensure ethical behaviour? Are there national guidelines? Are there ethics gatekeepers in your own organization to whom you could turn for guidance?

References

Cooper, J. and Urquhart, C. (2005) The Information Needs and Information-Seeking Behaviours of Home-Care Workers and Clients Receiving Home Care, *Health Information and Libraries Journal*, **22** (2), 107–16.

Digital Curation Centre (2013) *Research Data Management*, www.dcc.ac.uk/news/research-data-management.

Edmondson, R. (2011) *National Film and Sound Archive: the quest for identity: factors shaping the uneven development of a cultural institution*, PhD thesis, University of Canberra, www.canberra.edu.au/researchrepository/file/b433f19b-0f56-351a-c914-5aa319fb1300/1/introductory_pages.pdf.

Lawal, I. O. (2009) *Library and Information Science Research in the 21st Century: a guide for practising librarians and students*, Chandos Publishing, Oxford.

Nielsen, B. and Borlund, P. (2011) Information Literacy, Learning, and the Public Library: a study of Danish high school students, *Journal of Librarianship and Information Science*, **43** (2), 106–19.

Ohm, P. (2010) Broken Promises of Privacy: responding to the surprising failure of anonymization, *UCLA Law Review*, **57**, 1701–77.

Virginia Polytechnic Institute and State University (2013) *Protecting Confidentiality and Anonymity*, www.irb.vt.edu/pages/confidentiality.htm.

Recommended further reading

Israel, M. and Hay, I. (2006) *Research Ethics for Social Scientists*, Sage Publications, London.

Macfarlane, B. (2009) *Researching with Integrity: the ethics of academic enquiry*, Routledge, New York, NY.

Oliver, P. (2010) *The Student's Guide to Research Ethics*, 2nd edn, McGraw-Hill/Open University Press, Maidenhead.

Resnik, D. (2001) *What is Ethics in Research and Why is it Important?*, National Institute of Environmental Health Sciences, www.niehs.nih.gov/research/resources/bioethics/whatis.

Shapcott, R. (2010) *International Ethics: a critical introduction*. Polity Press, Cambridge, UK.

Stewart, C. N. (2011) *Research Ethics for Scientists: a companion for students*, Wiley, West Sussex.

Part 2

Doing research, evaluation and audit

6

Reviewing the literature

Michelle Maden

'When might I need to do a literature review?'

'Aren't all literature reviews the same?'

'Why do a literature review?'

This chapter aims to provide you with the skills to conduct an effective literature review. It will provide a brief overview on the different types of review, the importance of the literature search within the research process and approaches to the analysis and synthesis of the literature.

In particular, this chapter assumes that you already know how to search the literature (see recommended further reading) and focuses on providing practical guidance on the skills and tools required to synthesize and critique the literature.

Role of the literature review

The role of the literature review to inform the research process is well documented (Grant and Booth, 2009; Hart, 1998; Jesson, Matheson and Lacey, 2011; Rowley and Slack, 2004). Defined as 'a library desk-method involving the secondary analysis of explicit knowledge, so abstract concepts of explicit, tacit knowledge are explored' (Jesson, Matheson and Lacey, 2011, 9), the literature review helps to set your research, evaluation or audit in context and is an acknowledgement that you know what is happening within that context (Hall, n.d.a). Furthermore, the literature review can assist in supporting the development of a research proposal (see Chapter 4) in identifying potential research designs and the feasibility of adopting such approaches by assessing the strengths and weaknesses of the methodologies (see Chapters 7 and 8) adopted in previous studies. Examining the literature in this way will help to refine the research approach and aid in justifying the need for the research by identifying gaps within the literature.

Finally, when writing up your project (see Chapter 11) reference to the wider literature is required within the discussion of the project findings, setting your project findings in context with what has been done before. For example, you may want to state whether your findings confirm or contradict previous findings or contribute a new understanding or perspective to the subject. This can only be done with an awareness of the existing literature.

The excerpts in Case study 6.1 demonstrate how literature can be used not only to establish the background to the research, but also to inform the framework for data analysis and discussion sections. Linking back to the wider literature within the discussion relates the findings of the study back to previous work on this topic and demonstrates how the research has added to the evidence base.

Case study 6.1 Utilizing the literature to inform the research process

Quoted from Maden-Jenkins, M. (2011) Healthcare Librarians and the Delivery of Critical Appraisal Training: barriers to involvement, *Health Information and Libraries Journal*, **28** (1), 33–40.

Informing the literature review

In an evaluation of a pilot critical appraisal workshop for librarians, Booth and Brice verified two of their assumptions – that statistics were seen by librarians as a stumbling block for appraising a paper and that some knowledge of research methodology was required.

In a preliminary analysis of a systematic review examining the barriers and enablers of librarian application of critical appraisal skills, Brice and Booth report four categories of barriers: personal characteristics, environment, technical knowledge and role expectations . . .

Informing the methodology

Qualitative data were analysed using the thematic analysis constant comparison method . . . Themes identified by Booth and Brice as barriers in the training and implementation of critical appraisal were also used as a framework for the analysis in order to confirm/refute their findings.

Informing the discussion

The results confirm previously identified themes relating to barriers to librarian involvement in critical appraisal (role expectations, environmental, knowledge and personal characteristics). The reporting of barriers relating to statistical issues suggests an underlying assumption that in order to be involved in delivering critical appraisal training librarians must be involved with the statistical content; however, the results reported in an earlier paper also demonstrate that librarians can be involved in delivering critical appraisal training without delivering statistical aspects. ▪

Defining the topic

Writing a literature review can be a difficult task for students and those new to research (Webber, 2002; Todd and Kirk, 1995). One tool designed to assist with the thought process in defining the topic for review is concept mapping (often referred to as mind mapping). Defined as 'tools and organizational strategies for making explicit and overt visual representations of concepts and their interrelationships' (Todd and Kirk, 1995, 335), concept maps can aid in defining and scoping the topic prior to conducting the search, to establish key themes to explore within the literature review. They can also assist in identifying search terms and organizing the structure of the review (Rowley and Slack, 2004; Webber, 2002; Hall, n.d.b; Buzan and Buzan, 2006; see also Chapter 10).

Using a visual approach, the topic area under review is placed in the centre of the page and key themes to be explored are linked to the topic (Webber, 2002). Figure 6.1 on the next page displays a concept map based on a literature review that examined the attitudes, barriers and levels of involvement of librarians in the delivery of a training programme. The review takes a broader approach of examining all fields of librarianship to set the context for the role and extent of health library professionals' involvement in critical appraisal.

Visually representing the key theme and sub-themes often makes the process of identifying associations and links between the literature more explicit and transparent. The concept maps are dynamic tools that can be extended and enhanced as the literature is identified, helping to formulate new ideas and foster links between concepts as you begin to synthesize the literature (see Figure 6.4).

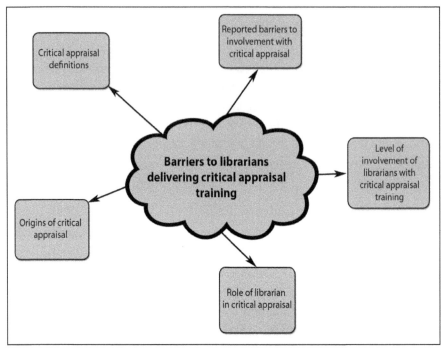

Figure 6.1 *Concept map defining topic prior to literature search*

Defining the type of review

Before beginning the search process it is essential to define the type of literature review you are undertaking, as this will determine the process and rigour with which the review is undertaken (Grant and Booth, 2009). A literature review can form part of a larger piece of work (e.g. a research proposal, or the introduction section of an academic paper or dissertation), be a piece of work in its own right (e.g. a book chapter or review paper) or a research methodology in its own right (e.g. a systematic review). The extent of how far literature reviews have developed in the library and information sector is demonstrated by Grant and Booth (2009). In a typology of reviews they used a framework to examine the methodology of reviews and identified 14 types of review. Key differences between three of the most common types of review can be seen in Table 6.1.

Although there are many different types of review, their underlying purpose is the same, to set the project in context, justify the project approach and give credibility to the project findings.

Before starting a literature review it is useful to read similar types of

Table 6.1 *Selection of commonly used review methodologies (taken from Grant and Booth, 2009, 91–108)*

Label	Description	Search	Appraisal	Synthesis	Analysis
Literature Review	Generic term: published materials that provide examination of recent or current literature. Can cover wide range of subjects at various levels of completeness and comprehensiveness	May or may not include compre-hensive searching	May or may not include quality assessment	Typically narrative	May be chronological, conceptual, thematic, etc.
Scoping Review	Preliminary assessment of potential size and scope of available research literature. Aims to identify nature and extent of research evidence (usually including ongoing research)	Complete-ness of searching determined by time/scope constraints. May include research in progress	No formal quality assessment	Typically tabular with some narrative commentary	Characterizes quantity and quality of literature, perhaps by study design and other key features. Attempts to specify a viable review
Systematic Review	Seeks to systematically search for, appraise and synthesize research evidence, often adhering to guidelines on the conduct of a review	Aims for exhaustive, compre-hensive searching	Quality assessment may determine inclusion/ exclusion	Typically narrative with tabular accompan-iment	What is known; recommend-ations for practice. What remains unknown; uncertainty around findings, recommend-ations for future research

reviews around the topic area or sector to get an understanding of the structure for your literature review. This is particularly important if you are thinking of submitting your work to a journal, in which case scan recent reviews within the journal you are thinking of submitting to. The journal may even provide guidelines for writing up the review.

Critiquing your literature search

Reviewing or critiquing your search strategy as well as the results retrieved is crucial in identifying errors that may impact on the accuracy of the search (McGowan, Sampson and Lefebvre, 2010) and result in the exclusion of relevant literature. Common errors include inappropriately combining terms and concepts with AND/OR, and incorrect spelling. A simple spelling error may result in zero results being retrieved. Searching on your terms/phrases line by line, rather than combining terms all on one line should alert you more quickly to potential spelling errors.

In response to concerns over the quality of searches reported in systematic reviews, checklists for reviewing the search are available (McGowan, Sampson and Lefebvre, 2010; Craven and Levay, 2011). Although established for the purpose of critiquing systematic review searches, the same principles apply to assessing any type of search strategy for accuracy.

Documenting your search strategy

One requirement common to writing up literature reviews, e.g. as part of a dissertation or a systematic review, is to include a record of the search strategy either as an appendix or as supplementary material to a published study. Regardless of the type of literature review you are undertaking, it is good practice to document your search strategy. In doing so the search is not only explicit but transparent and reproducible, thus serving to increase the robustness of your methodology (Craven and Levay, 2011). Given the importance of the literature search in performing a systematic review, more detailed guidance on documenting a systematic review search is available elsewhere (Booth, 2006a; Booth, Papaionnou and Sutton, 2011).

Key details to record include the resources searched (including database platform), the web addresses, the date the search was performed, the search terms and the number of references located. Using such a template encourages consistency in the way in which searches are recorded across multiple sources (Craven and Levay, 2011), an example of which can be found in Figure 6.2.

Be careful when transcribing the search strategy; it is often better to copy and paste terms direct from the databases with the minimum of editing, thus reducing the possibility of transcribing error. To ensure the accuracy of the transcribed search it is useful to repeat the search directly from the transcribed copy back into the databases, thus highlighting any transcription errors.

Search strategy recording template

Title: Healthcare librarians and the delivery of critical appraisal training: barriers to involvement

Databases (platform)	Date searched	Version	No. retrieved
LISTA (EBSCOHost)	01/04/2012	Mid 1960s -	303
CINAHL (EBSCOHost)	03/04/2012	1981-	38
LISA (EBSCOHost)	01/04/2012	N/A	285
Library Literature and Information Science Index - H.W.Wilson (EBSCOHost)	01/04/2012	N/A	63
Medline (HDAS NHS Evidence)	03/04/2012	1950-	109
Zetoc (zetoc.mimas.ac.uk/)	04/04/2012	N/A	223

Database search strategies:

LISTA

#	Search terms	No. retrieved
1	DE "MEDICAL librarians" OR DE "HOSPITAL librarians"	477
2	DE "LIBRARIANS" OR DE "ACADEMIC librarians" OR DE "ACQUISITIONS librarians" OR DE "ADULT services librarians" OR DE "BLACK librarians" OR DE "BOOKMOBILE librarians" OR DE "CATALOGERS" OR DE "CHILDREN'S librarians" OR DE "CHRISTIAN librarians" OR DE "ELECTRONIC resource librarians" OR DE "GAY librarians" OR DE "JEWISH librarians" OR DE "LGBT librarians" OR DE "LIBRARIANS as authors" OR DE "LIBRARIANS with disabilities" OR DE "MALE librarians" OR DE "MAP librarians" OR DE "MINORITY librarians" OR DE "MUSEUM librarians" OR DE "MUSIC librarians" OR DE "NATIONAL librarians" OR DE "PART-time librarians" OR DE "PUBLIC librarians" OR DE "REFERENCE librarians" OR DE "SCHOOL librarians" OR DE "SERIALS librarians" OR DE "SPECIAL librarians" OR DE "SYSTEMS librarians" OR DE "TECHNICAL services librarians" OR DE "TRANSGENDER librarians" OR DE "WOMEN librarians" OR DE "YOUNG adult services librarians"	24476
3	librarian*	106769
4	information specialist*	2540
5	1 or 2 or 3 or 4	108264
6	critical* ND apprais*	140
7	critical* ND assess*	114
8	critical* ND analys*	359
9	critiqu*	1204
10	6 or 7 or 8 or 9	1799
11	5 and 10	303

CINAHL

#	Search terms	No. retrieved
1	(MH "Librarians+")	4728
2	librarian*	8161
3	information specialist*	97
4	1 or 2 or 3	8214
5	critical* ND apprais*	1566
6	critical* ND assess*	664
7	critical* ND analys*	1411
8	critiqu*	3940
9	5 or 6 or 7 or 8	7402
10	4 and 9	38

Search Strategy Protocol Version1 1MM 01/04/12   Page 1

Figure 6.2 *Search strategy recording template*

Analysing, critiquing and synthesis

Writing a literature review can be a daunting task, particularly for those new to research. The focus really is on the term 'review'. The review should not simply be a descriptive account of previous work but a critique and synthesis, comparing and contrasting the existing literature and identifying key themes, concepts, theories, research approaches, key findings, methodological strengths and weaknesses, and gaps within the literature.

The purpose of the review will define to some extent the depth of analysis and synthesis required (Jesson, Matheson and Lacey, 2011). A review written as part of a dissertation or as a piece of work in its own right, e.g. a systematic review, will require greater coverage and depth in relation to the analysis and synthesis of the literature than one written as an introduction to a project report or journal article.

The remainder of this chapter aims to offer an understanding of what is involved in the analysis and synthesis of the literature and how this process may be undertaken. Further recommended reading on analysis and synthesis can be found at the end of this chapter.

Analysing the literature

Initially you may be faced with a vast array of literature and the first decision to take is where to begin. The key questions to address when determining whether to include the literature relate to relevance and value; is it relevant to the topic area? How does it inform the topic of study? (Jesson, Matheson and Lacey, 2011).

The next step is to start to develop a coherent and analytical overview of the literature. Analysis involves not only making sense of the literature through an identification of the key features relevant to the aims of your review, e.g. type of literature, key findings, strengths and weaknesses, and gaps, but also involves offering an interpretation of the literature based on your assessment of these features.

The type of analytical approach adopted will depend upon the nature of the literature you are reviewing. Approaches adopted include chronological, conceptual, thematic, gap analysis, etc. (Grant and Booth, 2009). Thematic analysis of the literature is often adopted in LIS reviews involving reading the individual studies and highlighting the key features to code and categorize.

Some categories and themes you may have already identified as key areas to explore within the review. Table 6.2 demonstrates how the SPICE framework (Setting, Perspective, Intervention, Comparison, Evaluation; Booth 2006a) can be used to identify categories to consider. Other categories and themes may emerge as you read the literature, and so the SPICE framework can act as a basis from which to allow your data analysis to develop.

In addition, if you are undertaking a review of empirical research a critique of the research methods must also be undertaken.

Table 6.2 *Using an adaptation of the SPICE framework to generate categories and themes*

SPICE	Categories identified within the literature	Themes
Setting	Countries of origin; Field in which the studies were undertaken (e.g. health/academic librarianship); Type of healthcare setting (e.g. acute, primary care, mental health)	Geography
Perspective	Origins of librarian involvement in critical appraisal How librarians are involved in critical appraisal (active vs. supportive role; training vs. summary writing); Responsibility for delivering critical appraisal e.g. clinical/academic librarian Delivery of critical appraisal training e.g. alone or in collaboration Appropriateness of librarian involvement in critical appraisal	Historical perspective Role of librarian in critical appraisal Level of librarian involvement Role of librarian in critical appraisal
Intervention	Definitions of critical appraisal Type of critical appraisal content delivered by librarians; Method of delivery e.g. group session, one-to-one support; No. of training sessions delivered; Length/frequency of training sessions	Definition Level of librarian involvement
Outcome	What prevents librarians from getting involved in critical appraisal?	Theoretical (perceived) vs. actual barriers

Critiquing the literature

Critiquing the literature will help to shape the decisions you take relating to your own research approach. Booth (2007, 75) defines critical appraisal, as a form of critique, as 'an enabling mechanism, a focus for systematic exploration of the strengths and weaknesses of a research study.' Critiquing the literature will help you identify what types of research have been conducted and involves making an assessment of both the strengths and the weaknesses of a study. It adopts a holistic approach, taking into consideration both the actual findings of the study (and whether they agree or conflict with each other) and the methodological conduct of the research. Was the methodology appropriate? If the methods are flawed it can signal caution that the results will also be flawed.

Assessing research in this way can help you avoid taking findings at face value while avoiding a purely negative viewpoint; instead, by critiquing the literature you will gain a balanced assessment and critical understanding taking into account any bias (Jesson, Matheson and Lacey, 2011).

One way of structuring your critique of a paper is to use a checklist, providing a series of questions that act as a prompt when reading. These can be particularly useful if you are not that familiar with particular research designs. Booth categorizes checklists into three types:

1 Question-led, which focus on common types of questions asked, e.g. CRiSTAL (Booth and Brice, 2003), ReLIANT (Koufogiannakis, Booth and Brettle, 2006).
2 Study design-led, which focus on the specific research methodology, e.g. Critical Appraisal Skills Programme.
3 Generic checklists that focus on broad approaches to methodology, e.g. qualitative, quantitative or mixed-method designs (Glynn, 2006; Suarez, 2010; Long et al., 2002a, 2002b).

If you are new to critiquing literature, there are some pre-appraised sources freely available on the internet. For example, the journal *Evidence Based Library and Information Practice* (2013) publishes evidence summaries with a commentary reflecting on methodological issues. Other examples within the LIS literature provide guided examples through the appraisal process (Suarez, 2010; Booth and Brice, 2004) and published systematic reviews will report on the quality of methodological issues (e.g. Brettle et al., 2011).

Synthesizing the literature

Synthesis is about bringing the literature together in a logical manner in order to complete the analysis with an overarching assessment, taking into account all the literature reviewed. As with analysis there are various approaches to synthesizing the literature that may depend upon the type of the literature you are working with (Booth, Papaionnou and Sutton, 2011). Qualitative literature may lend itself to three forms of analysis:

1 Thematic analysis: identifying patterns across the identified literature.
2 Meta-ethnography: involving induction and interpretation, following a similar approach to the data analysis used in the studies being synthesized (see Chapter 9).

3 Meta-synthesis: the bringing together of findings on a chosen theme that results in an analysis greater than the sum of its parts.

Quantitative literature may be synthesized narratively, providing a written account of connected themes, possibly also incorporating meta-analysis, in which the results of several studies are combined to demonstrate greater significance to the question being addressed (Booth, Papaionnou and Sutton, 2011).

Regardless of the approach, there are several key points to remember. A purely descriptive account of the literature and individual study-by-study presentation should be avoided. Try to summarize, critically compare and contrast *across* the literature, looking for where there is agreement and disagreement. Reading several literature reviews around your topic area will provide further examples of the synthesis process.

Hart (1998) and Hall (n.d.b.) outline the key questions to consider when comparing and contrasting the literature (see Figure 6.3). Specifically, think about the extent to which the literature addresses the aims of the review; what are the key findings and based on an assessment of the methodological issues, how does this impact on the interpretation of the literature?; what are the implications of the results of the review for practice/research?; are there still questions that remain unanswered?

What are the origins/definitions of the topic?
What key areas have been explored?
What are the key theories, concepts and ideas emerging?
What are the main areas for debate about the topic?
What are the main methodological approaches, and to what extent are the methods valid, reliable and applicable to your context?
What are the key findings and do they agree or conflict with each other?
What gaps exist within the literature that you want to explore in your research (justification of your own research)?

Figure 6.3 *Key questions to ask of the literature. (Taken from Hart (1998) and Hall (n.d.b.))*

As mentioned earlier in this chapter, concept mapping can be used to start to explore visually how the literature may be synthesized and linked together under common themes. Building on the general themes in Figure 6.1, Figure 6.4 illustrates how a concept map can be extended as your familiarity with the literature grows. Through your analysis of the literature it will also be possible to represent relationships between themes (shown by a dotted arrow).

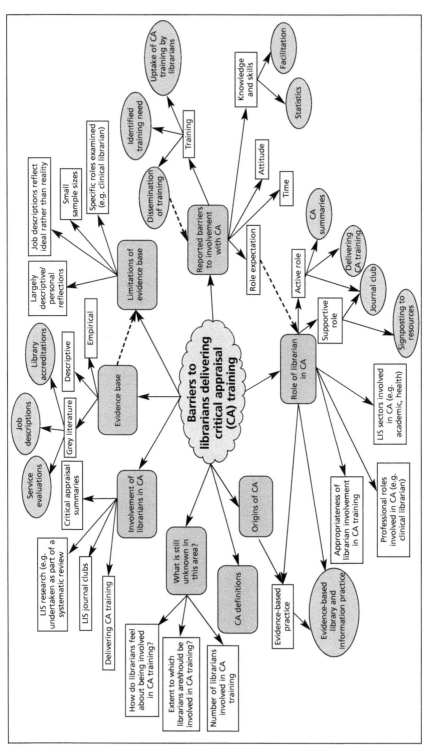

Figure 6.4 Extended concept map illustrating literature analysis and synthesis

Managing references

Managing your references with reference management software (see Chapter 10) assists in organizing an efficient collection of reference material and enables you to embed your references within your literature review as you write, automatically recreating a reference list (of papers specifically cited in your review) or bibliography (a list of supplementary reading) in the reference style of your choice; a key consideration when you come to write up your project findings and need to tailor your reference style in line with the author guidelines of your chosen journal (see Chapter 11). You can also share your references with others, a useful feature when you are collaborating with a team of researchers.

Structuring your literature review

While the structure for writing up the main sections of a review remains the same regardless of its purpose, what may differ slightly is the content within each of these sections. Table 6.3 on the next page offers generic guidance for structuring three common types of review.

The Preferred Reporting Items for Systematic Reviews (PRISMA) (www.prisma-statement.org) statement outlines the standards for reporting systematic reviews.

Academic conduct and style

Acknowledging the work of others is an important part of the research process and demonstrates rigour in the review process. Good practice when writing up a literature review is to ensure that you attribute the work appropriately so that it is clear what is your own work and what is the work of others. This includes citing work within its original context and accurately referencing the work. Chapter 11 explores issues relating to writing up your project findings in more detail.

Summary

This chapter has considered the variety of roles literature reviews can play within a research project, from providing context through to informing data analysis and the discussion of your project findings. It has highlighted how the purpose and type of literature review you are undertaking will inform the approach you take and introduced the subjects of concept analysis,

Table 6.3 *Structuring your literature review*

	Review written to inform research/dissertation	*Standalone literature review*	*Systematic review**
Abstract	Forms part of the background section only within a structured abstract	Concise summary of the review. Tends to be narrative	Structured abstract outlining background, methods, results and conclusion
Introduction	Background to topic. Why is this literature review important? Why is it needed?		Background to topic. Provide the rationale and justification for undertaking a systematic review
Main body	Examples include: 1. Thematic, using themes identified in analysis 2. Chronological		Aims/objectives Methods: Outlines approaches to searching, data selection, data extraction, quality assessment, data synthesis Results: Outlines characteristics of included studies, quality assessment, findings Discussion: Synthesis and summary of results
Summary/conclusion	Summarize the literature, linking back to review aims. Provide the rationale and justification for your own research. Should contain no new thoughts	Summarize the literature, linking back to review aims. Should contain no new thoughts	Answer review aims/objectives clearly. Highlight gaps and areas for further research. Should contain no new thoughts
* See PRISMA, Booth et al. (2011)			

critiquing the literature and information synthesis. Finally, advice is given on how to structure and document your searches and project report.

Points for reflection

- Think about the purpose of your review. Is it to inform empirical research, a dissertation or a standalone review (e.g. literature review, systematic review)? This will determine the scope and structure of the review.
- Use concept mapping to assist you in defining your project idea.
- Use a framework such as SPICE to formulate your search strategy.
- Examine the literature to determine what method of analysis and synthesis would be most appropriate.

References

Booth, A. (2006a) Clear and Present Questions: formulating questions for evidence based practice, *Library Hi Tech*, **24** (3), 355–68.

Booth, A. (2007) Who will Appraise the Appraisers? The paper, the instrument and the user, *Health Information and Libraries Journal*, **24** (1), 72–6.

Booth, A. and Brice, A. (2003) Clear-cut? Facilitating health librarians to use information research in practice, *Health Libraries Review*, **20** (1), 45–52.

Booth, A. and Brice, A. (2004) Appraising the Evidence. In Booth, A. and Brice, A. (eds), *Evidence-based Practice for Information Professionals: a handbook*, Facet Publishing, London, 104–19.

Booth, A., Papaionnou, D. and Sutton, A. (2011) *Systematic Approaches to a Successful Literature Review*, SAGE Publishing, London.

Brettle, A., Maden-Jenkins, M., Anderson, L., McNally, R., Pratchett, T., Tancock, J., Thornton, D. and Webb, A. (2011) Evaluating Clinical Librarian Services: a systematic review, *Health Information and Libraries Journal*, **28**, 3–22.

Buzan, T. and Buzan, B. (2006) *The Mind Map Book,* 5th edn, BBC Active, Harlow.

Craven, J. and Levay, P. (2011) Recording Database Searches for Systematic Reviews – what is the value of adding a narrative to peer review checklists? A case study of NICE interventional procedures guidance, *Evidence Based Library and Information Practice*, **6** (4), 72–87.

Critical Appraisal Skills Programme, *Appraising the Evidence*, www.casp-uk.net/find-appraise-act/appraising-the-evidence.

Evidence Based Library and Information Practice, http://ejournals.library.ualberta.ca/index.php/EBLIP.

Glynn, L. A (2006) Critical Appraisal Tool for Library and Information Research, *Library Hi-Tech*, **24** (3), 387–99.

Grant, M. J. and Booth, A. (2009) A Typology of Reviews: an analysis of 14 review types and associated methodologies, *Health Information and Libraries Journal*, **26** (2), 91–108.

Hall, H. (n.d.a) *Writing up your Dissertation*, http://drhazelhall.files.wordpress.com/2013/01/2013_hall_diss_write_up.pdf.

Hall, H. (n.d.b) *Writing a Literature Review*, http://www.slideshare.net/HazelHall/phd-lit-reviewtraining.

Hart, C. (1998) *Doing a Literature Review,* Sage Publications, London.

Jesson, J., Matheson, L. and Lacey, F. M. (2011) *Doing Your Literature Review: traditional and systematic techniques*, Sage Publications, London.

Koufogiannakis, D., Booth, A. and Brettle, A. (2006) ReLIANT: Reader's guide to the Literature on Interventions Addressing the Need for Education and Training, *Library Information Research*, **30** (94), 44–51.

Long, A. F., Godfrey, M., Randall, T., Brettle, A. and Grant, M. (2002a) *HCPRDU Evaluation Tool for Quantitative Studies*, University of Leeds, Nuffield Institute, http://usir.salford.ac.uk/12969/.

Long, A. F., Godfrey, M., Randall, T., Brettle, A. and Grant, M. (2002b) *HCPRDU Evaluation Tool for Qualitative Studies*, University of Leeds, Nuffield Institute, http://usir.salford.ac.uk/12970/1/Evaluation_Tool_for_Qualitative_Studies.pdf.

Maden-Jenkins, M. (2011) Healthcare Librarians and the Delivery of Critical Appraisal Training: barriers to involvement, *Health Information and Libraries Journal*, **28** (1), 33–40.

McGowan, J., Sampson, M. and Lefebvre, C. (2010) An Evidence Based Checklist for the Peer Review of Electronic Search Strategies (PRESS EBC), *Evidence Based Library and Information Practice*, **5** (1), 149–54.

Rowley, J. and Slack, F. (2004) Conducting a Literature Review, *Management Research News*, **27** (6), 31–9.

Suarez, D. (2010) Evaluating Qualitative Research Studies for Evidence Based Library and Information Practice, *Evidence Based Library and Information Practice*, **5** (2), 75–85.

Todd, R. J. and Kirk, J. (1995) Concept Mapping in Information Science, *Education for Information*, **13**, 333–47.

Webber, S. (2002) Mapping a Path to the Empowered Searcher. In Graham, C., *Online Information 2002: Proceedings, 3–5 December 2002*, Learned Information Europe, 177–81.

Recommended further reading

Booth, A. (2006b) 'Brimful of STARLITE': towards standards for reporting literature searches, *Journal of the Medical Library Association*, **94** (4), 421–30.

Booth, A. (2007) Who will Appraise the Appraisers? The paper, the instrument and the user, *Health Information and Libraries Journal*, **24** (1), 72–6.

Booth, A. (2008) Unpacking Your Literature Search Toolkit: on search styles and tactics, *Health Information and Libraries Journal*, **24** (1), 72–6.

Booth, A. and Brice, A. (2004) Appraising the Evidence. In Booth, A. and Brice, A. (eds), *Evidence-based Practice for Information Professionals: a handbook*, Facet Publishing, London, 104–18.

Booth, A., Papaionnou, D. and Sutton, A. (2011) Systematic Approaches to a Successful Literature Review, SAGE Publications, London.

Brettle, A. and Grant, M. J. (2004) *Finding the Evidence for Practice: a workbook for health professionals*, Churchill Livingstone, Edinburgh.

Cooke, A., Smith, D. and Booth, A. (2012) Beyond PICO: the SPIDER tool for qualitative evidence synthesis, *Qualitative Health Research*, published online 24 July,

http://qhr.sagepub.com/content/early/2012/07/22/1049732312452938.abstract.

Grant, M. J. and Booth, A. (2009) A Typology of Reviews: an analysis of 14 review types and associated methodologies, *Health Information and Libraries Journal*, **26** (2), 91–108.

HEALER (2013) *Step 2: review the literature*,

http://researchflowchart.pbworks.com/w/page/30400765/Step%202%3A%20 Review%20the%20Literature.

Jesson, J., Matheson, L. and Lacey, F. M. (2011) *Doing Your Literature Review: traditional and systematic techniques*, Sage Publications, London.

Rowley, J. and Slack, F. (2004) Conducting a Literature Review, *Management Research News*, **27** (6), 31–9.

7

Qualitative approaches

Alison J. Pickard

'How am I supposed to collect qualitative data? It all sounds a bit scary, I know where I am with the numbers we collect.'

'I don't have time to collect lots of detailed accounts of what people do.'

'Is qualitative data any use to me? I'm not sure what I would do with it even if I had it.'

Qualitative approaches to research, evaluation and audit are concerned with the 'why' and the 'how' of what people do. This approach to research aims to explore issues or questions in a particular context and provide 'thick description' of both the issues or questions and the environment in which they occur. Ryle (1971) separates actions into layers – the first layer, or 'thin description', tells us what was done and how often it was done. The second layer, or 'thick description', emerges once we begin to explore the context in which it was done, how it was done and why it was done. This level of detail not only allows for deeper understanding but it also allows for transferability of the findings from one context to another if those contexts are sufficiently similar. Transferability is the qualitative equivalent of generalization. For this reason context is important in qualitative research and wherever possible the research should be carried out in the natural setting of research participants, in order to witness the framework of their own multi-layered environment. This makes it an ideal approach for practitioner research, as you are already embedded in your context and you can bring understanding and insight to what goes on there. In qualitative research you, as the researcher, are central to the whole process and are able to use all of your knowledge and understanding of a situation to investigate the question and interpret the findings. (For further discussion on the nature and purpose of qualitative research see Denzin and Lincoln, 2011.)

Designing qualitative research

A qualitative research study starts out with a broad map of the research question or topic you want to explore, the context in which you will be exploring it and an indication of how you intend to explore it. Your research question will usually come from something that you've noticed in everyday practice or in the literature you've been reading. Qualitative research is reflective: it is an ongoing process of reflection, question generation, data gathering, analysis and interpretation. The purpose is to understand individual realities and apply this understanding in order to suggest ways forward. Any research study needs to be planned in sufficient detail to allow you to map out the territory in terms of who will be involved, what will be involved and how long it is expected to take (see Chapter 4). The basic design of qualitative research conducted within the boundaries of trustworthiness – transferability, credibility, dependability and confirmability – is illustrated in Figure 7.1.

The major components of qualitative research are:

- the literature review (see Chapter 6)
- fieldwork in a natural setting to capture the context
- the 'human as instrument' in order to understand and interpret that context
- purposive sampling
- emerging data collection
- grounded theory.

Qualitative fieldwork takes place in the setting being investigated whenever possible. This does not always mean you have to be permanently located in a research site, but it does mean that you will need to understand the setting and have some experience of it. The research 'instrument' refers to the actual tool used to collect data. In quantitative research the instruments could be questionnaires, transaction logs or tally counters. In qualitative research, *you* would be the primary instrument – usually supported by interview guides, observation prompt, field logs and written questions – but *you* are at the heart of the data collection. Tacit knowledge is important when you are trying to make sense of a situation: maybe you are investigating an issue in your own workplace or in a context very similar to your own.

> Since human experience is the topic of qualitative research, a human researcher is best able to respond and adapt to the data being gathered.
>
> Cook and Farmer, 2011, 8

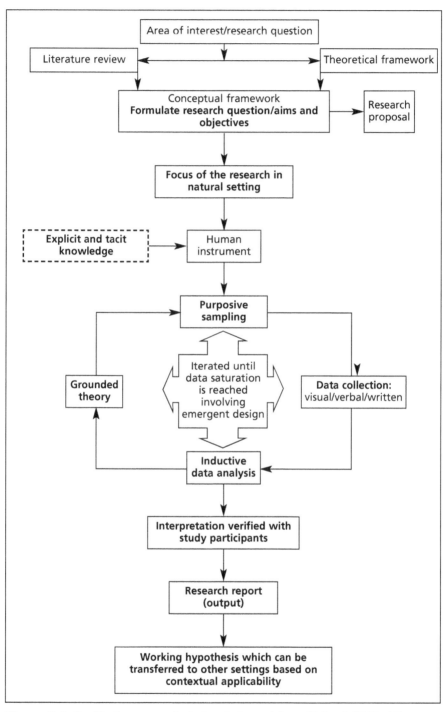

Figure 7.1 *Qualitative research design (adapted from Pickard, 2013, 19)*

Purposive sampling offers a number of different approaches; your choice will relate directly to your research objectives and is a strategic decision based on who you need to question. With purposive sampling nothing is random: each research participant is selected based on the contribution they can make to your research question. In Case study 7.1 McKnight applied a priori criteria sampling to identify her research participants (see Pickard, 2013, for an example of a sampling grid). Other approaches include snowball sampling, maximum variation, stakeholder sampling, extreme or deviant case sampling, typical case sampling, critical case sampling and pragmatic case sampling (see Given, 2008). Grounded theory (Glaser and Strauss, 1967) puts the emphasis on data gathering early in the research process to allow you to identify and map the territory, formulate your plans, adapt data collection during the study and inform continued sampling. Almost all qualitative research uses grounded theory to some extent. The term refers to developing theory that is grounded in the data you collect rather than a theory that is hypothesized and then tested; see Chapter 9 for a discussion of inductive and deductive analysis.

The term 'qualitative data' is used to describe a wide variety of data, from the few lines you may harvest from an open-ended question in a questionnaire to the thick description and rich narrative of an in-depth study of people and cultures (usually termed 'ethnography'). This chapter focuses on the core tenets of qualitative research and the most frequently applied methods and techniques for gathering data. How they are used and adapted are decisions that you as the researcher will take based on the purpose and scope of your research.

This first case study, 7.1, provides an example of the basic tenets of qualitative research; fieldwork in a natural setting, the human as instrument, purposive sampling, emerging data collection, and grounded theory.

Case study 7.1 An example of qualitative research carried out in a natural setting

---

McKnight, M. (2007) A Grounded Theory Model of On-Duty Critical Care Nurses' Information Behavior: the patient-chart cycle of informative interactions, *Journal of Documentation*, **63** (1), 57–73.

Purpose

Critical care nurses' work is rich in informative interactions. Although there have been *post-hoc* self-report studies of nurses' information seeking, there have been no observational studies of the patterns of their on-duty information behavior. This paper seeks to address this issue.

Design/methodology/approach

This study used participant observation and in-context interviews to describe 50 hours of the observable information behavior of a sample of critical care nurses in a 20-bed critical care unit of a community (non-teaching) hospital. The researcher used open, *in vivo* and axial coding to develop a grounded theory model of their consistent pattern of multimedia interactions.

Findings

The resulting Nurse's Patient-Chart Cycle describes their activities during the shift as centering on a regular alternation between interactions with the patient and with the patient's chart (in various record systems), clearly bounded with nursing 'report' interactions at the beginning and the end of the shift. The nurses' demeanor markedly changed between interactions with the chart and interactions with the patient. Their attention was focused on patient-specific information. They had almost no time or opportunity to consult published sources of information while on duty.

Originality/value

Libraries often provide nurses with information services that are based on academic models of information behavior. Clinical information systems are designed more for medico-legal record keeping than for nursing care. Understanding the reality of nurses' on-duty information behavior may guide librarians and systems designers in the provision of more appropriate systems and services.

In this study the researcher had considerable tacit knowledge gained from over 18 years' experience as a hospital librarian. The purposive sample of six was selected using a priori criteria; gender, education, and experience. Field notes were collected during participant observation as the researcher accompanied each nurse 'for one shift providing a total of 50 hours of field work'. Observations were made 'on weekdays (7 am to 7 pm), weekday nights (7 pm to 7 am), weekend days and weekend nights'. This allowed the researcher to immerse herself in the context and interpret the behaviour she witnessed within the natural setting of the research participants. It is not hard to see how this could be translated into a practitioner-based investigation; you would come to the study with considerable knowledge that could be applied at all stages of the research.

Qualitative research methods

A 'research method' is the overall strategy applied to a research study and not necessarily related to the individual data collection techniques you might use to collect data as part of that strategy. There are some methods or strategies that imply a particular technique or set of techniques for gathering data, but not always. For example, if your method was a case study you may use various combinations of techniques such as interviews, focus groups, questionnaires or observations in that case study. As 'methods' represent an overall strategy, what follows is a series of examples of methods to illustrate how they can be designed and applied using a variety of qualitative data collection techniques.

An ethnography is the study of people in their everyday lives; it involves you as the researcher 'participating, overtly or covertly, in people's daily lives for an extended period of time, watching what happens, listening to what is said, asking questions – in fact, collecting whatever data are available to throw light on the issues that are the focus of the research' (Hammersley and Atkinson, 1995, 1). Practitioner research offers an ideal opportunity to engage in an ethnographic study of your own 'back yard', a context in which you are already immersed. This is particularly useful when you are trying to understand the bigger picture of group and individual behaviour, how people act and interact.

Case study 7.2 An example of ethnography

Whipple, M. and Nyce, J. M. (2007) Community Analysis Needs Ethnography: an example from Romania, *Library Review*, **56** (8), 694–706.

Purpose

The purpose of this paper is to demonstrate the importance of using qualitative research methods, such as ethnography, in community analysis within the library and information science (LIS) community.

Design/methodology/approach

The authors review the LIS literature on community analysis up to May 2004, critique a representative case study and compare its results to what emerged from the research carried out in rural Romania summer of 2004. Students and faculty from Emporia State University and Ball State University in May 2004 gathered qualitative data on the rural information infrastructure and the information needs and of residents in the Romanian community of Lunca Ilvei. The research team used ethnographic methods to collect data and found this method to be effective in the analysis and understanding of the community's information behavior.

Findings
Community analysis in LIS has relied primarily on quantitative methods. While quantitative methods can give the researcher some information about a given community, these methods cannot always produce community sensitive and appropriate statements. Ethnography can produce this kind of data which can be used to assess and plan library services.

Research limitations/implications
The argument rests on a single village study. However, the paper's review of the literature and its analysis of a key example of community analysis strengthen the argument.

Originality/value
As libraries strive to serve communities and remain relevant to their users research methodologies, like ethnography, that are effective in revealing information needs, wants, behaviors, and fulfilment need be accepted as legitimate and distributed throughout the library community. ▓

This example demonstrates how ethnography can be used to explore the real-life context of users and help us to align our services to that context. Here the researchers moved into the village: for 'two weeks, while staying in the homes of local residents, the research team observed and took part in community life'. As well as observations they also interviewed 45 local residents; every afternoon and evening the team got together to reflect on their observations and findings during the day. Clearly this method of research is costly and time-consuming; however, the wealth of understanding that can be achieved through ethnographic investigation is rich, detailed and most importantly, highly effective in understanding your users.

A case study allows in-depth exploration at the level of the individual, a group, an organization, a service, or a location. A 'case' is defined as a 'bounded system'. Merriam explains that the 'case is a unit, entity, or phenomenon with defined boundaries that the researcher can demarcate or "fence in"' (1998, 27). A case study approach is particularly useful when you want to focus on a particular aspect of a service, or an individual user or group of users. It is also possible to conduct more than one case study and carry out a cross-case analysis to identify any common themes or extreme differences between cases. (See Stake, 1995 for more detail.)

Case study 7.3 An example of case study approach

Pei-Yi, L. and Shan-Ju, L. C. (2011) Elderly Participation in Public Library Voluntary Services: a case study of Taipei Public Library, *Journal of Educational Media & Library Sciences*, **49** (1), 3–38.

This study aims to explore the participation of the elderly in voluntary services in public libraries. The subjects for this study have been chosen from the elderly volunteers of the Taipei Public Library. The research questions attempt to investigate the following: the motivations and purposes of elderly participation in volunteer services, the factors that influence their choices of entering the public library service and the experience of volunteer services. This study uses a semi-structured interview and a small questionnaire to collect data. In order to obtain a comprehensive understanding of the research subjects and to interpret the research results appropriately, the findings have been supplemented with the background information of research subjects collected from personal profile forms to achieve the relevance to the volunteer services experience of elderly participation. The total of 30 elderly volunteer aged from 56 to 85 have been interviewed. Based on the research findings, the authors propose a framework for understanding elderly volunteers participating in public library services, and offer suggestions to voluntary service units of public libraries and elderly volunteers.

In this case study the researchers have identified a group and an organization (elderly volunteers of the Taipei Public Library). Within the bounded system of the case, the researchers applied semi-structured interviews and a small questionnaire; this is an example of how a method may not necessarily dictate a particular data collection technique.

The example in Case study 7.4 is one where the method was designed around a specific data collection technique, as the technique is intrinsic to the application of the method. The Delphi method was developed to gather *expert* opinion on a particular topic, usually as a means of taking forward agendas.

The Delphi method has a very clearly defined design (see Pickard, 2013, 149–56).

- Identify an expert panel that can inform the discussion on the issues at the heart of the investigation.

- Design an appropriate question template, usually with open-ended questions that allow members of the panel to construct their own meanings.
- Round One: The questions are sent out to all members of the expert panel at the same time, the responses are collated and summarized by the researcher and the summaries are returned to all panel members.
- Round Two: All panel members are sent an anonymized synthesis of ideas, comments and viewpoints taken from all responses. Panel members are asked to review the statements and assign a rank to their level of agreement or disagreement with each statement.
- Round Three: A synthesis of the second list, ranked and with the additional comments. Panel members are asked to rank the additional comments in the same way as they did the first list. Rounds can be reiterated until the researcher feels consensus has been reached, or the findings are stable, or a predefined number of rounds that was set at the outset has been reached.
- Processing: This is ongoing, as data will be processed, interpreted and synthesized after each round.
- Reporting: Findings are presented but it is usual for the panel to remain anonymous unless there is agreement otherwise.

Case study 7.4 An example of a Delphi study

Smiraglia, R. P. (2010) A Research Agenda for Cataloging: the CCQ editorial board responds to the year of cataloging research, *Cataloging & Classification Quarterly*, **48** (8), 645–51.

The cataloging and classification community was called to highlight 2010 as 'The Year of Cataloging Research,' and specifically was challenged to generate research ideas, conduct research, and generally promote the development of new research in cataloging. *Cataloging & Classification Quarterly* has become the most influential journal of research in cataloging and classification since its inception in 1981. The idea behind the research reported here was to give the CCQ editorial board an opportunity to present its point of view about research for cataloging. A Delphi study was conducted in three stages during the 2009-2010 academic year. Members were asked to define the key terms 'cataloging,' 'evidence,' and 'research,' and to develop a research agenda in cataloging. The results reveal a basic core definition of cataloging perceived as a dynamic, active process at the core of information retrieval. An eight-point research agenda emerges that is forward-looking and embraces change, along with top-ranked calls for new empirical evidence about catalogs, cataloging, and catalog users. ■

The study in the example was designed to establish a consensus on the definition of cataloguing and establish a research agenda for the future. The experts identified for the study were members of the editorial board of *Cataloging & Classification Quarterly*.

Data collection techniques

Qualitative data collection is extremely varied and can include almost any data that is not numerical, gathered using a variety of techniques that directly involve you and the research participant in a mutual shaping of the data. The emphasis here is on the role you play in interpreting the data, not just during the analysis phase but also during data collection.

Observation

What makes research observation so different from the observation you do every day to make sense of what goes on around you? Research observation is about gathering evidence of the 'here and now'; the purpose is to witness, record and analyse natural behaviour in a natural setting. This can sometimes be rather tricky. Imagine if a researcher was watching you. Would this affect your behaviour? The answer is probably yes. The presence of any observer in a situation is highly likely to affect that situation to some degree. The aim is to limit this effect and keep the situation as close to normal as possible. 'Observer effect' diminishes over time, and so prolonged engagement in the field can play a significant part in maintaining the natural feel of the situation. This is ideal for observing your own setting, as your presence is usual and unlikely to cause any disruption to the everyday pattern of events. The difficulty for you is in remembering that the usual may have a lot to offer in terms of understanding the context. Familiarity can make it difficult to decide what is noteworthy and what is not.

Patton (2002) identifies three types of observation; participant, non-participant and semi-participant:

- Participant observation is the traditional approach used in ethnography. You become, or already are, an insider and 'live' the experience of the research participants.
- Non-participant observation is about watching the behaviour of individuals or groups and taking no part in the activities.
- Semi-participant observation requires you to become an 'interested

expert', someone who is there to watch but also to ask questions and get involved in the activities taking place.

There are two issues here. One is your potential to alter the situation and bring too much influence on natural behaviour; the other is the likelihood that you will miss a lot of detail by taking a narrow focus or getting too involved. It helps here to be very clear about what you came to watch, taking field prompts in with you as an *aide memoire* is useful as long as you ensure that these prompts do not blinker you to behaviours which are important but not on your list. Delamont (2002) provides an excellent guide to educational qualitative research but it is also a very practical text for anyone entering the field to engage in qualitative investigation. What to look at should be guided by the purpose of your research – what was your research question? It could be that taking a broad approach to begin with will alert you to salient issues that need to be watched in more detail. For example, how do groups interact in the space you are watching? How do individuals move around and use that space? Does anyone spot the huge sign pointing to the new display of graphic novels in the corner?

Case Study 7.5 illustrates a study of how preschool children use the public library. The sample for the study was 30 girls within 3 months of their 4th birthday. The researcher assumed the role of a student, the children were familiar with this concept and thought nothing of her note-taking during the observations.

Case study 7.5 An example of participant observation

McKechnie, E. F. (2000) Ethnographic Observation of Preschool Children, *Library and Information Science Research,* **22** (1), 61–76.

Interviews and questionnaires are not suitable for use with young children whose language skills are not well developed. Effective alternatives may be found in methods associated with ethnographic field observation. Using examples from an ethnographic study of public library use by 30 preschool girls, describes 3 methods appropriate for studying the information-seeking behaviour and library use of preschool children: audio-recording of naturally occurring talk, participant observation, and key informant diaries. Discusses selected issues important for ethnographic field research with young children including gaining access and informed consent, observer effect, and young children's understanding of research. Data arising from naturally occurring talk and actions of the children show that these methods are unique in reflecting the perspective of the children themselves.

Observation note: Chloe had built a very high tower from the blocks. She then began to search for and retrieve more blocks from the floor. This went on for quite a while, in a repeated pattern of search, retrieve, sit and build. Another child (female, about two years old) was now playing with a large wooden truck on the floor in the picture book area near Chloe. The other child's mother suggested that she gather up some of the wooden blocks on the floor, put them in the back of the truck and drive them around. The other child gathered up some blocks. Instead of putting them in the truck, she carried them over to the table where Chloe was building with the same type of blocks, carefully put them on the floor beside Chloe and looked up at her. Chloe picked up the 'gift' and the girls smiled at each other. (Later in the visit, Chloe used the wooden truck to move around her materials for other building projects.)

Extract from the article (p. 66) ▨

Note taking is the traditional form of recording observational research; however, the use of video has a long history and is prevalent in usability studies, where user interaction with technology is recorded and analysed later. Whichever approach you take, the aim is to leave the field with the data and work with those data as soon as possible after exiting the field site. Too much distance between the actual event and your interpretation and analysis of that event can be problematic. Figure 7.2 provides an example of a briefing sheet which can be used prior to entering the field for known variables such as the subject, location and date. It can then be used either during the observation or immediately upon exiting the field. The purpose of the sheet is to provide you with a structure for note taking but not to act as a blinker to what is seen; you can provide yourself with prompts but you must remain open to what you are witnessing. Where you observe is dictated by the purpose of the study and gaining access to field sites; this may be relatively simple if you are investigating your own 'back yard',

CODE NAME OF SUBJECT...
LOCATION...
DATE............................
TOPIC...[e.g. what was the subject searching for?]
SETTING [e.g. what was the position of the subject in the room? How many people were using the room? Was it quiet or noisy? Level of activity?]

OBSERVATION [e.g. what did the subject do? How was it done? Was there any interaction with others? What did the subject say? Was there any change in mood during the observation?]

Facts written in blue / interpretations written in pencil.

Figure 7.2 *Observation briefing sheet (adapted from Pickard, 2013, 231)*

otherwise access will need to be negotiated. Also think about exiting the field: you need to plan your exit from the outset and make participants aware of when this will happen.

Focus groups

Focus groups are an excellent way of exploring topics from multiple viewpoints in a single data-gathering exercise. The focus group technique can be used to gather general background on a topic; stimulate debate and creativity; gather perceptions of services or products; uncover how your research participants relate to and talk about the topic of your study; confirm your interpretations of data already gathered; and gain feedback on your emerging research findings. This technique encourages discourse between research participants and allows them to test their own perceptions and possibly reflect on their standpoint in light of what others are saying. A focus group can be used at the outset of a study to map the territory. Focus groups can aso be used during the study as central data-gathering techniques and at the end of a study to confirm the researcher's interpretations and to evaluate any findings.

Organizing and moderating a focus group is no simple task therefore you must be prepared and plan the event well in advance.

In advance:

- Identify your participants.
- Select and book a location.
- Prepare and send out invitations which include: the purpose of the focus group and who you are; a brief synopsis of the topic for discussion; logistics such as date, time, expected duration and location; and any ethical considerations.
- Consider what equipment you will need, such as an audio or video recorder, pens, flipchart, briefing sheet and any disclaimer.
- Prepare a briefing sheet for yourself.

On the day:

- Prepare the room in such a way that participants can see and hear each other and you have an appropriate place in the setting.
- Set out your equipment.
- Open the discussion with a brief introduction – this provides every participant with the opportunity to speak from the outset.

- Open up the discussion and then begin the moderating process.
- Keep the discussion on track.
- Probe for more detail when appropriate.
- Do not be tempted to 'jump into the silence' – try to say as little as possible.
- Remember to thank everyone when the discussion is over and if they are involved in another element of the research take this opportunity to remind them of the next stage.

(Source: Pickard, 2013, 245–6)

Discussion is the central purpose of a focus group but there are ways of interacting with the group to maximize involvement and stir creativity if that is what you need. Using the basic premise of a focus group, it is possible to be creative about how you organize and run the event. It is possible to apply different approaches to 'round table discussions' that include activities to engage the participants. The 'World Café' technique focuses on 'conversations that matter' and involves greater numbers than are commonly associated with research focus groups. The level of discourse is increased by facilitating conversations in small groups then getting those groups to change tables and share emerging ideas (Brown et al., 2005). These conversations produce a considerable amount of data and the structure of the event facilitates meaningful dialogue. This technique translates very well into a research data-gathering technique and is an excellent example of how to be creative when organizing and running focus groups. Focus groups are about collective exploration of a topic; be clear about what you want to achieve and then be creative about how you can best achieve it.

In Case study 7.6 Ganster identified eight undergraduate participants to discover how the library could best support them. This focus group included an introduction and an open discussion but also the use of individual and group activities to encourage more creative thinking. This approach is rarely used but it is a very useful one in getting participants to think critically about the questions being asked. (For another example of encouraging group activity see Pickard, Gannon-Leary and Coventry, 2010; the appendices in this report provide details of the activities used during a round table event.)

Case study 7.6 An example of the use of focus groups

Ganster, L. (2011) Reaching Out to International Students: a focus-group approach to developing web resources and services, *College & Undergraduate Libraries*, **18** (4), 368–84.

Librarians at the State University of New York at Buffalo implemented the Resources for International Students Web guide to support library outreach to a multicultural and multilingual audience. A focus group helped librarians to understand the needs of new international students and tailor Web resources accordingly. In addition to creating awareness of international student cultural challenges, this article presents focus group guidelines to assist in the planning process of library services and resources. ▨

Interviews

Interviews are a major source of qualitative data and can range from the very structured, formal interview with detailed questions to the very informal, purposeful conversation led by the interviewee, with you taking a back seat once the direction, focus and central themes have been established. The purpose of an interview is to explore what the research participant knows, thinks and feels about an aspect of your research. A conversation is a two-way process, it is an interaction and works best when it is allowed to flow. Interviews are about constructing meaning and making sense of what is inside, and on, the mind of the interviewee. Kvale and Brinkmann (2009) identify seven stages of the interview process: thematizing, designing, interviewing, transcribing, analysing, verifying and reporting. Aim to analyse the data straight after the interview and before the next. This allows for reflexive action: maybe you need to change some of the questions for the next interview. Replication has no place in qualitative research unless it enhances your data collection, as there will be no attempt made to quantify your findings; each interviewee might add an entirely new perspective on the question.

Begin by clarifying the themes of your research: what is it you are interested in and are themes connected in any way? Structuring your themes is important, as you want to establish a natural flow to the conversation and enable your interviewee to stay focused on your themes. Once you have your themes you can start to design your interview questions and construct an interview guide. An interview guide is recommended over a list of questions, as it is easier to allow the conversation to flow and encourage the interviewee to share as much as you can. You need to steer the conversation but be very careful not to shut down a line of enquiry by cutting off your interviewee too abruptly. Table 7.1 provides some examples of how to start qualitative questions and how to recognize questions that may not be appropriate. In order to get to the heart of a topic you might start with an open question, ask a closed question to identify a fact and then ask a reflective question to clarify your own understanding. Avoid leading questions and multiple questions.

Table 7.1 *Types of qualitative questions*

Type	Example
Open questions	*Encouraging a conversation:* how . . ., who . . ., what . . ., when . . ., where . . .,describe . . ., explain . . ., 'in what way . . .', 'could you tell us about . . .'
Probing questions	*These are the same as open questions but used to follow up on answers already given:* 'could you tell me more about . . .', 'how would you . . .', 'where would that be likely to . . .'
Hypothetical questions	*Pose a theoretical situation:* 'imagine if you did have a massive increase in demand for . . . How would you handle the situation?'
Reflective question	*Clarifying your interpretation of what was said:* 'Would I be right in thinking that you . . .'
Closed questions	*Factual questions that can be answered in a word:* 'how long have you worked here?', 'do you agree with . . .?'
Leading questions	*Pushing towards the answer you want:* 'Surely you don't agree with limiting open hours?' 'Of course, you would want to provide the best service possible, wouldn't you?'
Multiple questions	*Asking more than one thing in the same question:* 'What do you think of self-service? Do you agree with it, and if not, why, and what do you think users might feel about this?'

When interviewing you need to establish a rapport with your interviewee, making them feel comfortable and relaxed. Body language has a huge part to play in interviewing; how you feel reflects directly back to the interviewee and they will respond to the signals you are sending. Piloting the interview is really important, not just to test your questions but also to rehearse your approach and become comfortable with your questions. There is no substitute for knowing your topic really well; this gives you confidence to ask questions and confidence to allow the conversation to develop. Think about the environment – where are you interviewing? Will it affect how the interviewees feel? Always remember to be realistic about how much time you request for the interview. We all appreciate being given time back but none of us like to have time taken away from us, and so it better to overestimate how long it will take than to overrun. You will need to consider your analysis before conducting the interview (see Chapter 9). When using unstructured interviews pre-coding is almost impossible. You will be sensitized to salient themes and you may already have the first set of categories established from your literature review but there is no doubt that the data you come back with from your interview will contain data that do not fit neatly into any predefined categories – indeed, that is the hope with qualitative research.

Researcher diaries

Your diary has a central role to play in qualitative research; it is a source of data as well as a record of events, and so its importance cannot be overstated. A diary can be maintained in two forms: first as a record of logistics in order to provide a step-by-step account of the path taken by the research and secondly as a reflexive journal which contains notes on recurring ideas, questions, concerns, discussions and points when major decisions are reached about the direction of the research. Your diary is more than a private record, it is essential to the research process (Stake, 1995). The diary is vital when it comes to establishing the trustworthiness of the research and would form a major component of the audit trail. A reflexive diary is very personal to the researcher and you must find your own way of maintaining a trail of events during the research activity; an example of which was given in Chapter 2. One approach to recording any reflexive or reflective activity is to break events down into three parts:

- description of the event
- interpretation of the event
- outcome.

This is a very broad outline, and that is intentional: all that needs to be recorded in a personal diary can fall under these three major headings. The whole purpose of the diary is to provide a personal, private arena where you can record developments and rehearse emerging themes. Figure 7.3 on the following page shows two excerpts from a researcher's diary that demonstrate how a particular issue in the research developed over time. The excerpts are chronological but not consecutive, as other things happened in between these two events, but it demonstrates how a development in the research can be traced back and recorded.

Participant diaries

The excerpt in Figure 7.3 illustrates not only how a researcher's log can be used but also how difficult it can be to encourage research participants to

This week I was dismayed when I went around the schools to collect the participants' diaries. Fourteen had made no entries at all, the reasons they gave were: 'I haven't done any research projects.' 'I forgot what to do', 'it interferes with my work', 'It takes up too much time.', 'I can't be bothered.' and 'I don't want to walk around with a great big yellow book, I feel stupid' [Researcher Log, p.102] . . . I've now had focus group meetings at each site to decide what could be done about the problem with the diaries. I explained that what was needed was a detailed account of searches carried out when I couldn't be present. Very productive discussions followed and participants identified ways in which they thought the Search Log could be a more effective tool. The suggestions I've had are: a hand written diary in their own words, a database using Microsoft Access, a diary kept in a Microsoft Word file. One participant requested an audio tape so he could describe his actions, not sure I can get one of those but I'm going to try – time to redesign the diary I think. [Researcher Log, p. 219].

Figure 7.3 *Excerpt from a researcher's log*

maintain a diary as part of your data collection. The experience described here was one where allowing the research design to 'roll and cascade' was highly effective. After participants rejected the very formal diaries they were encouraged to create their own diaries. This allowed them to decide on an approach they were more comfortable with and encouraged them to provide useful information in the new formats. Participant diaries can be used to:

- collect information about activities done outside of scheduled observations
- gather personal reflections on a topic
- provide 'life story' narrative or log of moves and choices made during a particular activity.

The purpose of the diary will dictate the format but the participant will dictate how much information is recorded, how much depth is provided and how much personal interpretation included, as well as how much is left out.

Some things to consider when preparing diaries:

- Think about the format (e.g. paper or electronic, written or oral).
- Provide some instructions in the diary so that it is at hand when the participant needs it.
- Give an example of the type of data you are hoping for but be very careful not to lead your participants towards content.
- Some headings or prompts could be included.
- Include a brief checklist of the type of things you are interested in (but

make it clear that it is not an exclusive list).

- Use language that your participants will understand – avoid jargon.
- Indicate relatively short bites of time or units of activity you want them to record.
- Include some open questions which would help to clarify the type of behaviour or activity you are interested in.
- Build in regular feedback sessions.
- Be prepared to redesign the diary if necessary.

In Case study 7.7 the researchers asked for autobiographical diaries to be maintained by 231 participants – there was a team of researchers involved in this project, otherwise this much data would have been impossible to analyse. The researchers acknowledge the potential drawbacks of participant diaries but even with these caveats it is still a source of rich data that would be difficult to harvest in any other way.

Case study 7.7 An example of a study using participant diaries

---

Black, A. and Crann, M. (2000) In the Public Eye: a mass observation of the public library, *Journal of Librarianship and Information Science,* **34** (3), 145–57. Taken from the abstract.

Reports results of a study which aimed to apply the technique used to gather data for the Mass Observation Archive (MOA) to the study of user behaviour in the public library. The study was designed to provide an open access public commentary on the public library and reveal what the public library does well, what it does badly and what it means to both its users and non-users . . . The data for the study was obtained from the written testimony of 231 contributions (64 men and 167 women) gathered from UK volunteers in response to the request for observation on public libraries and was gathered by the 'autobiographical diary' method, as employed by the MOA...The discourse analysis which was applied to the data was used to reveal specific aspects of library use, including: general impressions; cuts in services; social exclusion; commercialization; use of computers; public place/private space issues; library staff; and buildings, design and ambience. ▪

Managing qualitative data

Research data management is vitally important in any research activity: the nature of qualitative data is such that they require careful handling from the outset, and it is not a retrospective activity. Qualitative data can come in many forms; audio and video recordings, written transcripts, photographs and artefacts. It is important to set up a system for managing your data from the outset of the project, since this puts you in a strong position to establish the trustworthiness of your research (Pickard and Dixon, 2004). One technique is that of the audit trail, demonstrating the process of recording, storing and analysing and making accessible the evidence trail in qualitative research. Table 7.2 illustrates an example of an audit trail which was provided to demonstrate the steps taken during a research study and the evidence that was available to demonstrate how the findings were developed. The trustworthiness of the research is dependent upon how transparent the process is.

Summary

This chapter has identified the major tenets of qualitative research and provided an overview of the research methods and data collection techniques associated with the qualitative approach. Where appropriate, guidelines have been suggested for the design and implementation of these techniques within individual projects. If you want to answer those 'why' and 'how' questions in order to probe in depth into attitudes, behaviours, perceptions and the meanings behind those activities then your research is most likely going to be qualitative. Remember that a single data collection technique is rarely sufficient to provide suitable evidence for theory; triangulation by the use of more than one data collection technique is always recommended.

Case studies and examples have been provided to help illustrate points and demonstrate how theory has been put into practice. The suggested further readings and web resources provide support, advice and guidance on all of the topics covered in this chapter.

Points for reflection

- Look back at the most recent audit or evaluation research that was carried out in your organization, explore the data and highlight any findings that encourage you to ask questions such as: 'But why is that happening?' 'How did users develop that pattern of behaviour?' 'Why do we get so few . . .?' Now think about how you would go about discovering any answers to those questions.

Table 7.2 *Qualitative research audit trail (Source: Pickard, 2002. This design follows that of Edward S. Halpin as cited in Lincoln and Guba, 1985, Appendix A.)*

Classification	File type	Evidence

Raw Data	1. Electronically recorded material
	   Audiotape transcripts
	   Researcher's journal
	   Participant diaries
	   Minutes from tutorials
	2. Field notes
	   Interview records
	   Observation notes
	   Participant diaries
	3. Unobtrusive measures
	   Public records
	   Policy documents
	   Private records
	   Samples of individual work
		a. Dialogue of social interactions
		b. Interview transcripts
		c. Descriptions of events, feelings and responses of participants
		d. Descriptions of environments, participant characteristics, behaviours of individuals
		e. Written work of individuals
		f. Procedures and policies
		g. Daily routines
		h. Personal reflection

Data reduction and analysis	1. Electronically recorded material
	   Field note transcripts
	   Descriptions
	   NUD*IST index tree
	2. Summaries
	   Units of information:
	   Themes
	   Ideas behaviours
	   Concerns
	3. Theoretical notes
	   Emerging hypotheses
	   New concepts .
		a. Summary of interview transcripts
		b. Building of categories for analysis
		c. Developing themes for further investigation
		d. Coded transcripts
		e. Memos in NUD*IST database

Data reconstruction and synthesis	1. Index tree
	   Themes
	   Relationships
	2. Description of cases
	   Participant profiles
	   Interpretations
	   Discussion of emerging themes
	3. Cross-case analysis
	   Presentation of themes
	   Connections with previous research
	   Integration of concepts within conceptual framework
	4. Findings
	   Suggested ways forward
	   Reflection
		a. NUD*IST hierarchy of categories
		b. Links across and through hierarchical structure
		c. In-depth description of individual participants
		d. Explanations of connections
		e. Final thesis

Process notes	1. Methodology
	   Procedures, routines, strategies.
	2. Trustworthiness
	   Credibility
	   Dependability
	   Confirmability
		a. Daily activities
		b. Notes from supervisory meetings
		c. Decision-making
		d. Sampling
		e. Peer debriefing
		f. Member checks
		g. Prolonged engagement
		h. Triangulation checks

- Think about the role and function of one aspect of your work. What is it you want people to know and understand about it? Are those things easily counted? If not, how can you probe more deeply and, once you have, how can you share that story?
- At the next opportunity you have at work, stop for a few minutes and watch the activity going on around you. Take a little time to note what you see. Later, when you have finished work, look back at your notes and write out the story of what you observed. Notice the amount of rich data that is available to you every day and think about how this could inform what you do and how you do it.

References

Black, A. and Crann, M. (2000) In the Public Eye: a mass observation of the public library, *Journal of Librarianship and Information Science*, **34** (3), 145–57.

Brown, J., Isaacs, D. and World Café Community (2005) *The World Café: shaping our futures through conversations that matter*, Berrett-Koehler, San Francisco, CA.

Cook, D. and Farmer, L. (eds) (2011) *Using Qualitative Methods in Action Research: how librarians can get to the why of data*, Association of College and Research Libraries, Chicago, IL.

Delamont, S. (2002) *Fieldwork in Educational Setting: methods, pitfalls and perspectives*, 2nd edn, Routledge, London.

Denzin, N. K. and Lincoln, Y. S. (eds) (2011) *The Sage Handbook of Qualitative Research*, 4th edn, Sage Publications, London.

Ganster, L. (2011) Reaching Out to International Students: a focus-group approach to developing web resources and services, *College & Undergraduate Libraries*, **18** (4), 368–84.

Given, L. M. (ed.) (2008) *The Sage Encyclopaedia of Qualitative Research Methods, Vol. 2*, Sage Publications, Thousand Oaks, CA, 697–98.

Glaser, B. G. and Strauss, A. L. (1967) *The Discovery of Grounded Theory: strategies for qualitative research*, Aldine De Gruyter, New York, NY.

Hammersley, M. and Atkinson, P. (1995) *Ethnography: principles in practice*, 2nd edn, Routledge, Oxford.

Kvale, S. and Brinkmann, S. (2009) *InterViews: learning the task of qualitative research interviewing*, 2nd edn, Sage Publications, London.

Lincoln, Y. S. and Guba, E. G. (1985) *Naturalistic Inquiry*, Sage Publications, London.

McKechnie, E. F. (2000) Ethnographic observation of preschool children, *Library and Information Science Research*, **22** (1), 61–76.

McKnight, M. (2007) A Grounded Theory Model of On-Duty Critical Care Nurses'

Information Behavior: the patient-chart cycle of informative interactions, *Journal of Documentation*, **63** (1), 57–73.

Merriam, S. B. (1998) *Qualitative Research and Case Study Applications in Education*, Jossey-Bass, San Francisco, CA.

Patton, M. Q. (2002) *Qualitative Research and Evaluation Methods*, 3rd edn, Sage Publications, London.

Pei-Yi L. and Shan-Ju L. C. (2011) Elderly Participation in Public Library Voluntary Services: a case study of Taipei Public Library, *Journal of Educational Media & Library Sciences*, **49** (1), 3–38.

Pickard, A. J. (2002) *Access to Electronic Information Resources: their role in the provision of learning opportunities to young people. A constructivist inquiry*, unpublished doctoral dissertation, Northumbria University, Newcastle upon Tyne.

Pickard, A. J. (2013) *Research Methods in Information*, 2nd edn, Facet Publishing, London.

Pickard, A. J. and Dixon, P. (2004) The Applicability of Constructivist User Studies: how can constructivist inquiry inform service providers and systems designers?, *Information Research*, **9** (3), Paper 175, http://InformationR.net/ir/9-3/paper175.html.

Pickard, A. J., Gannon-Leary, P. and Coventry, L. (2010) *JISC Users' Trust in Information Resources in the Web Environment: a status report*, JISC, http://ie-repository.jisc.ac.uk/470/2/JISC_User_Trust_final_report.pdf.

Ryle, G. (1971) *Collected Papers, Volume II: Collected Essays, 1929–1968*, Hutchinson, London.

Smiraglia, R. P. (2010) A Research Agenda for Cataloging: the CCQ Editorial Board responds to the Year of Cataloging Research, *Cataloging & Classification Quarterly*, **48** (8), 645–51.

Stake, R. E. (1995) *The Art of Case Study Research*, Sage Publications, London.

Whipple, M. and Nyce, J. M. (2007) Community Analysis Needs Ethnography: an example from Romania, *Library Review*, **56** (8), 694–706.

Recommended further reading

Corbin Dwyer, S. and Buckle, J. (2009) The Space Between: on being an insider-outsider in qualitative research, *International Journal of Qualitative Methods*, **8** (1), 54–63.

Linstone, H. A. and Turoff, M. (eds) (2002) *The Delphi Method: techniques and applications*, http://is.njit.edu/pubs/delphibook/index.html.

Shenton, A. K. (2004) Strategies for Ensuring Trustworthiness in Qualitative Research Projects, *Education for Information*, **22**, 63–75.

Useful websites

Library and Information Research Group (LIRG), www.lirg.org.uk.

LIS Research Coalition, http://lisresearch.org.

The Qualitative Paradigm: School of Computing, Dublin City University, www.computing.dcu.ie/~hruskin/RM2.htm.

Qualitative Research Web Sites: Ronald J. Chenail, Nova Southeastern University: www.nova.edu/ssss/QR/web.html.

Qualpage: Resources for qualitative research: GlobalQuig at the University of Georgia, www.qualitativeresearch.uga.edu/QualPage.

8

Quantitative approaches

Christine Urquhart

'How can quantitative research help improve my library service?'

'I'm not good with numbers and quantitative research is all about statistics, right?'

'You mean that the information I already collect about my service can be used for "quantitative research"?'

Introduction

You might be surprised to learn that you are already doing some quantitative research as part of your library practice: you just don't label it as such. Think of the range of routine statistical collections that your organization makes – customer statistics and resource usage figures, for example. On their own these may not be very meaningful, but what happens if you compare your statistics now with statistics for a year, or two years, ago? Or how your organization compares with another organization elsewhere? Longitudinal changes in customer usage may be telling you something about the quality of the service, or the effect of increased or reduced staff inputs, but we have to be careful about linking cause and effect. One of the key messages of the examples discussed later in the chapter is the care you need to take to avoid reaching mistaken conclusions. You may want to believe that the changes are the result of reduced resourcing, or the effect of your changes in an information literacy programme but beware – there may be other reasons. This chapter will help you understand what can, and cannot, be achieved through quantitative research. The emphasis will be on some examples to illustrate some of the principles of quantitative research. You may need to consult a basic statistics textbook as well for further explanation of some of the principles of statistical analysis, and some of the highlighted terms. Chapter 9 offers an outline of some of the main ideas.

If you are familiar with the type of data being collected routinely, you are probably also aware of some of the problems in the collection and analysis of such data. Can you be sure of the reliability of the data collection? For example, are all the staff counting the items in the same way? If you are benchmarking your activity against that of another organization, are they counting in the same way that you are? Do you share the same interpretations of what it is you are counting? Next, is the data collection robust? For example, if you are counting things manually, how easy is it for someone to cheat, or make some figures up? And just as bad, or worse, how likely is it for the library system to go down, or for some other computer problems to occur – which may affect data collection?

Measures and indicators

One important idea to get straight is the difference between measures and indicators. Confusion about this underlies some of the reasons why people mistrust quantitative research. Fundamentally, quantitative research often makes us uncomfortable, as the figures seem to be telling us something we do not believe. Sometimes the figures are correct, of course, and the message is uncomfortable, but often our problem is that the figures are presented as unambiguous representations of concepts. For example, we might want to measure 'customer satisfaction'. We can ask a sample of customers about their level of satisfaction, but we know from experience of running the service that the answers depend on their expectations, their lifestyle, and when we ask for their views. Alternatively, we take the 'proof of the pudding is in the eating' approach and conclude that if customers are satisfied they will use the service and that increased satisfaction should be reflected in increased service use. Service use is a measure, but we are using it as an indicator of our concept of customer satisfaction. What makes a customer satisfied is likely to change, of course, particularly with the changes in the way we do things in an internet age. It is perfectly justifiable for library services to make changes to the way they measure satisfaction, but those changes can seem suspicious to outsiders, who might suspect we are simply trying to fiddle the figures. Changes in our indicators can make assessment of changes in satisfaction very difficult, if not impossible, to assess. Most quantitative researchers expect to find the same measures used in a pre-test, or previous test, as those used post-test, or in a later test. There are some ways around this problem of keeping relevant with measures. The first is to use several indicators together to get nearer the concept of customer satisfaction. The second is to devise a battery of questions designed to test some views on what might influence customer satisfaction (based on theory and previous research), and work out what the new dimensions of satisfaction are.

What questions are suitable for quantitative research, evaluation or audit?

Quantitative research, evaluation or audit usually requires counting of numbers (amounts) or counting along a scale (e.g. a satisfaction scale). As stressed in the previous section, we need to be very careful that what we are counting relates to what we are trying to measure. For funders and policymakers, numbers often seem to be convincing, and quantitative research offers the possibility of assessing quickly whether a policy is working through measurements of some sort. Is there a change? How large is the change? How big is the problem? How many staff are necessary to handle the scale of current activities?

One of the main concerns in quantitative research is deciding whether the differences you might find, in, for example, a trial of two different interventions, are actually meaningful. Speaking in statistical terms, you'll need to assess the significance of the findings. To do this, we need to approach the research carefully, aware that there may be other factors that have made a difference (apart from our intervention), and aware that the sample of participants we had for the intervention may have been less representative of the population than we would have hoped. Let's look at the way one quantitative research study was designed (Case study 8.1), to explain how questions suitable for quantitative research are identified.

Case study 8.1 Identifying questions suitable for quantitative research

---

Xie, B. (2011) Older Adults, E-Health Literacy, and Collaborative Learning: an experimental study, *Journal of the American Society for Information Science and Technology (JASIST)*, **62** (5), 933–46.

The theory-driven Electronic Health Information for Life-Long Learners via Collaborative Learning (eHILLL-CL) intervention, developed and tested in public libraries, aims to improve older adults' e-health literacy. A total of 172 older adults participated in this study from August 2009 to June 2010. Significant differences were found from pretest to posttest in general computer/Web knowledge and skill gains and in e-health literacy ($p<0.001$ in all cases; effect sizes: 0.5–2.1; statistical power: 1.00 even at the 0.01 level) and three attitude measures ($p<0.05$) for both computer anxiety and attitudes toward the aging experience in physical change, and $p<0.01$ for attitude toward the CL method; effect sizes: 0.2–0.3; statistical power: 0.4–0.8, at the 0.05 level). No significant difference was found in other variables. Participants were highly positive about the intervention and reported positive changes in health-related behavior and decision making. Group composition (based on gender, prior familiarity with peers, or prior computer experience) showed no significant impact on CL outcomes. These findings contribute to the CL and health literacy literatures and infer that CL can be a useful method for improving older adults' e-health literacy when using the specific strategies developed for this study, which suggests that social interdependence theory can be generalized beyond the younger population and formal educational settings. ▦

Xie wanted to test whether a collaborative learning approach for e-health literacy training in public libraries would work for older adults. The paper describes the justification for collaborative learning, and discusses some of the gaps in the evidence. These gaps include the transferability of findings for younger people to an older population, knowledge about what actually makes collaborative learning effective, deciding on suitable outcome measures, effect of gender and effect of previous computer experience. These gaps influenced the research questions that were asked, and the hypotheses that were set up for testing. One of the hypotheses tested was 'General computer/internet knowledge increases significantly from pre-intervention (the baseline) to post-intervention'. The null hypothesis is that there is no difference (in computer/internet knowledge, in this case), and conventionally this is the hypothesis that is held, unless the statistical tests show that we should shift to the alternative hypothesis, that there is a difference. There is always a risk that even if the results indicate we should accept that there is a difference, the null hypothesis was the correct one. The meaning of p, usually the significance level of 5% (0.05) is the risk we take in rejecting the null hypothesis in favour of the alternative hypothesis when in reality the null hypothesis is the correct one.

Some statistical tests assume that the sample distribution of responses (e.g. results on a computer/internet general knowledge test) are distributed in a particular way, and the tests do not work well with data that are not distributed that way. Sometimes the tests used, such as the t-test used by Xie, behave well even if the distribution is a bit skewed from the ideal for testing.

Many tests assume a normal distribution, the 'bell-shaped curve', which is what you would get when measuring the heights of staff in your organization. There are a few people at the extremes (very tall, or very short) but most are distributed in the middle, and the mean (average height) will be at the middle of the bell shape (see Chapter 9).

In the research by Xie, 111 participants completed both the pre- and post-tests. The results, e.g. for computer/internet knowledge, show a significant change. The average or mean score for pre-test was 3.36, post-intervention the score was 4.13. Not everyone scored 3.36 pre-test – there was a spread of scores around 3.36 which is expressed as the standard deviation of 1.24, and similarly post-intervention a standard deviation of 1.15. The t-test calculations demonstrated that there was a significant difference, indicating that obtaining scores like these would be very unlikely in the event of there actually being no difference in the pre- and post-intervention scores. This being the case, these results are interpreted as indicating that some other factor, and very probably the experimental intervention, influenced the participants' scores. Therefore, it appears that the intervention brought about the improvement in scores at post-test compared with at pre-test. It is worth noting that effect size and sample size each have some bearing on the outcome of the t-test. If you do not expect to find a large difference (in the averages before and after the intervention) you will need a larger sample than you would need if the difference between the averages before and after is expected to be large.

Collecting the data

For evaluation and audit, the obvious source of data is the organization itself, and what your library and the parent organization collect as routine statistics, or occasional supplementary surveys. For the Association of Research Libraries project on library assessment, Hiller, Kyrillidou and Self, (2008) collected a wide range of data from the 24 libraries visited and the list (Figure 8.1 overleaf) provides some reminders of the possible sources of quantitative data that could contribute to evaluation, audit and research.

Before discussing the list in more detail, it is worth noting that almost all the libraries studied by Hiller, Kyrillidou and Self noted difficulties in using data effectively, and around three-quarters cited problems in data collection and/or data analysis. Common sense indicates that trying to integrate different types of data will be difficult. Data may have been collected at different times, and that makes comparisons more difficult. Changes in the

- Standardized surveys regularly conducted (e.g. LibQUAL+™)
- Use statistics, e-metrics – data mining on the usage metrics for e-resource collections
- Usability testing (human–computer interaction testing, with some quantitative analysis)
- Customer surveys (presumably with some qualitative data but likely to be quantitative as well)
- Process analysis/improvement studies (these are more likely to be systems analysis studies but may include some quantitative data, e.g. on traffic flows for people or items being processed)
- Space/facility analysis (again, likely to be based around systems analysis but with some quantitative data).

Figure 8.1 *Possible sources of quantitative data*

definition of the data to be collected, different interpretations – all these cause problems whenever trying to do simple adding, or subtracting, operations.

As an example of some of the pitfalls, compare the following sets of statistics, and the different values quoted:

- Percentage of adults using public libraries (January to December 2009): **38%** (Source: *Taking Part* survey, cited in Sproston and Purdon, 2010. This figure includes physical and remote online usage.)
- Members of a public library (2008–9): 35.6 million (based on an estimate of **58%** of the population holding a library card).

(Source: LISU, 2012)

There is quite a large difference between 58% and 38%, even supposing that members of a public library will include children, who are not included in one estimate. The initial lesson to be learnt from these sets of statistics is that library 'usage' needs to be very carefully defined. The *Taking Part* survey does appear to reflect a usage pattern that we might expect to be representative today – some physical visits, and some online usage. The second figure for 'members of a public library' is based on an estimate of 58% of the population holding a library card, but that does not mean that they use the library card, of course. In addition, the LISU table cites two sources for the data, and the same estimate of 58% has been applied for all years from 2000/01 to 2010/11 (a decision which is not justified in the notes).

The next question to ask is about the way the data have been collected.

Case study 8.2 Quantitative data collection

Sproston, K. and Purdon, S. (2010) Taking Part and Active People Surveys: an independent evaluation, Department for Culture, Media and Sport (DCMS), London, 7.

> *Taking Part* has been funded by DCMS, Sport England, Arts Council England, the Museums, Libraries and Archives Council, and English Heritage since 2005. It is a face-to-face continuous survey of adults aged 16 and over, and children aged 5–15. The interview lasts around 45 minutes, and information is collected on participation in sport, arts, museums and galleries, libraries, archives, and heritage. Until recently, its key objective has been to provide robust measurement for DCMS's Public Service Agreement (PSA) and Departmental Strategic Objective (DSO) targets (on increasing participation in culture and sport). With a large sample size (14,452 adults and 2,500 children aged 11 to 15 in 2008–2009) it allows detection of small changes in the population's participation levels.

A footnote provides us with the information that the data are collected through the use of showcards to list the activities.

The extract presented in Case study 8.2 claims that the sample size is large – but are you surprised that 17,000 individuals are sufficient to give a good picture of what is happening among a population of 50 million individuals? (In case you wonder, I have checked the Office of National Statistics website to obtain a rough estimate of the population of England). This is probably an appropriate point to deal with some of the strange behaviour of sampling statistics. These rules apply whether you are intending to conduct a research project or simply doing a straightforward evaluation. The hard work is partly done for you when you can use software available on the web to find out how many people you need to survey to be sure that the percentage you obtain is a good 'ballpark' figure. I used the Creative Research Systems (2012) calculator and found that, for a sample size of 17,000, and a population of 50 million, the confidence interval is quite small (plus or minus 1%). Essentially this means, for a 99% confidence level (as confident as you can be with statistics):

> We can be 99% confident that – if we had repeated the *Taking Part* survey again in 2009 – we would find that the percentage of adults using public libraries would range between 37% (38–1) and 39% (38+1).

Unfortunately many library surveys are done in hundreds, not thousands, and often, as we shall see later, our confidence intervals (here, the plus or minus one percentage point) are often much larger.

Returning to the first item on the list of quantitative data sources (standardized surveys), the moral of the story is to use the results of standardized surveys, particularly if the sample size is large, but be careful to check how the data have been collected and whether any estimation factors have been applied, before assuming that the standardized survey data can be used for your own setting.

Returning to the LISU figure of 58% – it seems strange, and perhaps coincidental, that a Pew Internet Research study (Miller, Purcell and Rainie, 2012), cites a figure of 58% of Americans aged 16 or over, for the percentage having a library card. Again, looking at how the data have been collected, the Pew Internet Research study is based on 'nationally representative' telephone surveys of the population, using mobile phone and landline samples, and the surveys are conducted in both English and Spanish. The main 2011 sample involved 2986 Americans. This does not seem a large number but if you feed the numbers into the sample size calculator, using an estimate of 312 million for the US population, and click on the 99% confidence level, the confidence interval is 2.36. This means, using the same model as above:

> We can be 99% confident that – if we had repeated the telephone survey again in 2012 – we would find that the percentage of Americans holding library cards would range between 55.6% and 60.4% (I have rounded the percentage to the first figure after the decimal point).

For most practical purposes, that range of just under five percentage points either way is very respectable. For many surveys, it is worth trying to get a response from at least 300 respondents, preferably 400 if you can, to ensure that your confidence interval is around plus or minus 5 percentage points.

Statistical compilations – LISU and benchmarking

The other lesson to draw from the above discussion is that LISU statistics are not useless, but, as with all the other statistics cited in the paragraphs above, please read the small print in the notes sections. LISU resources include a selection of statistical information for and about the library domain in the UK. LISU also collates and prepares for publication the annual management statistics of SCONUL (Higher Education and National Libraries) and UCISA (Universities and Colleges Information Systems Association). LISU undertake many consultancy projects and tailored statistics for particular user groups or settings may be available in some of the special reports.

If you are interested in, or worried by, the problems of variations in the way routine library statistics are collected, then a LISU report by Greenwood and Creaser (2006) on data collection is worth reading. Some of the differences in compiling the returns made the comparisons between the library services very difficult, as like was not really being compared with like. For example, this was evident in the way staff are counted – the degree of centralization of some support services may not be truly reflected in the returns different public libraries made to CIPFA (Chartered Institute of Public Finance and Accountancy). Even seemingly simple metrics, such as visitor counts, depend on where the visitor counter is located in the library, and the report concluded that a standardized method of counting and calibration was necessary for automatic counters.

The value of many benchmarking exercises is often the discussion over what to measure and how, to ensure that the benchmarking comes up with genuinely valid comparisons. The M25 consortium of academic libraries is aiming to provide a benchmarking repository. The aim (which is similar to exercises conducted by the Medical Library Association in North America) is to encourage the libraries to enter their data, and to use that data for strategic planning. By using a standard format, a comparison between years is possible (for the member library) and comparisons among other (anonymized) libraries helps to query reasons for differences in apparent performance. Sometimes the differences may be associated with the way the library is organized and how its resourcing is accounted for by the parent organization. If those responsible for the benchmarking can sort out the data collection method differences and resolve discrepancies, then it should be possible to come up with some meaningful comparisons. Benchmarking is not just about showing that library A does more than library B, the real learning is how library A does what it does, compared to library B, and how both justify the decisions made.

E-metrics and web analytics

There is – thankfully – more collaborative activity on data collection for libraries now. Academic libraries need to develop standard tools for the measurement and analysis of e-metrics – the usage figures associated with downloads of e-resources – and Project COUNTER has helped the academic and national libraries, working with the resource vendors and aggregators, to develop COUNTER-compliant statistics so that it is possible to make comparisons. At the same time, many academic libraries have been developing repositories of their own scholarly outputs. One of the reasons for developing a repository is to showcase university research, increasingly important when research funders want evidence that research reports are made available. The IRUS-UK project (Needham and Stone, 2012) is a national aggregation service that provides standards-based statistics for all content downloaded from participating UK institutional repositories (IR)s. The service will collect usage data from participating repositories, process the data into COUNTER-compliant statistics and then present statistics back to originating repositories to be used in a variety of ways. One aim is to obtain a true picture of the impact of research outputs at the article or item level – total usage rather than having to add up usage on a publisher site, and then compare this with usage, perhaps calculated a different way, on the repository site.

Some of the repository managers have been using open source web analytic tools such as Google Analytics to detect and quantify usage (see Chapter 10). Black (2009) describes many other uses of Google Analytics beyond usage statistics. The use of web transaction logs is not straightforward. Black (2009) provides warnings about the IP address of the requesting machine (sometimes the user's computer but sometimes the proxy server of the internet service provider) and the problem of caching (the page may be used again but it is the version cached on the user's machine, not the one on the web server hosting the site). Black used the AWStats log file analysis program, an open source program. Using this program she was able to calculate:

- overall usage and repeat visits (noting how visit is defined for this analysis)
- timing and duration of visits
- access routes (direct or through a search engine, and proportion of each)
- most popular content.

The message is that usage statistics need to be handled carefully – check the meaning of what is being measured, the definitions involved, and what the transaction logs actually represent.

Bibliometrics and web metrics

Bibliometrics is a method (with supporting meta-theories) that arose from information science. Many of the quantitative and qualitative methods we use are borrowed from other disciplines – bibliometrics is our own (Milojević and Sugimoto, 2012). Much of the research using bibliometric techniques has focused on measurement of scientific activity and productivity (scientometrics), or scholarly communication, or webometrics (Thelwall, 2009). Altmetrics is a new term coined to describe attempts to measure the totality of scholarly impact, which now includes activity on online reference management systems such as Mendeley and Zotero, social media such as Twitter and scholarly blogs. 'Altmetrics aren't citations, nor are they webometrics; although these latter approaches are related to altmetrics, they are relatively slow, unstructured, and closed.' (Priem et al., 2010). Bibliometric techniques are likely to be of interest to any libraries involved in research support services and the specialist libraries supporting research organizations. Researchers (and obviously their funders) are interested in the impact of their research, and many national research assessment exercises are likely to make some use of bibliometric techniques.

A wide range of questions can be answered through bibliometric research (Urquhart, 2006). For library managers some of the principles behind the techniques may be applied to management problems such as the obsolescence of electronic journals. Analysis of the transaction logs of Emerald Insight (mainly management and business journals) and Blackwell's Synergy, over specific time periods, showed that the download half-life was one year (Nicholas et al., 2006). In other words, of a dataset that included nine months of 2003, over 50% of downloads were for articles published in 2002 or 2003. Explanation of patterns is made more complex by the availability of older material through electronic archives (which may encourage more downloading and citation), different policies and models on open access.

Citation analysis methodologies have been reviewed (Hoffmann and Doucette, 2012) to provide guidance on how to use citation analysis to detect patterns of use. For example, by examining the sources cited in a key journal for a group of users (e.g. nurses) it is possible to assess whether a library service is meeting the needs of nurses – who might well want access to some of the sources cited in the articles they read. Citation analysis can be used to study types of resource cited, age of cited resources, frequency of citation to journal titles, and library holdings. Mapping studies of the nursing literature have been conducted by the Nursing and Allied Health Resources section of the Medical Library Association. This sort of study is important for nursing libraries, as the range of resources that nursing researchers may need is quite large. It is obviously much easier to make the case for including a journal in a database or library collection if there is evidence to show that it is cited frequently. Citation analysis can be a time-consuming process and Hoffmann and Doucette recommend judicious use of sampling and other methods to complement citation analysis before making management decisions.

When have enough data been collected?

One of the most common questions people have when thinking about quantitative research is about the size of a sample – how many should be surveyed to get as true a picture of opinion, experience, skills or knowledge as possible? From earlier sections you might be thinking that if 17,000 people are required to pinpoint, quite accurately, opinions on the use of public libraries in a population of 50 million – that's nearly 3000 times greater than 17,000 – then it should not be too difficult to get a large enough sample for a library user population of say, around 10,000 students. Unfortunately sample size estimations do not work on a nice proportional basis.

One of the aims of any survey is to generalize from the sample. It is not normally possible to investigate the entire population, and it should be stressed here that when statisticians talk about populations they do not necessarily mean people. If you were assessing information literacy skills on a particular test, the population of interest is all the possible test results that could be produced, rather than the individuals doing the tests. If the aim is to generalize, we want as representative a sample as possible. It is easier to get sample bias (an unrepresentative sample) with smaller samples, as Case study 8.3 shows.

Case study 8.3 The significance of sample size

Imagine you are pooling three sets of information literacy test results – one group of 10 outstandingly proficient results, one group of 10 very poor results, and one group of 10 middling results. If you took a sample of 8, you could end up with 8 from the outstandingly proficient or from the very poor results sets. If the sample size was 15, then the sample would have to include more than one set of results, and we are more likely to get a representative sample. If the sample size was 20, then your chances of getting a representative sample are better still, although there is a small chance that you could be biased high (10 outstandingly proficient + 10 middling) or biased low (10 very poor + 10 middling). If you reflect on the possible combinations, you should begin to see that you actually need quite a large sample here to be reasonably sure of getting a representative sample. ▦

Sample size and confidence intervals

If your population is 10,000 students (for a survey of student satisfaction with library services), how many students do you think you need to survey to get a representative sample? We are going to assume at this stage that it is possible to randomly sample, so that all the students have the same chance of being selected. At this point you should use a sample size calculator on the web (see Chapter 10). Assume that we would be happy with a confidence interval of plus or minus 5, so that we could say, for example, that 75% (plus or minus 5%) of students were happy or very happy with library services, with a 95% confidence level. For the calculator select the 95% confidence level, put in the population of 10,000, and then press calculate. The answer should be 370. Now imagine that a colleague in a much smaller institution wants to do a survey. Obviously their resources are much more limited. If you need to sample 370 students, how many students would need to be sampled in an institution of 1000 students? The result – 278 students – might surprise you, but think back to problem of the small sample discussed in Case study 8.3.

Case study 8.4 Sample size and confidence intervals

Bridges, L. M. (2008) Who Is Not Using The Library? A comparison of undergraduate academic disciplines and library use, *Libraries and the Academy*, 8 (2), 187–96.

This study examines the differences in undergraduate library use by academic discipline at Oregon State University (OSU). In the winter of 2006, an online questionnaire about physical and virtual library use was distributed to 3,227 OSU undergraduates; 949 responses were received. Chi-square tests were used to distinguish differences between user groups. The results indicate that students in the Agricultural Sciences College use the physical library less than students in the Liberal Arts College, Health and Human Sciences College, and the Sciences College; students from the Engineering College use the virtual library less than students from the Liberal Arts College. ▦

As an example from the literature, Bridges attempted to examine the relationship between academic discipline and library use at Ohio State University. A random sample of around 22% of the undergraduate students (n=14,443) at the Corvallis site was targeted and 949 responses were received. Plugging the figures into the sample size calculator indicates that – overall – the size of the sample was more than sufficient to give, say, a percentage (plus or minus 5%) of the students that used the library regularly. The research team describe how they compared the percentages of freshmen, sophomores, juniors and seniors in their sample with the percentages of each student group in the population, and – as far as it is possible to judge – the proportions are reasonably similar. The problems come when trying to compare the academic disciplines, as the eight subject colleges varied in size, and for the smaller colleges we might be running into the small numbers and sample bias problem. Using the sample size calculator, and assuming that a subject college had 1000 students, we can see that for a confidence level of 95% we would need a sample of 400 students from that population of 1000 students, to be able to state that x% of a particular college (plus or minus 5%) used the library regularly. For a population of 2799 students (estimated College of Engineering figure) the sample size required would be 538, and the sample size obtained was 205 students, under half what ideally is necessary.

This example illustrates one of the problems for many library evaluations. Determining what is feasible and what can be answered with some degree of certainty requires careful planning. In this case, the sample obtained was large enough to give a clear indication of views on usage for the undergraduate body as a whole, and (probably) the changes for particular year groups. With all the benefits of hindsight, to answer the question about the effect of academic discipline, the researchers might have thought carefully about what they really needed to know, and how they might have grouped the disciplines to avoid some of the small sample bias problems. The sample size for the College of Engineering students (n=205), for a population of 2799 students, actually gives a confidence interval of 6.6% (and confidence level of 95%). For many practical purposes this might be sufficient, although not as rigorous as desirable.

Yang and Hofmann (2011) examined progress toward the Next Generation Catalogue (NGC) in North American colleges and universities. To do this, they took a 10% sample of the population of colleges and universities, which worked out at 260, and from these 233 OPAC interfaces were examined. A checklist of items that characterize NGC was used to assess these OPAC interfaces. The authors state that the findings can be extrapolated to the population, and if you use the sample size calculator, at the 95% confidence level, you will find that the confidence interval is plus or minus 6%. (There is a mistake in the published paper, incidentally, as the authors have assumed that 6% is the entire interval, and it is 12%, (plus 6% one way, minus 6% the other).

Chances of interventions being effective – and confidence intervals

The example of 'average values' and confidence intervals in Case study 8.5 is outside the library and information science research field, but the theme of the topic is relevant to most of us: the use of a website with learning tools, information and some interactive elements, to support health promotion in the workplace.

Case Study 8.5 Average values and confidence intervals

Robroek, S. J., Lindeboom, D. E. and Burdorf, A. (2012) Initial and Sustained Participation in an Internet-Delivered Long-Term Worksite Health Promotion Program on Physical Activity and Nutrition, *Journal of Medical Internet Research,* **14** (2), e43.

Background
Determinants of participation in health promotion programs are largely unknown. To evaluate and implement interventions, information is needed regarding their reach as well as regarding the characteristics of program users and non-users.

Objective
In this study, individual, lifestyle, and health indicators were investigated in relation to initial, and sustained participation in an Internet-delivered physical activity and healthy nutrition program in the workplace setting. In addition, determinants of program website use were studied.

Methods
Determinants of participation were investigated in a longitudinal study among employees from six workplaces participating in a two-year cluster randomized controlled trial. The employees were invited by email to participate. At baseline, all participants visited a website to fill out the questionnaire on lifestyle, work, and health factors. Subsequently, a physical health check was offered, followed by face-to-face advice. Throughout the study period, all participants had access to a website with information on lifestyle and health,

and to fully automated personalized feedback on the questionnaire results. Only participants in the intervention received monthly email messages to promote website visits during the first year and had access to additional Web-based tools (self-monitors, a food frequency questionnaire assessing saturated fat intake, and the possibility to ask questions) to support behavior change. Website use was monitored by website statistics measuring access. Logistic regression analyses were conducted to identify characteristics of employees who participated in the program and used the website.

Results

Complete baseline data were available for 924 employees (intervention: n=456, reference: n=468). Lifestyle and health factors were not associated with initial participation. Employees aged 30 years and older were more likely to start using the program and to sustain their participation. Workers with a low intention to increase their physical activity level were less likely to participate (Odds Ratio (OR)=0.60, 95% Confidence interval (95%CI), 0.43-0.85) but more likely to sustain participation throughout the study period (ORs ranging from 1.40 to 2.06). Furthermore, it was found that smokers were less likely to sustain their participation in the first and second year (OR=0.54, 95%CI 0.35-0.82) and to visit the website (OR=0.72, 95%CI 0.54-0.96). Website use was highest in the periods immediately after the baseline (73%) and follow-up questionnaires (71% and 87%). Employees in the intervention were more likely to visit the website in the period they received monthly emails (OR=5.88, 95%CI 3.75-9.20) but less likely to visit the website in the subsequent period (OR=0.62, 95%CI 0.45-0.85).

Conclusions

Modest initial participation and high attrition in program use were found. Workers with a low intention to change their behavior were less likely to participate, but once enrolled they were more likely to sustain their participation. Lifestyle and health indicators were not related to initial participation, but those with an unhealthy lifestyle were less likely to sustain. This might influence program effectiveness. Regular email messages prompted website use, but the use of important Web-based tools was modest. There is a need for more appealing techniques to enhance retention and to keep those individuals who need it most attracted to the program. ▪

The research design was a randomized control trial (a cluster randomized design to be exact, with six workplaces involved). There were 456 participants in the intervention arm, 468 in the control arm. All had access to the website, and personalized feedback on the lifestyle questionnaire available. Only the intervention group received monthly e-mail messages in the first year of the intervention, and this group also had more tools available to them on the website. All participants had a physical health check at the start of the study. The results showed that 6% of the participants did not visit the website throughout the study period, 18% visited the website once, 13% twice, and 64% three times or more. The range of website visits during the whole two-year study period was 0–46, with a median of 3 visits (interquartile range: 2–6 visits). The median here is an 'average' value that is worked out by putting all the values for the number of visits in order (see Chapter 9). The reason that a median is a better estimator of the 'average' is that the distribution is likely to be lumpy (not an even bell-shaped curve) and that a few large values at the extreme end will distort the calculation of the mean value if you simply added up all the values and divided them by the number of data items. The 'interquartile range' means the middle group. If you divided the set of values into four quarters, then the interquartile range covers the 25% of values below the median and the 25% of values above the median. This range (2–6) and the actual range of website visits (0–46), together with the median of 3 visits, suggests that most participants did not exceed 6 visits – only a very small number visited much more than that.

Another of the findings is that in the period of 4–12 months after baseline, participants in the intervention condition, who received monthly e-mail messages during this period, were more likely to visit the website (OR=5.88, 95%CI 3.75-9.20, adjusted for company). OR means 'odds ratio', and is calculated in the following way:

- Of the 456 participants in the intervention arm, 123 visited the website (and 333 did not).
- Of the 468 participants in the control group, 28 visited the website (and 440 did not).
- The odds of an intervention group participant visiting the website is 123/333, and the odds of a control group participant visiting the website is much lower, at 28/440.
- The ratio of those two sets of odds is the odds ratio (and again, plug the figures into an online odds ratio calculator to check). In this case, the intervention group is almost six times more likely than the control group to visit the website. Please note that – even so – only around a quarter of the intervention group (123/456) actually visited the website!

In fact, the values I got were a little different from the figures cited in the article, but this could be something to do with the way I had to back-calculate the figures from some percentages quoted in the paper. The moral is that it is always worth checking the calculations if you need to use the figures for your own purposes. The problem about large samples is getting them, of course, and often it is better to do a more tightly controlled study of a smaller sample, to help increase the response rate, and use some other complementary qualitative research method, to explain what is happening.

The confidence interval estimates how sure (to a 95% confidence level) we can be about the odds ratio. The calculation can be done using an odds ratio and confidence interval calculator available on the internet (see Chapter 10), but the same principles apply as before – smaller samples will have larger confidence intervals, and with larger samples we can be more confident that our result was about right, as the confidence interval is smaller. See Chapter 9 for more information about confidence intervals. In summary, first think carefully about the questions you want to ask, and work out what is feasible. It is very tempting to try to do subgroup analysis, to try to profile users, but remember the problems about small samples, the likely sampling bias and the way the confidence interval increases.

General guidance on survey instruments

Before setting out to design a questionnaire, it's worth checking whether anyone else has done a similar study. There is no point in making extra work for yourself, if other groups have already done the hard work of developing and testing a questionnaire. Obviously you should check whether the questionnaire worked, and whether the researchers checked the internal validity of the questionnaire. There are many validated questionnaires that should work and measure what they claim to measure, particularly for psychological behaviours.

Sometimes some alterations made be required for your particular setting. Lu and Adkins (2012) describe how they modified the Bostick Library Anxiety Scale to make it more suitable for their research subjects – international graduate students. Sensibly, they retained as much of the original scale as possible, but added one more category, on language and cultural barriers. To check whether the test was internally reliable they used Cronbach's alpha test. Cronbach's alpha measures whether the items in each of the subscales (e.g. language and cultural carriers) were measuring the same general concept and whether the instrument as a whole was measuring the same general concept (in this case library anxiety).

Are there simple statistics?

The answer is yes, and the commentary on some of the examples cited in this chapter should encourage you to challenge some of the statistics presented in your professional journals. If you think they look strange, you could be right. Check whether the tables and text match – they should, but reviewers may have missed something.

Statistics revels in the unusual names often attached to tests, and you can do a simple Google search to check the details of a test named in an article. The important thing to check is the conditions of use – when it is appropriate to use the test, and what the restrictions are on the distribution of the data. Many tests are only valid when used on the 'normal' distribution (the bell-shaped curve – see Chapter 9).

The challenge for some library and information science research is that the sample distribution is not necessarily normal. You may have heard of the 80:20 rule – that 80% of the usage (of services such as libraries) comes from 20% of the population, and that sort of distribution is like a mountain peak with a steep slope on one side (conventionally the left hand side, looking at it) and a very long gradual slope down on the right hand side. There are quite a few skewed distributions like that in library and information science research.

There are statistical tests that do not demand normal distributions, called 'non-parametric tests'. They will often work with much smaller samples than the sample sizes that I have quoted earlier, and you can even do them with paper and pencil.

Case study 8.6 What to do in the absence of normal distribution

---

Price, T., Urquhart, C. and Cooper, J. (2007) Using a Prompt Sheet to Improve the Reference Interview in a Health Telephone Helpline Services, *Evidence Based Library and Information Practice*, **2** (3), 27–42.

Objective

The study examined whether a prompt sheet improved the reference interview process for health information advisers working at NHS Direct, a 24 hour telephone helpline that provides confidential health care advice for the public in England.

Method

A randomized control trial was conducted at eight NHS Direct sites across
England in 2003-04. Newly recruited health information advisers (n=30), full
and part-time, were randomly allocated to a control group (n=15) or
intervention group (n=15), and 26 completed the study. Existing health
information advisers were involved in the planning and design of the
intervention. The prompt sheet included prompts for demographic
information, reason for call, condition/treatment plan, existing knowledge of
caller, special needs of the caller, handling a call empathetically, conclusion.
Testing of reference interview expertise was done at the end of basic training,
and two months later, using the same ten test questions that were based on
common questions received by NHS Direct. A relevance framework for possible
responses was drawn up for each question for scoring test responses, with
more relevant responses scoring higher than less relevant responses.

Results

The average score of prompt (experimental) and non-prompt (control)
participants increased on the second test, for each of the 10 questions. The
prompt group improved significantly more overall than the control group.
There was variation within the groups. Sixteen health information assistants
showed a net increase in their score over all ten questions (10 experimental
group, six control group). The post-test score for an individual on a particular
question did sometimes decrease from the pre-test score, but all 26 improved
on at least one question. Previous call handler experience did not appear to
influence the extent of improvement, but length and type of experience in the
post may have an influence.

Conclusion

The trial demonstrated the benefit of a simple and inexpensive prompt sheet
for some, though not all, newly recruited health information advisers to
improve their reference interview technique. ■

Often a pre-test, post-test design of scores on a knowledge test would use a
t-test, but in Case study 8.6 the randomized sample was small (26 completed
the study) and the distribution was unlikely to be normal. Instead, non-
parametric tests were used to examine whether the prompt sheet was
effective, and what might be making the difference.

Another study that used non-parametric statistics (Taheri and Hariri,
2012) compared the indexing and ranking of XML-based content objects

containing MARCXML and XML-based Dublin Core (DCXML) metadata elements by general search engines (Google and Yahoo!)

Summary

Quantitative research requires careful planning before going ahead with data collection. Thankfully, many library and information professionals now see the value of collaborative data collection, and more datasets are being made available for use by collaborating members or for everyone to access. If there is an available dataset that fits your needs, then use it, rather than wasting time doing your own data collection exercise. Try to get expert statistical advice before you start, but be prepared to question that advice. Similarly, use 'tried and tested' questionnaires or interview schedules wherever possible, as these give you a good basis for comparing your findings with those obtained by other researchers. The examples described in the chapter should help you reflect that you are probably doing quantitative research or audit already, without realizing it. Make the most of the routine statistics that are collected, and remember the difference between a measure and an indicator. Last but not least, do not be afraid to play with the numbers and statistics, and make the most of any software that helps you to display the results well.

Points for reflection

- Think about the kinds of information/data you already collect as part of your work. Having read this chapter, how has it changed the way you view the potential use you can put it to? In what way? Do you need to be more careful about the consistency of data collection?
- What statistical or quantitative research terminology is new to you? Check that you understand the meaning of some of the terms highlighted in italics in the chapter, such as randomized, sample distribution, metrics, indicators, median, mean, confidence intervals, non-parametric statistics.
- How will you approach the critical reading of an article or report that uses quantitative methods? What are some of the key points you need to check about sampling and testing? Have the authors presented confidence intervals to help you assess the transferability of the findings?

References

Black, E. L. (2009) Web Analytics: a picture of the academic library website user, *Journal of Web Librarianship*, **3** (1), 3–14.

Bridges, L. M. (2008) Who is Not Using the Library? A comparison of undergraduate academic disciplines and library use, *Libraries and the Academy*, **8** (2), 187–96.

Creative Research Systems (2012) *Sample Size Calculator*, www.surveysystem.com/sscalc.htm.

Greenwood, H. and Creaser, C. (2006) *Best Practice in Data Collection: report of a benchmarking exercise for Leicestershire Library Services and Warwickshire Library and Information Services*, Occasional Paper no. 36, Loughborough University, LISU.

Hiller, S., Kyrillidou, M. and Self, J. (2008) When the Evidence is Not Enough: organizational factors that influence effective and successful library assessment, *Performance Measurement and Metrics*, **9** (3), 223–30.

Hoffmann, K. and Doucette, L. (2012) A Review of Citation Analysis Methodologies, *College and Research Libraries*, **73** (4), 321–35.

LISU (2012) *Trends in UK Library and Publishing Statistics*, Loughborough University.

Lu, Y. and Adkins, D. (2012) Library Anxiety Among International Graduate Students, *Proceedings of ASIST 2012, October 28–31*, Baltimore, MD.

M25 Consortium, www.m25lib.ac.uk.

Miller, C., Purcell, K. and Rainie, L. (2012) *Reading Habits in Different Communities*, http://libraries.pewinternet.org/2012/12/20/reading-habits-in-different-communities.

Milojević, S. and Sugimoto, C. R. (2012) Metrics and ASIS&T: an introduction, *Bulletin of the American Society for Information Science and Technology*, www.asis.org/Bulletin/Aug-12/AugSep12_Milojevic_Sugimoto.html.

Needham, P. and Stone, G. (2012) IRUS-UK: making scholarly statistics count in UK repositories, *Insights*, **25** (3), 262–7.

Nicholas, D., Huntington, P., Jamali, H. R. and Tenopir, C. (2006) What Deep Log Analysis Tells Us About the Impact of Big Deals: case study OhioLINK, *Journal of Documentation*, **62** (4), 482–508.

Price, T., Urquhart, C. and Cooper, J. (2007) Using a Prompt Sheet to Improve the Reference Interview in a Health Telephone Helpline Service, *Evidence Based Library and Information Practice*, **2** (3), 27–42.

Priem, J., Taraborelli, D., Groth, P. and Neylon, C. (2010) Altmetrics: a manifesto, http://altmetrics.org/manifesto.

Robroek, S. J., Lindeboom, D. E. and Burdorf, A. (2012) Initial and Sustained Participation in an Internet-Delivered Long-Term Worksite Health Promotion

Program on Physical Activity and Nutrition, *Journal of Medical Internet Research,* **4** (2), e43.

Sproston, K. and Purdon, S. (2010) *Taking Part and Active People Surveys: an independent evaluation,* Department for Culture, Media and Sport (DCMS), London.

Taheri, S. M., and Hariri, N. (2012) MARCXML and Dublin Core's Metadata Elements by General Search Engines, *The Electronic Library,* **30** (4), 480–91.

Thelwall, M. (2009) *Introduction to Webometrics: quantitative web research for the social sciences,* Morgan and Claypool, Synthesis Lectures on Information Concepts, Retrieval, and Services, 2009, Vol. 1, No. 1, San Rafael, CA.

Urquhart, C. (2006) *Solving Management Problems in Information Service,* Chandos Publishing, Oxford, 46–52.

Xie, B. (2011) Older Adults, E-health Literacy, and Collaborative Learning: an experimental study, *Journal of the American Society for Information Science and Technology (JASIST),* **62** (5), 933–46.

Yang, S. Q. and Hofmann, M. A. (2011) A Study of the OPACs of 260 Academic Libraries in the USA and Canada, *Library Hi-Tech,* **29** (2), 266–300.

Recommended further reading

LISU (2013) Publications, www.lboro.ac.uk/microsites/infosci/lisu/pages/publications/publications.html.

9

Data analysis

Jenny Craven and Jillian R. Griffiths

'What is data analysis? In fact, what is data?'

'Statistics are just plain scary!'

'Can't I get someone else to do this bit?'

What is data analysis?

Data analysis is a vital step in the research process. Whatever method has been applied to data collection, at some point it will be necessary to translate raw data into usable information. Analysis is usually undertaken after all the data have been gathered, but it may also be undertaken during the collection period or as part of a pilot study to ensure the most appropriate method of collection is selected. Whichever approach is undertaken, it is important to remember that without data, no analysis can take place, and that the quality of your analysis will depend, to a great extent, on the quality of your data. As Robson puts it: 'No data – no project' (Robson, 2002, 385).

What comes before?

Before data analysis can commence it will be necessary to go through a number of stages. These have been discussed in earlier chapters, but in summary, before the analysis stage, you should have undertaken the following activities:

- identifying research problems
- searching the existing literature base
- critical appraisal of the literature

- developing the questions and/or hypothesis
- applying a theoretical base
- sampling strategies
- data collection techniques.

You should now be ready to start analysing your data.

Types of analysis: quantitative and qualitative

There are a variety of approaches to conducting research (see Chapter 1) but in general research tends to use an inductive or deductive approach.

An inductive approach seeks to build up a theory that is adequately grounded in a number of relevant cases and involves comparing concepts or categories emerging from one stage of the data analysis with concepts emerging from the next stage. These comparisons form the basis of the emerging theory. The researcher continues with this process of comparison until no new significant categories or concepts can be identified (see Lacey and Duff, 2001, 7; Robson, 2002; Strauss and Corbin, 1998).

A deductive approach begins with general ideas (such as theory, laws, or principles) and from this a specific hypothesis is formed, which can be tested in order to support the general ideas. This approach seeks to use existing theory to shape the approach to aspects of data analysis. It involves attempting to build an explanation while collecting and analysing the data.

Data analysis can include a variety of approaches: for example, analysing responses to an interview or focus group questions, written responses to an online questionnaire, diary entries, document analysis or observation notes. Data is collected in text and numbers, or can be turned into text or numbers, and is generally split into two types, quantitative and qualitative.

Deductive research is often associated with quantitative experiments or surveys, and inductive research with qualitative interviews or ethnographic work. However, this is not a hard-and-fast rule, as experimental research may use quantitative or qualitative data or a combination of both. For example, in a study of the information-seeking behaviour of visually impaired people in electronic library environments, numerical data, such as time taken to complete a task, surveying the page, and the number of keystrokes performed was logged, as well as open interview questions to capture user perceptions relating to the task undertaken (Craven, 2003).

The following sections will describe quantitative and qualitative data analysis in more depth.

What is quantitative data analysis?

Quantitative data analysis is a systematic approach to investigations during which numerical data is collected, or the researcher transforms what is collected or observed into numerical data. It often describes a situation or event; answering the 'what' and 'how many' questions a researcher may have about the situation under investigation.

A quantitative approach is often concerned with finding evidence to either support or contradict an idea or hypothesis you might have. A hypothesis is where a predicted answer to a research question is stated, for example, you might state that if you give a student training in how to use a search engine it will improve their success in finding information on the internet. You could then go on to explain why a particular answer is expected – you put forward a theory. Most often when a researcher is interested in hypothesis testing they will conduct an experiment to gather their data.

A quantitative approach is also concerned with generalizability or external validity. This involves the extent to which the results of a study can be generalized (or applied) beyond the sample to the larger population. In other words, can you apply what you found in your study to other people (population validity) or settings (ecological validity).

For example, a study of postgraduate Masters students in a UK university that found one method of teaching statistics was superior to another may not be applicable with first-year undergraduate students (population) in an American university (ecological validity).

Reliability or internal validity is concerned with repeating a piece of research in order to establish the reliability of its findings. Reliability is the consistency and dependency of a measure. Sometimes it is referred to as the repeatability or the test-retest reliability. This means that a reliable test should produce the same results on successive trials.

Case study 9.1 An example of a review of studies considering reliability and validity

---

Walsh, A. (2009) Information Literacy Assessment: where do we start?, *Journal of Librarianship and Information Science*, **41** (1) 19–28.

Abstract: Interest in developing ways to assess information literacy has been growing for several years. Many librarians have developed their own tools to assess aspects of information literacy and have written articles to share their experiences.

This article reviews the literature and offers readers a flavour of the methods being used for assessment: those which are popular within the field and also illustrative examples from some of the case studies found, particularly where they show how the reliability and validity of the methods have been considered. It does not aim to be an exhaustive list of case studies or methods, but a representative sample to act as a 'jumping off point' for librarians considering introducing assessment of information literacy into their own institutions. ▧

This case study article presents a useful summary of information literacy research studies, with a particular focus on reliability and validity considerations.

Quantitative data may be obtained in a variety of ways and from a number of different sources (see Chapter 8). Many of these are similar to sources of qualitative data (see Chapter 7).

This section of the chapter will focus on understanding the concepts behind statistical analysis before discussing descriptive statistical techniques in detail. Inferential statistics are introduced but please refer to the references included in the bibliography for detail regarding particular approaches.

An example study will be used throughout this section to enable you to see the different results obtained from applying different statistical approaches.

Hypothesis testing in quantitative research

In hypothesis testing we generally have two hypotheses:

1 A null hypothesis (which usually indicates no change or no effect)
2 An alternative hypothesis (which is usually our experimental hypothesis).

The evidence from the sample is taken to support either the null or the alternative hypothesis.

When a researcher is interested in hypothesis testing they will conduct an experiment to gather their data. For our example, we take one sample from a population of students, give them some training in how to search and then ask them to find some specific information. We ask another sample of students to search for the same specific information but don't give them training – and we see which group did better through a variety of different measures, some subjective and some objective. So, does the data we gather contain evidence that agrees with the alternative (experimental) hypothesis or the null hypothesis? In testing a hypothesis we never actually prove or disprove it; all we ever get is evidence from a sample that either (a) supports a hypothesis or (b) contradicts a hypothesis.

The hypothesis contains concepts that need to be measured. To do this we need to:

- translate concepts (the research idea/s) into measurable factors
- take these measurable factors and treat them as variables. (A variable is something that can be changed, such as a characteristic or value. So what does that mean? Anything that can vary can be considered a variable. For instance, age can be considered a variable because age can take different values for different people or for the same person at different times. Similarly, country can be considered a variable because a person's country can be assigned a value.)
- identify measurement scales to quantify variables.

In order to do this we need to take into account causality.

Causality: cause and effect in quantitative research

This is essentially concerned with showing how things come to be the way they are. To do this we need to identify and further understand our variables:

- **Independent variable** – the variable that is deliberately manipulated by the researcher
- **Dependent variable** – the variable that is measured to find out the effect of the manipulated (independent) variable
- **Control variables** – may be potential independent variables, but are held constant during the experiment.

In this instance our experimental (or alternative) hypothesis is that if we give students more training it will take less time to search and conversely if we give less training it will take more time to search – we have a cause (training) and effect (time taken). The null hypothesis is that there will be no change or effect.

So, we conduct an experiment where students are timed whilst searching for information to assess the speed of their searching behaviour; some were given prior search training.

- **Independent variable** (the variable that is deliberately manipulated by the researcher) = **training,** which we can manipulate by varying training given to different students.
- **Dependent variable** (the variable that is measured to find out the effect of the manipulated variable) = **time taken** to find information, which we can measure by timing how long to search.
- **Control variables** For example, searching behaviour may be affected by previous use, age, educational level, and even time of day. Some of these may be controllable, but others may not be, e.g. degree of frustration.

Independent variables are assumed to have a causal impact on the dependent variable – training is therefore assumed to have a causal impact on the length of time taken to find the information.

Case study 9.2 An example of variables within a research study

---

Getz, I. and Weissman, G. (2010) An Information Needs Profile of Israeli Older Adults, Regarding the Law and Services, *Journal of Librarianship and Information Science*, **42**, 136.

Based on Nicholas' framework for assessing information needs, this research aims to construct a profile of both Israeli older adults and their information needs regarding laws and social services. Data were collected by questionnaires answered by 200 older adults, born in Europe, Asia and Africa, who attended social clubs for older adults. The results indicated that older adults primarily require information for dealing with changes in their lives. They do not know enough about the laws and services existing for their benefit. Significant correlations were found between the age, educational level, self-reported health status and the subjects in which they are interested. ■

Case study 9.2 focuses particular attention on identifying the independent variables of the study.

Case study 9.3 An example of variables within a research study

---

Marton, C. and Choo, C. W. (2012) A Review of Theoretical Models of Health Information Seeking on the Web, *Journal of Documentation*, **68** (3), 330–52.

Purpose
By selectively reviewing theory-driven survey studies on internet health information seeking, the paper aims to provide an informal assessment of the

theoretical foundations and research methods that have been used to study this information behaviour.

Design/methodology/approach

After a review of the literature, four theory-driven quantitative survey studies are analyzed in detail. Each study is examined in terms of: theoretical framework; research variables that form the focus of the study; research design (sampling, data collection and analysis); and findings and results of hypothesis testing and model testing. The authors then discuss the theoretical models and analytical methods adopted, and identify suggestions that could be helpful to future researchers.

Findings

Taken as a whole, the studies reviewed point strongly to the need for multidisciplinary frameworks that can capture the complexity of online health information behaviour. The studies developed theoretical frameworks by drawing from many sources – theory of planned behaviour, technology acceptance model, uses and gratifications, health belief model, and information seeking models – demonstrating that an integration of theoretical perspectives from the health sciences, social psychology, communication research, and information science, is required to fully understand this behaviour. The results of these studies suggest that the conceptual models and analytical methods they adopted are viable and promising. Many relationships tested showed large effect sizes, and the models evaluated were able to account for between 23 and 50 percent of the variance in the dependent variables.

In Case study 9.3, particular attention is paid to identification of independent and dependent variables and presenting research variables of reviewed studies (see Marton and Choo, 2012, table 2).

Descriptive and inferential statistics

At the very beginning of your research it is critical to identify what you are trying to find out. It sounds simple, but pinning down exactly what you want to do will help you choose the data collection and analysis tool most appropriate for you. So, ask yourself:

- 'Am I trying to describe what happens with the participants in my sample?' *or*

- 'Do I want to be able to generalize my results to the wider population?' By 'generalize' we mean the degree to which the conclusions in your study would hold for other persons in other places and at other times.

If you want to describe what happens with your sample of participants then you will most likely use descriptive statistics (see Descriptive statistics below). And if you follow this approach then an online survey service would be a good tool to use, as it will update the frequency analysis each time a participant completes your questionnaire. Frequency analysis gives a simple summary of the number of responses to each question.

If you want to be able to generalize your results to a wider population you will need to use inferential statistics (see Inferential statistics, page 158). With these, you are trying to reach conclusions that extend beyond the immediate data of your study. For instance, we use inferential statistics to try to infer from the sample data what the wider population might think, whilst we use descriptive statistics simply to describe what's going on in our data.

Coupled with this you will also need to identify your variables in terms of levels of measurement, thinking of them as nominal, ordinal or scale (interval/ratio). This is necessary, as certain statistical tests can only be used with specific types of data to produce accurate results. Looking at these in more detail:

- **Nominal** (categories). Values on this scale are just labels, e.g. for the variable Gender the scale of measurement would be based on the labels of Male or Female.
- **Ordinal** (ranks). Values have inherent logical order but may have uneven or hard-to-define labels. So, we can say that we are more, or less, satisfied with something but we cannot exactly say by how much more. e.g. Very dissatisfied/Dissatisfied/Neutral/Satisfied/Very satisfied.
- **Scale, Interval and Ratio** variables are often treated as one:
  — Interval (scale). This ranks the order of items that are measured and allows you to quantify and compare the sizes of differences between them. For example, amongst pupils undertaking a spelling test, a score of 8 out of 10 will be higher than 6 and the difference between them is 2 points. Interval variables normally have an arbitrary minimum and maximum point, so for example, scoring 0 on the spelling test does not represent an absence of any spelling knowledge and nor does a score of 10 represent perfect spelling knowledge.

— Ratio (scale). This also has a logical order, equal intervals and a true zero, e.g. physical quantities, such as mass, length or energy are measured on ratio scales.

Descriptive statistics

Descriptive statistics are concerned with summarizing and describing the results from your research: they describe what the data shows. As well as reporting basic frequency analysis (adding up responses and reporting them as values – 5/42 participants – or percentages – 12%), you may also wish to undertake summary statistics.

Table 9.1 may help you to choose which method to use in analysing the measure of central tendency (the average) and the measure of dispersion (spread). Use of descriptive statistics can be seen in a wide variety of studies, for example Korobili et al., 2011; Ferebee and Davis, 2011 (who also undertook some inferential analysis); Johnson, Griffiths and Hartley, 2001 (which also presents some use of correlation analysis); Griffiths and Glass, 2011; Griffiths, 2012.

Table 9.1 *Measure of central tendency and the measure of dispersion*

Type of data	Measures of central tendency – *average*	Measure of dispersion – *spread*
Nominal	Mode	Verbal descriptions only
Ordinal	Mode and Median	Range
Interval/Ratio	Mode, Median and Mean	Statistical measures of deviation, especially standard deviation

Mean, median, mode

The arithmetic mean is the standard average, often simply called the 'mean'. It is often confused with the median (the middle value) and the mode (the most occurring or likely value).

The mean is the arithmetic average of a set of values, or distribution, and works well for data that is evenly distributed. However, for skewed distributions (where the frequency is higher on one side than the other) the mean is not necessarily the same as the middle value (median), or the most likely (mode). For example, mean income is skewed upwards by a small number of people with very large incomes, so that the majority have an income lower than the mean. In such an instance the mean is not a good representation of the average income.

By contrast, the median income is the level at which half the population is below and half is above and the mode income is the most likely income, and favours the larger number of people with lower incomes. So, for skewed distributions the median or mode are often more intuitive measures of such data than the mean because they better represent the average. An example of the use of the mean and the median can be seen in Nicholas, Huntington and Williams (2001), whilst Koehler (1999) presents results using the mean, median and standard deviation.

Mean

To calculate the arithmetic mean you must add up all the data, and then divide this total by the number of values in the data. For example, ten students are timed whilst searching for information on the internet. What is the arithmetic mean time taken to search?

> 1 minute + 3 minutes + 4 minutes + 4 minutes + 5 minutes + 5 minutes + 6 minutes + 7 minutes + 8 minutes + 10 minutes = 53 minutes
> There are 10 values, so you divide the total by 10:
> **53 ÷ 10 = arithmetic mean = 5.3 minutes.**

Median

The median time taken for searching in the case of our ten students is calculated by putting the values in order, then finding the middle value. If there are two values in the middle then you find the mean of these two values. So the time taken by each of the ten students to search for information in minutes:

> 1, 3, 4, 4, (5, 5,) 6, 7, 8, 10
> The middle values are marked in brackets, and they are both 5. Find the mean of these values:
> **5 + 5= 10 ÷ 2= 5. So the median is 5.**

Mode

The mode time taken to search in our example is the value that appears the most often in the data. It is possible to have more than one mode if there is more than one value that appears the most. So the time taken by each of the ten students to search for information in minutes:

1, 3, 4, 4, 5, 5, 6, 7, 8, 10
The values that appear most often are 4 and 5. They both appear more frequently than any of the other data values. **So the modes are 4 and 5.** Where multiple modes occur another measure of central tendency may be preferred.

The range

The interquartile range gives a more reasonable indication of the dispersion of the distribution than using the full range and is often used along with the median to describe the observations of a study.

To find the range, you first need to find the lowest and highest values in the data. The range is found by subtracting the lowest value from the highest value. So, the time taken by each of the ten students to search for information in minutes may be ordered as:

1   2   3   4   5   6   7   8   9   10
The lowest value is 1 and the highest value is 10. Subtracting the lowest from the highest gives:
10 – 1 = 9. So the range is 9 minutes.

The range is a basic method of dispersion and relies on just two values, the extremes, of our set of values. These could be outliers, untypical of other values in the sample. So, we could use a fairer measure of dispersion that avoids any outliers and use a range based on the quartiles of the distribution. Using this we can calculate the interquartile range, the distance between Q1 and Q3. Just as the median is the value which cuts the observations in two, so the quartiles are the values that cut the observations into four equal parts, as Figure 9.1 on the following page illustrates.

With our data in order of magnitude, let's work out the median, the lower quartile, the upper quartile and the interquartile range.

The median (**Q2**, the middle value) = 1/2 × (n+1)th value, where n is the number of data values in the data set, thus:

Q2 is 1/2 × (10+1) = 0.5 × 11 = the 5.5th value

The Lower Quartile, **Q1**, is the median of the lower half of the data set = 1/4 × (n+1)th value, where n is the number of data values in the data set, thus:

Q1 is $1/4 \times (10+1) = 0.25 \times 11$ = the 2.75th value

The Upper Quartile, **Q3**, is the median of the upper half of the data set = $3/4 \times (n+1)$th value, where n is the number of data values in the data set, thus:

Q3 is $3/4 \times (10+1) = 0.75 \times 11$ = the 8.25th value

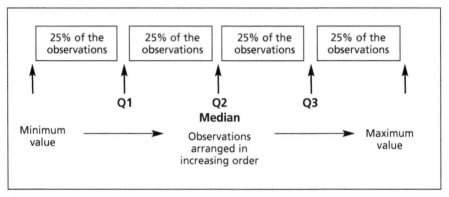

Figure 9.1 *The interquartile range*

Where a quartile is between values then calculate the average of those values, so the average between values 5 and 6 for **Q2**, the average between values 2 and 3 for **Q1** and the average between values 8 and 9 for **Q3**. Figure 9.2 shows the position of Q1, Q2 and Q3 in our data set and how the averaging is worked out to produce a value for each.

Therefore, the interquartile range, **IQR**, = Q3 – Q1, 7.5 – 3.5 = **4 minutes.**

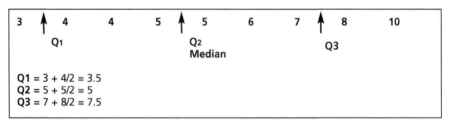

Figure 9.2 *Establishing values for Q1, Q2 and Q3*

Standard deviation

The standard deviation takes into account *all* the values in a distribution – the range takes into account only two (lowest and highest), while the interquartile range takes into account only the middle 50%, and shows the dispersion of values around the arithmetic mean. The larger the dispersion, the larger the standard deviation. It shows how much variation or dispersion exists from the average (mean, or expected value). A low standard deviation indicates that the data points tend to be very close to the mean, whereas high standard deviation indicates that the data points are spread out over a large range of values.

To calculate the standard deviation we take the deviation of each value from the arithmetic mean, then calculate an average from these deviations. So, with our example data **1, 3, 4, 4, 5, 5, 6, 7, 8, 10:**

$53 \div 10$ = Arithmetic mean = 5.3 minutes

As you can see from Table 9.2, there is a problem with this approach. The negative values and the positive values cancel each other out, so in order to

Table 9.2 *Calculating the standard deviation, positive and negative values*

Value (time taken to search in minutes)	Deviation
1	1–5.3 = –4.3
3	3–5.5 = –2.3
4	4–5.3 = –1.3
4	4–5.3 = –1.3
5	5–5.3 = –0.3
5	5–5.3 = –0.3
6	6–5.3 = 0.7
7	7–5.3 = 1.7
8	8–5.3 = 2.7
10	10–5.3 = 4.7
TOTAL MEAN	0.0 0.0

find the dispersion around the mean we must remove the negative signs and we do this by squaring the deviation – this removes the negatives and makes them positive. The steps we therefore need to go through are:

- find the arithmetic mean
- find the deviations from the mean
- square the deviations from the mean
- add these values together
- divide this sum by the number of items in the distribution
- find the square root of the result.

Divide the sum of the deviation squared, which is **60.1** as shown in Table 9.3, by the number of items in the distribution: **60.1 ÷ 10 = 6.01**. And then find the square root of this = **2.45**. This is the standard deviation from the arithmetic mean. Actually, this is a slight simplification. Statisticians advise that a more useful standard deviation statistic is produced by, in the above calculation, dividing the sum of the squared deviations (**60.1**) by **9** rather than **10**; in other words, one should divide by one fewer than the number of items (**10 − 1 = 9**).

Table 9.3 *Calculating the standard deviation with deviation squared*

Value (time taken to search in minutes)	Deviation	Deviation squared
1	1–5.3 = **–4.3**	18.49
3	3–5.5 = **–2.3**	5.29
4	4–5.3 = **–1.3**	1.69
4	4–5.3 = **–1.3**	1.69
5	5–5.3 = **–0.3**	0.09
5	5–5.3 = **–0.3**	0.09
6	6–5.3 = **0.7**	0.49
7	7–5.3 = **1.7**	2.89
8	8–5.3 = **2.7**	7.29
10	10–5.3 = **4.7**	22.09
TOTAL	0.0	60.1

What does this tell us? Using the standard deviation, we have a way of knowing what is normal, and what exceeds or goes beyond a normal range. For our study we now know that anything beyond 2.45 minutes *over* the mean time of 5.3 minutes to search (so anything more than 7.75 minutes) is longer than normal and that anything beyond 2.45 minutes *under* the mean time of 5.3 minutes (so anything less than 2.85 minutes) is shorter than normal. An example of this applied to a study can be seen in MacFarlane et al. (2010).

Inferential statistics

Inferential statistics are often used to enable generalizations from a sample to be made to a population. They are concerned with using observations as a basis for making estimates or predictions, that is, inferences are applied to a wider situation than the one which has been studied. Inferential statistics help us determine whether the difference we find between our experimental and control groups is caused by the manipulation of the independent variable or by chance variation in the performances of the groups. If the difference has a low probability of being caused by chance variation, we can feel confident in the inferences we make from our samples to the populations they represent. Inferential statistical analysis is inextricably linked with how you have sampled your population – great care must be taken that a truly random probability sample has been obtained before you can undertake some types of inferential statistical analysis.

Key concepts include:

- **Standard normal distribution:** the normal distribution with a mean of zero and a standard deviation of one. Often called the bell curve because the graph of its probability looks like a bell (see Figure 9.3).
- **Hypothesis testing (also called significance testing):** a statistical procedure for discriminating between two statistical hypotheses – the null hypothesis (H0) and the alternative hypothesis (Ha, often denoted as H1).
- **Analysis of variance (ANOVA):** an inferential statistic that can be used to compare two or more means.

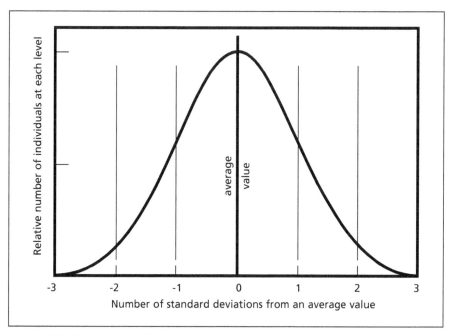

Figure 9.3 Normal distribution or bell curve

- **Statistical significance:** the extent to which the relationship can be generalized to the population (the characteristics of samples drawn from the population they represent will almost always vary somewhat from those of the true population).

The fundamentals of inferential statistics (and descriptive statistics) are covered in more depth in Byrne (2007), including techniques such as chi-square, correlation, and analysis of variance (ANOVA). This primer also provides advice on which test to use with different types of data.

It is also useful to note that software packages are often helpful in the analysis and presentation of data; for example spreadsheet packages, such as Microsoft Excel, can be useful in analysis and also for the creation of graphs when writing up and presenting the results in a report. Graphical presentation of statistics, for example pie charts, bar charts and summarizing findings into tables, is essential if the results of the study are to be communicated clearly to the reader of your report.

Statistical software packages are also available, of which SPSS is possibly the most well known (Pallant, 2010). This package enables you to analyse data more fully than using a spreadsheet. Although superficially it looks like a spreadsheet it does not work in the same way. You cannot, for example, sum a row of figures by inserting a formula in a cell. Instead, the data is entered in columns, with each column being set up as a separate, defined variable. The data is then worked on using the menus to provide output (tables, graphs, statistics) in a separate window. This software is very powerful and is particularly useful when handling large volumes of data and where inferential analysis is required.

Figure 9.4 shows a summary different statistical approaches you may take. For further reading about key statistical tests, when they can be used and with which type of data, please refer to Byrne (2007), 41–6.

How to find statisticians and how to talk to them!

Having worked through this section of the chapter, you will now be equipped to define your study, understand your variables and undertake descriptive statistical analysis. You will also have an understanding of the difference between descriptive and inferential approaches. However, there may be some instances where collaboration with a statistician would be beneficial. Finding a statistician, and knowing what to ask, will be critical in deciding on an approach in order to obtain the results that you require.

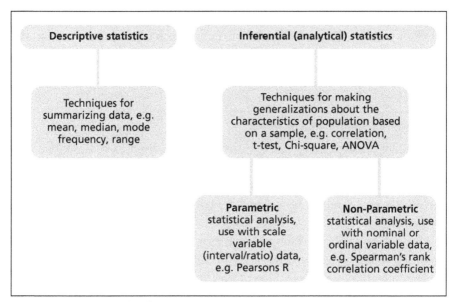

Figure 9.4 Summary of different statistical approaches

Think back to the earlier questions:

- 'Am I trying to describe what happens with the participants in my sample?'
  or
- 'Do I want to be able to generalize my results to the wider population?'

These questions will enable you to talk with a statistician with greater understanding of what may be achieved. Statisticians may be available in your organization, or you may need to seek one externally. Examples of organizations within the library and information science field that may be able to offer support include:

- Library and Information Research Group (LIRG) at www.lirg.org.uk
- IFLA Statistics and Evaluation Section at www.ifla.org/statistics-and-evaluation
- LIS Research Coalition at http://lisresearch.org
- LISU, based in the Department of Information Science at Loughborough University, at: www.lboro.ac.uk/departments/ls/lisu
- NIHR, the NHS National Institute for Health Research, at www.nihr.ac.uk/Pages/default.aspx.

Whether you choose to undertake some statistical analysis yourself, or whether you collaborate with a statistician, the outcome of rigorous research design, sampling and appropriate statistical approach is rich evidence to support, explain or clarify the situation you have been researching.

Analysing qualitative data

Qualitative research generates text or words that need to be described and summarized in order to answer a question. It typically involves the seeking of patterns and relationships between various themes that have been identified, or to relate behaviour or ideas to the characteristics of the participants.

Qualitative data comes in various forms, including interview transcripts, recorded observations, focus groups, ethnographic studies, texts and documents, diary entries or blogs (see Chapter 7). It should be noted that quantitative studies can also include some form of qualitative data, such as open-ended survey questions and semi-structured interviews, which will require analysis through qualitative approaches.

Before analysis can commence, data collected will most likely have to be transcribed. This is particularly true of focus groups and interviews, where the session has usually been recorded in some way. Typically, the transcription of data will take at least twice as long as the collection phase, and sometimes longer depending on the quality of the recording or note taking. Rabiee (2004, 657) has estimated transcription of a one-hour focus group 'could easily take 5–6 h to transcribe in full, leading to thirty to forty pages of transcripts'. Agencies do exist that will undertake transcription (a basic search on Google for 'data' AND 'transcription services' will provide some examples) but the feasibility of this will depend on resources available for the study. Thus, decisions need to be made before the analysis stage as to how data will be handled for analysis (see Chapters 7 and 8).

Qualitative data tends to generate a huge amount of text in the form of transcriptions, notes, observations or diary entries. Analysis can seem daunting when faced with this amount of data, and it is therefore important to organize it into an appropriate and manageable format. This can be as simple as using a highlighter pen, or as complex as using one of the highly sophisticated software analysis tools available (see below). How it is organized will depend very much on the amount of data, and method used for collecting it, but can be loosely grouped into a manual or electronic approach.

Manual

Sorting, categorizing and coding and analysing data can all be done manually, particularly if you are not dealing with large amounts of data. Manual management of data could be as simple as the use of Post-it notes or highlighter pens, or creating paper divisions into categories and sub-categories. Data can also be grouped manually and placed into a Microsoft Word table or similar; this allows use of the Search and Find functions to identify further categories, sub-categories and frequencies or repetition in the text.

Electronic

Large amounts of data can be added to a database and then key words filtered in order to sort the data into categories and themes. Although this would require previous knowledge of the creation and use of databases, the advantage of using a database is that data can be stored and queried in a number of ways. There are also a number of highly sophisticated tools that are collectively known as Computer Aided Qualitative Data AnalysiS (CAQDAS) tools; examples include NVivo (www.qsrinternational.com/products_nvivo.aspx) and Atlas-ti (www.atlasti.com). Tools such as these for doing research are discussed further in Chapter 10.

Qualitative data analysis process

The approach you take to your qualitative data analysis will depend on the overall aims of the analysis and your research question. For example, do you want the data to contribute to policy decisions, improving service delivery, or to share knowledge and increase understanding in a specific area?

Approaches to qualitative data analysis can be inductive or deductive, but generally, qualitative research uses an inductive process, developing theories from the data gathered.

Qualitative data analysis looks further than precise numerical evidence. It looks for categories such as descriptions, comments and behaviour. Common features of qualitative data analysis include:

- affixing codes to a set of field notes drawn from data collection
- noting reflections or other remarks
- sorting or sifting through the materials to identify similar phrases, relationships between themes, distinct differences between subgroups and common sequences

- isolating patterns and processes, commonalties and differences, and taking them out to the field in the next wave of data collection
- gradually elaborating a small set of generalizations that cover the consistencies discerned in the data base
- confronting those generalizations with a formalized body of knowledge in the form of constructs or theories.

(Source: Miles and Huberman, 1994)

With the above features in mind, a number of stages can be identified in the process of analysing qualitative data:

Familiarization with the data

Following data collection, the first stage of analysis is familiarization with the data. This can be achieved by 'listening to tapes, reading the transcripts in their entirety several times and reading the observational notes taken during interview and summary notes written immediately after the interview'. (Rabiee, 2004, 657). During this process it may become apparent that further data need to be collected before moving to the next stage.

Developing themes and coding text

Having familiarized yourself with the data, the next stage is to form ideas or themes arising from it. At this stage, statements, keywords and quotes that relate to the research question can be isolated and grouped under thematic headings. For an example, Thomas and Harden (2008) provide a good description of the application of thematic analysis to bring together and integrate the findings of multiple qualitative studies (of the barriers to, and facilitators of, healthy eating amongst children).

Data can be further examined to look for patterns and to identify any new and emerging themes. This stage usually involves some kind of coding process, which organizes text according to the thematic headings identified.

Data can be coded according to categories and sub-categories identified by reading and re-reading the data collected. Categories and sub-categories provide information relevant to the topic studied and are used to help explore and clarify the research question. Codes can be based on:

- themes, topics
- ideas, concepts

- terms, phrases.

There are different approaches to coding. For example, a framework analysis approach extracts themes from the literature to form a structure on which to map codes (Aharony, 2011; Beverley, Bath and Barber, 2007).

Alternatively, a more grounded theory approach can be adopted, where coding is applied to themes that emerge from the data collected (Saumure and Shiri, 2008). This is known as open coding, and is applied according to what each piece of data is an example of. For example, a focus group discussion on 'Making use of computers in the library' could include examples of activities such as courses taken, computer clubs, use of software and using sources of information.

As well as open coding, other types of coding applied to grounded theory include axial coding, which interconnects categories identified by open coding, and selective coding, which establishes the core category of categories. For further reading on grounded theory and coding, see Robson (2002, 492–9). See also Learn Higher and Manchester Metropolitan University (2008).

Typically, information that could be incorporated about a code will include:

- why you have created the code
- some detail of what the code is about and what the coded text reveals
- why you have changed a code
- thoughts and questions about the analysis that occur to you as you code.
                                        (Source: Taylor and Gibbs, 2010)

Coding can be flat or non-hierarchical, like a list, where there are no sub-code levels. For example, in a study of the impact of IT facilities in public libraries (Craven and Brophy, 2006), library users were asked to describe any IT training they had received; the responses could be grouped as:

- college course
- school
- self taught
- library courses
- online courses
- no training
- computer programming
- database design

- web and graphic design
- word processing
- introduction to computers
- computers and the internet
- keyboard and mouse skills
- internet and e-mail
- using the internet for family history research.

Coding can also be grouped using a tree or hierarchical approach that has a branching arrangement of sub-codes. Ideally, codes in a tree relate to one another by being 'examples of . . .', or 'contexts for . . .', or 'causes of . . .', or 'settings for . . .', and so on. For example, using the same question as above, the responses can be grouped into the type of IT training, and where it was undertaken:

- college course
  — computer programming
  — database design
  — web and graphic design
  — word processing
- school
  — introduction to computers
- self taught
  — text books and manuals
  — online courses
- library courses
  — computers and the internet
  — keyboard and mouse skills
  — internet and e-mail
  — using the internet for family history research.

What can be coded, with keyword examples, is illustrated further in Table 9.4, with an example of a study of library and information research areas (adapted from Aharony, 2011, 31). For this study, 417 articles from research publications were examined and classified according to an existing classification scheme (Zins, 2007) to reflect the current state of research in the field of information science. Categories were identified according to key topics from the classification scheme, with keywords assigned to each category. A note of caution, however: coding can be highly subjective and therefore care must

Table 9.4 *Examples of what can be coded (adapted from Aharony, 2011, 31).*

Category	Examples
Foundations of information science	Historical notes
Methodology used	Bibliometric analysis; qualitative analysis; webometrics; chi-square method
Information/learning society	The virtual scholar; web usage studies; information literacy; information theory
Information technology	Meta search engines; search logs; information retrieval systems;
Data organization and retrieval	Information seeking; searching; browsing; search strategies; search terms
Information ethics and law	Ethics; legal information; open access publications; open source; copyright
User studies	Information needs; information need analysis; user behaviour; information behaviour; user studies
Social information studies	Disabled people; adolescent well-being; cultural aspects; health information; cancer information overload

be taken to ensure appropriate codes are developed and applied. This can be achieved through an initial peer review process, where two or more researchers code separately and then meet to discuss and agree on the codes applied and to set a framework or method for coding.

Case study 9.4 An example of how the coding structure that has been applied was also validated

---

Foster, A., Urquhart, C. and Turner, J. (2008) Validating Coding for a Theoretical Model of Information Behaviour, *Information Research*, **13** (4), http://informationr.net/ir/13-4/paper358.html.

Introduction

Many models of information behaviour are based on research done mostly, or solely, by one individual and the coding may not be easy for other researchers to use. The aim of the research was to develop and test a theoretical model of information behaviour, developed by one individual. The first objective was a review of the coding.

Method

A review of the literature on inter-rater reliability calculations indicated some possible methods to be used. We used one of these methods in a parallel coding experiment, and developed a simplified codebook after several rounds of parallel coding and team discussions.

Analysis

The analysis was iterative. Further review of the social sciences literature helped to resolve our differences of interpretation.

Results

Our team discussions were very useful. The inter-rater reliability calculations indicated only the large extent of initial disagreement. We simplified the codebook terms, and reduced the number of terms. The revised model suggests changes to the description of context, and the scale and intensity of information seeking activities.

Conclusions

Obtaining transferable definitions of information seeking activities is difficult but a team can debate meaning successfully. ■

This case study discusses some of the problems that can arise when trying to agree on the coding process. In particular, differences were noted in the personal interpretations of which codes should be applied, as well as the level of importance applied to concepts, so that certain codes would be ignored by some and applied by others. It was also noted that coders seemed to subconsciously operate within a reduced set of codes or showed preferences for certain codes rather than using the full range identified for the coding framework. The pilot coding work compared coding of two interview transcripts by two researchers; a third researcher then coded the transcripts and provided notes to help explain actions. The team discussed the findings and examined reasons for the similarities and differences between the codes applied. From this, an agreement was reached on a refined set of codes, which were checked against another set of interview transcripts to highlight any further queries.

Finding meaning from the data

In order to make sense of the data, analysis will focus on one or more of the following:

- words (i.e. from text transcripts, field notes, observations, etc.)
- context (tone and inflection)
- internal consistency (opinion shifts – for example, whether responses or opinions are consistent throughout; does the respondent contradict him

or herself at any point, or change his/her mind? This may happen in a focus group discussion if led by other group members)
- frequency and intensity of comments (counting, content analysis)
- specificity
- trends/themes
- iteration (data analysis is an iterative process moving back and forth).

(Source: Brennan, 2012)

Finding meaning from the data may include the grouping of events, places, or people with similar patterns, themes or trends; then noting any patterns or themes, comparing and contrasting data to establish similarities or differences between the data groups. It may also include looking at any interrelationships between the different parts of the data. Simple counts can be conducted to see if patterns or themes can be grouped according to frequency, although applying frequencies should be used with caution in qualitative research because there may be cases where just one mention of an issue occurs, but in that particular context it can be extremely important. For example, a study of the usability of a library website may elicit favourable responses, apart from one negative response from a respondent with a visual impairment, who uses screen reading technology to access the site, and experiences problems accessing a particular function of that site. This is just one comment, but it is an important one because it is likely to be representative of other people using similar technologies.

Questions may also emerge, such as: are there any deviations from the patterns or themes identified? What interesting stories emerge from the data? Are the findings in agreement with findings from other studies, and if not, can this be explained? Do the findings suggest that additional data need to be collected?

Case study 9.5 Example of a procedure used to identify broad-level trends in qualitative content analysis

---

Saumure, K. and Shiri, A. (2008) Knowledge Organization Trends in Library and Information Studies: a preliminary comparison of the pre- and post-web eras, *Journal of Information Science*, **34** (5), 651–66.

Abstract: Qualitative analyses were used to launch a preliminary exploration of the dominant knowledge organization (KO) trends in the pre- and post-web eras. Data for this study was assembled by searching the Library Information Science and Technology Abstracts database for articles that have used the term 'knowledge organization' or 'information organization' in their titles, abstracts or descriptors. Taken as a whole, these preliminary results suggest that the content of the KO literature has shifted since the advent of the web. Although classic KO principles remain prominent throughout both eras the presence of new content areas such as metadata denotes a shift in KO trends. In the pre-web era the literature was related in large part to indexing and abstracting. In contrast, cataloging and classification issues dominate the landscape in the post-web era. The findings from this paper will be of particular use to those interested in learning about upcoming trends in the KO literature. ■

In this case study, the authors provide an example of finding meaning from data using thematic analysis. Data for this study were collected by searching the LISTA database for articles that included the terms 'knowledge organization' or 'information organization' in their titles and abstracts. From the articles retrieved, broad level trends were identified, such as organizing corporate or business information, machine-assisted knowledge organization, librarians as knowledge organizers of the web, cataloguing and classification. The trends identified emerged from the data and no attempt was made to establish a framework for possible future trends. For each of the trends, the related data was imported into Microsoft Word for further analysis and from this, sub-trends were identified as well as their prominence within each era.

Reliability and validity

The nature of qualitative research means that, unlike quantitative data analysis, it can be criticized for being subjective or anecdotal, and it can be difficult to make systematic comparisons. For example, people give widely differing responses that are highly subjective. It is also dependent on skills of the researcher, particularly in the case of conducting interviews, focus groups and observation.

To avoid criticism, a strong emphasis should be placed on reporting the reliability and validity of the methods employed for analysis. This could include:

- describing the approach to and procedures for data analysis
- justifying why these are appropriate within the context of your study
- clearly documenting the process of generating themes, concepts or theories from the data audit trail

- referring to external evidence, including previous qualitative and quantitative studies, to test the conclusions from your analysis as appropriate.

Other points for consideration are:

- reflexivity: being aware of your own values, ideas and prejudgements as a researcher
- triangulation: use made of other data collection types i.e. different groups, interviews and diaries, observation, etc.
- respondent validation: feed back the findings from research to the participants in some way (e.g. transcripts or quotations) to check accuracy or consent for use. In some cases respondents may be asked to comment on the interpretation or drafts of the report; it is important at this stage to decide whether or not to allow new data to be introduced.
  (Sources: Dixon-Woods et al. , 2004; Lacey and Duff, 2001, 23–5)

Summary

This chapter began by emphasizing the importance of 'what comes before' the data analysis process, such as developing the research question or hypothesis, sampling strategies and data collection techniques (all of which have been covered in previous chapters in the book). 'What comes before' will influence whether the analysis undertaken will be quantitative, qualitative, or a combination of both.

The chapter then went on to look at quantitative and qualitative analysis in more depth. It provided examples of different approaches to analysing data, including coding and thematic analysis, statistical analysis, descriptive and inferential statistics, how to find meaning from your data, and interpreting results. Case studies and working examples were provided to help illustrate points and demonstrate how theory can be put into practice. Organizations that can provide advice and support are listed, together with suggestions for further reading and useful websites.

Points for reflection

- Before you start to think about analysis, have you decided on your data collection method? This will influence your data analysis methods.
- If you want to answer the 'what' and 'how many' questions you may have

about something, your data collection and analysis is most likely to be quantitative.
- If you want to explore people's attitudes, feelings and behaviours in greater depth, your data collection and analysis is most likely to be qualitative.
- Your research question or hypothesis will influence whether your quantitative analysis will include descriptive or inferential statistics, or whether your qualitative approach uses deductive or inductive processes.
- Help and advice on data analysis is widely available: see the suggested further reading and useful websites sections below.

References

Aharony, N. (2011) Library and Information Science Research Areas: a content analysis of articles from the top 10 journals 2007–8, *Journal of Librarianship and Information Science*, **44** (27), 27–35.

Beverley, C. A., Bath, P. A. and Barber, R. (2007) Can Two Established Information Models Explain the Information Behaviour of Visually Impaired People Seeking Health and Social Care Information?, *Journal of Documentation*, **63** (1), 9–32.

Brennan, M. (2012) *Qualitative Data Analysis*, presentation at Systematic Reviews of Qualitative Studies and Evidence, 16 February 2012, www.staff.ncl.ac.uk/david.harvey/AEF801/MBQual.ppt.

Byrne, G. (2007) A Statistical Primer: understanding descriptive and inferential statistics, *Evidence Based Library and Information Practice (EBLIP) Journal*, **2** (1), http://ejournals.library.ualberta.ca/index.php/EBLIP/article/view/168.

Craven, J. (2003) Access to Electronic Resources by Visually Impaired People, *Information Research*, **8** (4), Paper no. 156, http://informationr.net/ir/8-4/paper156.html.

Craven, J. and Brophy, P. (2006) Longitude II: assessing the value and impact of library services over time. In Brophy, P. Craven, J. and Markland, M. (eds), *Libraries without Walls: evaluating the distributed delivery of library services*, proceedings of an international conference held on 16–20 September 2006, organized by the Centre for Research in Library and Information Management (CERLIM), Manchester Metropolitan University, Facet Publishing, 119–24.

Dixon-Woods, M., Agarwal, S., Young, B., Jones, D. and Sutton, A. (2004) *Integrative Approaches to Qualitative and Quantitative Evidence*, Health Development Agency, London.

Ferebee, S. and Davis, J. W. (2011) Persuading Library Use in Technologically Structured Individuals, *Library Hi Tech*, **29** (4), 586–604.

Foster, A., Urquhart, C. and Turner, J. (2008) Validating Coding for a Theoretical

Model of Information Behaviour, *Information Research*, **13** (4), http://informationr.net/ir/13-4/paper358.html.

Getz, I. and Weissman, G. (2010) An Information Needs Profile of Israeli Older Adults, Regarding the Law and Services, *Journal of Librarianship and Information Science*, **42**, 136.

Griffiths, J. R. (2012) User Engagement with Evaluation of Digital Libraries: a case study of the DiSCmap project. In Dobreva, M., O'Dwyer, A. and Feliciati, P. (eds), *User Studies for Digital Library Development*, Facet Publishing, London.

Griffiths, J. R. and Glass, B. (2011) Understanding the Information Literacy Competencies of UK Higher Education Students, In Walton, G. and Pope, A. (eds), *Information Literacy: infiltrating the curriculum, challenging minds*, Chandos Publishing, Oxford.

Johnson, F. C., Griffiths, J. R. and Hartley, R. J. (2001) *DEvISE: a framework for the evaluation of internet search engines*, Library and Information Commission (LIC) research report 100, Resource: The Council for Museums, Archives and Libraries, www.cerlim.ac.uk/projects/devise.

Koehler, W. C., Jr. (1999) Classifying Web sites and Web Pages: the use of metrics and URL characteristics as markers, *Journal of Librarianship and Information Science*, **31** (1), 21–36.

Korobili, S., Malliari, A., Daniilidou, E. and Christodoulou, G. (2011) A Paradigm of Information Literacy for Greek High School Teachers, *Journal of Librarianship and Information Science*, **43** (2), 78–87.

Lacey, A. and Duff, D. (2001) *Trent Focus for Research and Development in Primary Health Care: qualitative data analysis*, Trent Focus Group.

Learn Higher and Manchester Metropolitan University (2008) *Analyse This!!! – Learning to analyse data*, online tutorial, http://learnhigher.ac.uk/analysethis/index.html.

MacFarlane, A., Al-Wabil, A., Marshall, C. R., Albrair, A., Jones, S. A. and Zaphiris, P. (2010) The Effect of Dyslexia on Information Retrieval: a pilot study, *Journal of Documentation*, **66** (3), 307–26.

Marton, C. and Choo, C. W. (2012) A Review of Theoretical Models of Health Information Seeking on the Web, *Journal of Documentation*, **68** (3), 330–52.

Miles, M. B. and Huberman, A. M. (1994) *Qualitative Data Analysis*, 2nd edn, Sage Publications, Thousand Oaks, CA.

Nicholas, D., Huntington, P. and Williams, P. (2001) Establishing Metrics for the Evaluation of Touch Screen Kiosks, *Journal of Information Science*, **27**, 61.

Pallant, J. (2010) *SPSS Survival Manual*, 4th edn, Oxford University Press.

Rabiee, F. (2004) Focus-group Interview and Data Analysis, *Proceedings of the Nutrition Society*, **63** (4), 655–60.

Robson, C. (2002) *Real World Research: a resource for social scientists and practitioner-researchers*, 2nd edn, Wiley.

Saumure, K. and Shiri, A. (2008) Knowledge Organization Trends in Library and Information Studies: a preliminary comparison of the pre- and post-web eras, *Journal of Information Science*, **34** (5), 651–66.

Strauss, A. and Corbin, J. (1998) *Basics of Qualitative Research*, 2nd edn, Sage Publications.

Taylor, C. and Gibbs, G.R. (2010) *How and What to Code*, http://onlineqda.hud.ac.uk/Intro_QDA/how_what_to_code.php.

Thomas, J. and Harden, A. (2008) Methods for the Thematic Synthesis of Qualitative Research in Systematic Reviews, *BMC Medical Research Methodology*, **8**, 45.

Walsh, A. (2009) Information Literacy Assessment: where do we start?, *Journal of Librarianship and Information Science*, **41** (1) 19–28.

Zins, C. (2007) Conceptions of Information Science, *Journal of the American Society for Information Science and Technology*, **58** (3), 335–50.

Recommended further reading

Bawden, D. (1990) *User-oriented Evaluation of Information Systems and Services*, Gower, Farnham.

Bryman, A. (2006) Integrating Quantitative and Qualitative Research: how is it done?, *Qualitative Research*, **6** (1), 97–113, http://qrj.sagepub.com/content/6/1/97.full.pdf+html?ijkey=bc35fb078bef9a40f2fd78d7900fd93eb839b097.

Burns, R. (2000) *Introduction to Research Methods*, Sage Publications, London.

Newton , R. R. and Rudestam, K. E. (1999) *Your Statistical Consultant: answers to your data analysis questions*, Sage Publications, London.

Rowntree, D. (1991) *Statistics Without Tears: a primer for non-mathematicians*, Penguin, London.

Shenton, A. K. (2004) Strategies for Ensuring Trustworthiness in Qualitative Research Projects, *Education for Information*, **22**, 63–75.

Stephen, P. and Hornby, S. (1997) *Simple Statistics for Library and Information Professionals*, 2nd edn, Library Association Publishing.

Strauss, A. and Corbin, J. (1998) *Basics of Qualitative Research*, 2nd edn, Sage Publications.

Thomas, G. (2011) How to Do Your Case Study: a guide for students and researchers, Sage Publications.

University of the West of England, *Data Analysis Online Learning Programme*, http://hsc.uwe.ac.uk/dataanalysis/.

University of the West of England, *Qualitative Analysis: what is it?*
http://learntech.uwe.ac.uk/da/qualitativeanalysis3.aspx.
Vaughan, L. (2001) *Statistical Methods for the Information Professional: a practical, painless approach to understanding, using, and interpreting statistics*, Information Today, Inc. for the American Society for Information Science and Technology, Medford, NJ.

Useful websites

IFLA Statistics and Evaluation Section, www.ifla.org/statistics-and-evaluation.
Learn Higher and Manchester Metropolitan University (2008) *Analyse This!!! – Learning to analyse data*, online tutorial,
http://learnhigher.ac.uk/analysethis/index.html.
Library and Information Research Group (LIRG), www.lirg.org.uk.
LIS Research Coalition, http://lisresearch.org.
LISU, based in the Department of Information Science at Loughborough University,
www.lboro.ac.uk/departments/ls/lisu.
NIHR, NHS National Institute for Health Research,
www.nihr.ac.uk/Pages/default.aspx.
University of Glasgow, *STEPS Statistics Glossary*,
www.stats.gla.ac.uk/steps/glossary/index.html.
University of Leicester, Online statistics,
www.le.ac.uk/bl/gat/virtualfc/Stats/descrip.html.
University of the West of England, *Data Analysis Online Learning Programme*,
http://hsc.uwe.ac.uk/dataanalysis/index.asp.

10

Tools to facilitate your project

Maria J. Grant

'I feel completely overwhelmed by the amount of "information" I've gathered. Help!'

'What tools are out there to help me manage all this data?'

'How can I keep track of what's going on in the wider LIS community?'

When doing a project, whether it's research, evaluation or audit, you can often feel overwhelmed by the amount of information generated and, particularly when you are new to project work, it can be difficult to know where to turn for support. The good news is that there are lots of tools and networks available to help you.

This chapter moves through the resources and tools available at each stage of the research, evaluation and audit process, discussing reference management software, concept mapping, alert services, RSS readers. Some of the more commonly used tools available are listed in each section. These are provided purely for illustration purposes and are not intended as recommendations.

Reference management software and associated applications

For many of us, literature searching is an integral part of the service we provide as part of our day-to-day practice. The end point for this service often manifests itself as a printed list of references or, more commonly, a file of downloaded references for the service user to manage, appraise and analyse. Like our service users, when using literature to inform our own practice we can employ tools to assist the management and manipulation of the literature. These can include reference management software packages and concept mapping tools, sometimes referred to as mind mapping.

Reference management software

Reference management software, also known as citation management software, enables you to upload records and keep track of the records you've found through your database searches. Each document listed in the database search results is given its own record within the software, usually with a notes field so that you can annotate the record in terms of its usefulness and relationship to the themes you've identified in the literature.

Reference management software packages can be embedded within word processing files to generate a reference list as you write your literature review, project report or journal article, and reduce the likelihood of a reference not being included in the reference list. This can be a real benefit when writing for publication in a journal, as a strength of this type of software is its ability to generate reference lists in a variety of formats, which can be easily changed to meet the different formats of a particular set of author guidelines. Additionally, if you are working as a part of a bigger writing team, many reference management software packages enable you to share your references with colleagues.

Commercial reference management software packages are numerous; the most commonly known ones include Biblioscape, Endnote, Reference Manager, Refworks and Sente. These can be bought as a standalone piece of software to use on a single computer, in a web-based format or as a phone application (app). Open source reference management packages include Mendeley and Zotero, which offer similar functionality. For research teams in which individuals are geographically separated, the use of virtual reference management software systems such as Endnote Web, which allow multiple user access, can be particularly valuable.

If you prefer to create your own bibliography or reference list, Referencing@Portsmouth is an interactive tool that assists in providing guided examples of the more popular referencing styles.

Concept and mind mapping tools

Having identified the literature for inclusion in your project report or article, your next step will be to identify the themes within the literature and how they relate to one another.

Concept and mind maps provide a way of visually displaying information around a single idea to develop an understanding of how themes relate to one another. The centre of each map represents the main concept, for example your research question, with associated ideas radiating out from the centre.

Mind maps can be as low tech or as sophisticated as your tastes and budgets permit, from hand-drawn maps, those created in word processing files (see Figure 10.1) and dedicated mind-mapping software such as FreeMind, iMindMap, MindMeister and Omnigraffle. As with the reference management software, mind-mapping software is available in a range of formats including those for purchase, free downloads (often in the form of a simplified version of the full software package) and smart phone applications (apps).

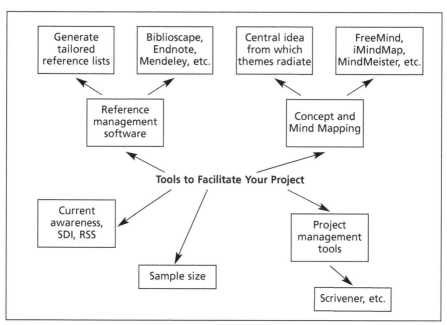

Figure 10.1 *Tools to facilitate your project*

Sample size and confidence interval calculators

In Chapter 8, the topic of quantitative methods was introduced. Part of the discussion centred on sample size and its role in enabling inferences to be made about a population. As indicated, it is possible to calculate sample size using pencil and paper, but for those of us less confident about our numerical skills, there are also a variety of online sample size calculators available, such as that shown in Figure 10.2. The calculators are relatively straightforward to use, but it's important to understand the underlying statistical concepts when using these tools (see Chapters 8 and 9) in order to properly interpret their outputs.

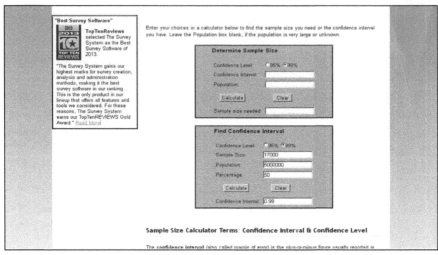

Figure 10.2 *A sample size calculator, Creative Research Systems, www.surveysystem.com/sscalc.htm*

Case study 10.1 Using a sample size calculator

In Chapter 8, the issue was raised of whether 17,000 participants was a large sample size for a survey collecting information on participation in sport, arts, museums and galleries, libraries, archives and heritage in the United Kingdom (UK).

Knowing that the population of the UK is approximately 50 million, a sample size calculator was used to determine the confidence interval for estimates of library usage for a 17,000 sample size. Given these population and sample sizes, the calculator returned a 99% confidence level in the survey result. This indicates that were the survey to be repeated with a similar sample size, estimates of library use would most likely vary by only 1% from those obtained. ■

Current awareness and selected dissemination of information

I suspect most of us are already familiar with current awareness and selected dissemination of information (SDI) tools and use them in providing our library and information service to users, but it's useful to remind ourselves that we can also use these tools for our own benefit.

When you've undertaken a database search, most providers enable you to set up an alert service (or SDI) that will periodically re-run your saved search strategy and automatically e-mail you the results. This can be extremely helpful in keeping you up to date with the latest published literature and, when you're busy with the day job, acts as a gentle prompt to re-engage with your own project work.

The majority of journals provide table of content (TOC) alerts that can help you stay in touch with recent literature. You subscribe to and receive an alert every time a new issue or article containing your specified keywords is published, either via e-mail or RSS (Rich Site Summary or Really Simple Syndication) feed readers. Depending on which sector (and indeed country) you work in, most people are familiar with JournalTOCs, ticTOCs and the British Library table of contents service, ZETOC.

Blogging, microblogging and RSS feeds

Blogging and microblogging are an accepted part of most people's professional practice and provide a (usually) informal forum for discussion and dissemination on dedicated topics. Blogs consist of online discrete entries (or 'posts'), typically presented in reverse chronological order, with an opportunity for readers to contribute or respond to the post, and can be a great way to let the world know about your project as it develops. Popular blog site providers include Blogger (provided by Google), Blogspot and WordPress. Microblogging, often in the form of a Twitter post, can also be an effective tool in letting people know about your work (including alerts to your latest blog post) and inviting discussion around a topic area.

In the example shown in Figure 10.3 on the next page, the blogger writes on the topic of helping librarians identify publishing and presentation opportunities. They provide calls for papers, presentations, participation, reviewers as well as links to related sites and the opportunity to comment on postings or contact the blogger direct.

If there are particular organizational websites, blogs or Twitter accounts whose output you wish to keep updated on, RSS feeds can be the way forward. RSS feeds update automatically and aggregate content from a range of sources into a single access point known as an RSS Reader. Content can be presented in full or summarized by headline. Commonly used RSS

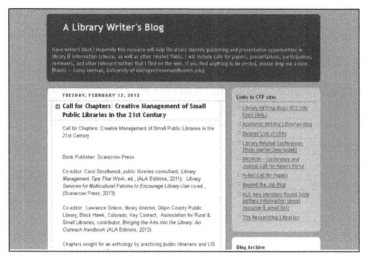

Figure 10.3 *A library writer's blog (http://librarywriting.blogspot.co.uk)*

Readers include Feedly, Mozilla Thunderbird, NetVibes, NewsBlur, Pulse and The Old Reader.

For a more interactive way of managing your social media you'll be pleased to know there are dedicated tools for the job. As demonstrated in Figure 10.4, these management systems use a dashboard format allowing you to bring together and interact with all your social media, e.g. Facebook, LinkedIn or Twitter, in a single place. The value of social media management tools is that they enable you to obtain an overview of your social media in a single place and disseminate your project updates in a coherent and time-efficient way. Examples of social media management systems include Hootsuite, MetroTwit, Tweetbot and Tweetcaster.

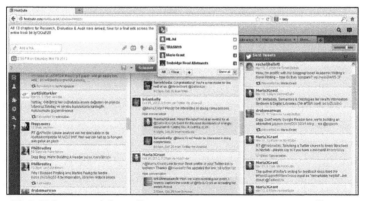

Figure 10.4 *Using a social media management system to co-ordinate your social media*

Wikis and project management tools

If your project involves lots of different contributors, wikis can enable you to work collectively by storing content at a central point to which you all have access. Content can be in the form of a web page or store for shared documents which, depending on the level of access granted by the wiki administrator, can permit users to add, modify or delete content. In Figure 10.5, a wiki was being used to co-ordinate a team involved in a literature review. The wiki was originally used to share database search results and later to keep track of where, if at all, papers were to appear in the review. Summaries of the papers appraised for the review were stored centrally on the wiki, while details of reviews and documents to inform the discussion were recorded and a copy of the final report written and edited collectively by team members.

Figure 10.5 *Example of a wiki being used to co-ordinate a systematic review*

There is a wide range of open access wiki software to choose from, often with contemporary packages to purchase with more advanced features. Once you've found software that you're happy with, it's a simple case of setting up an account and inviting members to join. Wiki software includes JotSpot, PBWorks and WikkaWiki.

If you are using a range of social networking tools to disseminate information about your project, you may also find Storify a useful piece of software. Storify enables you to bring multiple social networks together, reorder elements and add text to create an account of a project.

Given the range of tools already outlined, you're most likely at your limit regarding additional types of software packages to consider, so let's name just one more, the project management tool. Rather than have multiple applications and files to access, project management tools help you to organize all your notes, mind maps, PDFs and links to web pages, in a single place and point of access. Sections of your project report or journal article can be saved as discrete points in time and exported into a Microsoft Word document to bring everything together once the content has been finalized. An example of this type of software package is Scrivener.

Survey tools

Surveys are one of the most common types of investigative approaches adopted within the library and information sector, and with good reason: through customer feedback and questionnaires they can provide us with a potentially quick yet insightful view of the preferences of our users. Online surveys are commonplace and, ranging from open source, free reduced functionality software to off-the-shelf packages, all exist to match our budgets with the depth of investigation we wish to achieve. Examples include the Bristol Online Survey, RationalSurvey and SurveyMonkey. Figures 10.6 and 10.7 illustrate ways in which a survey tool can present an analysis of the same data.

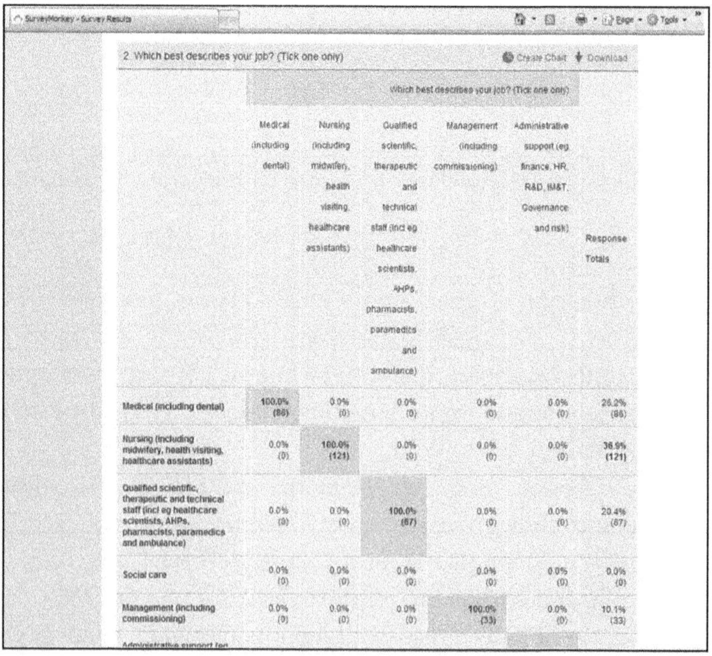
2. Which best describes your job? (Tick one only)

	Medical (including dental)	Nursing (including midwifery, health visiting, healthcare assistants)	Qualified scientific, therapeutic and technical staff (incl eg healthcare scientists, AHPs, pharmacists, paramedics and ambulance)	Management (including commissioning)	Administrative support (eg finance, HR, R&D, IM&T, Governance and risk)	Response Totals
Medical (including dental)	100.0% (86)	0.0% (0)	0.0% (0)	0.0% (0)	0.0% (0)	26.2% (86)
Nursing (including midwifery, health visiting, healthcare assistants)	0.0% (0)	100.0% (121)	0.0% (0)	0.0% (0)	0.0% (0)	36.9% (121)
Qualified scientific, therapeutic and technical staff (incl eg healthcare scientists, AHPs, pharmacists, paramedics and ambulance)	0.0% (0)	0.0% (0)	100.0% (67)	0.0% (0)	0.0% (0)	20.4% (67)
Social care	0.0% (0)	0.0% (0)	0.0% (0)	0.0% (0)	0.0% (0)	0.0% (0)
Management (including commissioning)	0.0% (0)	0.0% (0)	0.0% (0)	100.0% (33)	0.0% (0)	10.1% (33)

Figure 10.6 *SurveyMonkey analysis of participant employment – summary table*

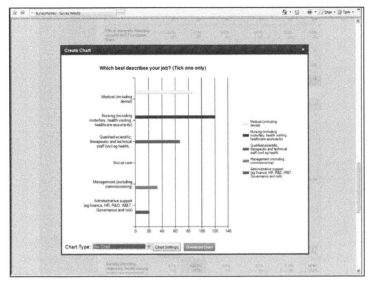

Figure 10.7 *SurveyMonkey analysis of participant employment – graph*

Data analysis tools

Chapters 7–9 explored the differences and the strengths of both qualitative and quantitative approaches to data collection and, as you might expect, these necessitate different tools to support their analysis.

Working on a basis similar to electronic folders, software exists to aid the analysis of qualitative and mixed methods data. Transcripts are loaded into the software and as you read you can highlight key words and concepts; the software then retrieves other sections from the transcripts where these words and concepts occur. Examples of qualitative analysis software packages include Ethnograph, NUD*IST and NVivo.

Depending on the size of your quantitative data set, you have a number of options. For small surveys, a software package such as a Microsoft Excel spreadsheet may be all you need for your data analysis, quantifying the number and types of response to a particular question (see Figure 10.8). For something slightly more sophisticated, for example looking for patterns of responses, or carrying out inferential analyses (as discussed in Chapter 9) you are likely to find a dedicated software package such as IBM SPSS Statistics more suitable for your needs (see Figure 10.9).

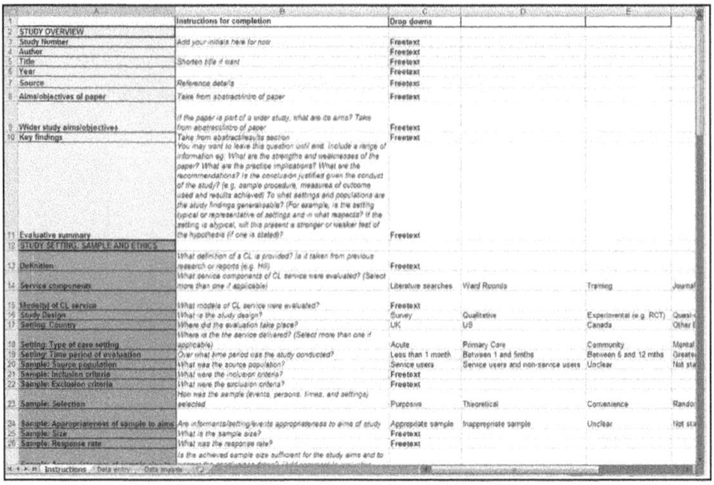

Figure 10.8 *Using a Microsoft Excel spreadsheet to analyse data within a systematic review*

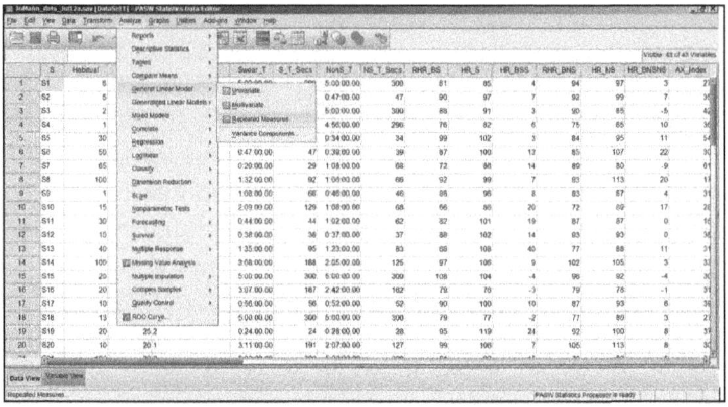

Figure 10.9 *IBM SPSS Statistics*

Analysing website usage

Although caution should be exercised when using web transaction logs (see Chapter 8), when used well these tools can provide detailed statistics on the usage of a website, time and duration of visits, how visitors to the site have accessed its content and the most popular content. Open access sources exist, with more sophisticated versions of the same product available to purchase. Commonly used web transaction logs include AWStats and Google Analytics.

Resources for writing

Publishers such as Wiley-Blackwell and Emerald are increasingly keen to support prospective authors in preparing manuscripts for journal submission by developing dedicated 'Author Services' web resources. These websites aim to assist writers with everything from finding a journal or English-language editing service through to providing style filters for use with reference management software packages and optimizing your article for retrieval by search engines. They are well worth a look.

Points for reflection

- Think about the type of project you are planning to undertake. Does it require a qualitative or quantitative approach? What kinds of data does this mean you will be collecting? How will you be analysing your data?
- What kind of budget do you have to support your project? Can you purchase pure built software packages or will you need to locate open access free examples of similar tools? Do an internet search to see what you can find that might meet your needs.

Recommended further reading

Bazeley, P. (2007) *Qualitative Data Analysis with NVivo*, 2nd rev. edn, Sage Publications, London.

Buzan, T. (2009) *The Mind Map Book: unlock your creativity, boost your memory, change your life*, BBC Active, London.

Field, A. (2009) *Discovering Statistics Using SPSS*, 3rd edn, Sage Publications, London.

Gahan, C. and Hannibal, M. (1998) *Doing Qualitative Research Using QSR NUD*IST*, Sage Publications, London.

Part 3

Impact of research, evaluation and audit

11

Writing up your project findings

Graham Walton and Maria J. Grant

'Writing is a luxury I don't have time for in my job!'

'Is there anyone who can help me get started?'

'How do I decide where to send my writing?'

Introduction

An integral part of completing a project, particularly one involving research or evaluation, is the process of reporting the work to the wider community. Becoming effective in writing research requires knowledge and skills that are transferable from the wide range of attributes and awareness already existing in the library and information science (LIS) practitioners' skills portfolio. The purpose of this chapter is to provide an insight into aspects of writing to ensure that, as a writer, you become familiar with both the pleasures and challenges of writing. Strategies to overcome the challenges of writing are provided and the complex and varied motivations for writing are explored.

Motivation for writing

In some professions the culture, professional framework, job responsibilities and support structures are highly influential in motivating writing activity. While this is true for academic libraries in countries such as the USA and Nigeria, where tenure and financial gain are factors, in general extrinsic motivators are unusual within the LIS sector. As neither career progression nor a permanent contract are linked with writing output for most librarians, it is down to you as an individual to identify what motivates and influences your approach to writing.

Writing is often a primarily solo activity, and so it can be helpful to have an understanding of a range of factors identified in the literature that motivate others to write up their work (Bradley, 2008; Clapton, 2010; Sullivan, 2011):

1 **Provides an outlet for project findings**: Having your work published enables you to share your ideas and findings with other LIS practitioners and helps inform their decision-making, strengthening and improving library services. The more project work that is written up the rate at which our available knowledge base, which we ourselves may wish to draw on, will continue to grow.

2 **Boosts individual's reputation**: By contributing to the knowledge base, your writing portfolio can contribute to your professional progression. It provides the opportunity to raise your personal profile within your own organization and the wider LIS community and demonstrates that you have a range of skills that can be used in different settings. Very often further opportunities arise that can be directly attributed to specific items of professional writing.

3 **Boosts reputation of LIS profession**: The value and importance of the LIS practitioner's role is not always understood or appreciated, especially within large organizations. Contributing high-quality writing outputs will go some way to redress this perception, in enabling you to be viewed on an equal footing to your other publication-active colleagues. This can especially be the case on occasions when your research findings and writing activity have wider relevance than purely to the LIS profession.

4 **Allows development of interest**: By embarking upon writing, you are sending out a clear message that this is an area which interests you and which you wish to enhance. Very often this involves setting the context for your chosen subject area with a literature review (see Chapter 6); this process alone can contribute to the knowledge base in your chosen area when written up and published. By writing about work projects you are also joining a community of like-minded people who share your interest in that area.

The above four aspects of intrinsic motivation are not discrete reasons for writing and, very often, you may find that you are influenced by a combination of some or all of the above.

Barriers to writing and how to overcome them

Having chosen to write, you have to have a sense of realism that as a writer you are likely to encounter various barriers as you seek to write an account of your ideas, theories and project outcomes. Knowing what these barriers may be in advance, together with a list of available coping strategies, will provide a better chance that they will be effectively overcome. It is possible to synthesize the work of various commentators (Bradley, 2008; Clapton, 2010; Shenton, 2005; Shenton, 2008; Sullivan, 2011) to identify three different barriers: limited time, skills and support gap and organizational constraints.

Limited time

A common challenge for the LIS practitioner is finding the time to write; other work-related tasks take priority and the delays in getting something ready for publication can be so great that the topic becomes so stale or out of date that continuing is not appropriate.

Facing time constraints is present at all levels in libraries, from library directors to people in their first professional post. One solution is to 'find/make' time by timetabling short bouts of writing within your working week (Murray, 2005; Silvia, 2007), for example, not opening your e-mails first thing but instead dedicating the first half hour of each day to writing.

Acknowledging that writing for publication is part of professional practice, having permission to write up your work from within your organization can also make a big difference. Either independently, or with a colleague or manager, take a critical look at your diary to identify activities that could realistically be rescheduled to free up a block of writing time without detrimentally impacting on other work commitment, thereby making time rather than waiting for the opportunity to arise.

Skills and support gap

Many practitioners, perhaps yourself included, claim they do not have the skills or confidence to write and be published (see Chapter 2); apprehension can sometimes be so great that the writing never even starts. This is perhaps ironic, given that our daily work focuses on information, its presentation and distribution. Writers wishing to become productive can be intimidated by the publishing process and having their work scrutinized by their peers.

Social networking (see Chapter 10) provides a relatively safe place to start sharing your thoughts. By becoming a member of professional discussion lists, experience can be gained on responding to current debate and topics in a measured and appropriate manner. A blog can be established which focuses on your specific research project, where updates and progress can be posted; the same applies for a Facebook account that can be set up to allow you to communicate about your research with interested parties. Sites such as LinkedIn are increasingly being used as a place for people to express views and enter into debate with like-minded people.

Sullivan (2011) has detailed a range of ways in which LIS practitioners can acquire the necessary skills. These can include:

1 **Formal classes/inductions:** For a structured approach to writing skills, formal classes can provide a good introduction (Fallon, 2009).
2 **Workshops:** Writing workshops are often offered by a range of professional bodies. They provide an opportunity to develop practical writing skills with others at similar stages in their writing careers.
3 **Editorial support:** Editors of journals are often only too happy to be approached to talk through with a prospective writer how their work can develop.
4 **Online and printed guides:** There are variety of books aimed at covering writing skills (Murray and Moore, 2006; Day, 2007; Belcher, 2009) including those designed specifically for LIS practitioners (Gordon, 2004; Langley and Wallace, 2010). A wide range of freely available online guides is also available (SkillsYouNeed, 2011; Fallon, 2010; MindTools, 2012).
5 **The peer review process itself:** Whether one is a referee or someone receiving feedback from a referee, the peer review process can be a great learning opportunity. As a referee you learn to read, formulate and communicate constructive feedback, while as someone receiving feedback you can learn to strengthen your writing by responding to comments and seeking to anticipate the types of questions a reader might pose having read your piece of writing.
6 **Writing groups:** These provide a collegiate and supportive environment in which writing is seen as a social activity that benefits from discussion between peers (Murray and Moore, 2006). Writers groups can be an effective way to develop your skills and confidence in writing and are becoming increasingly widespread, with examples of library-related writing groups in England (Grant et al., 2010); Ireland (Fallon, 2009) and the USA (Tysick and Babb, 2006).
7 **Writing with an experienced colleague:** Joining forces with some who

already has experience of publication can be a great way to learn how to write. They can help you with writing dilemmas, such as how to present your findings, help you make writing decisions, e.g. where to submit your writing, and generally lead by example (Murray, 2005).

Organizational constraints

It is very rare for a librarian's job description to include responsibilities for writing. Sometimes the culture and ethos of the organization does not appear to be supportive for professional writing (Bradley, 2008; Shenton, 2008) and addressing this potential barrier to your writing activity might well necessitate a change in organizational culture (see Chapter 13). As research has become more pervasive, so time barriers are removed and opportunities for research and collaboration are encouraged. However, if barriers to writing continue to persist in your organization, you can perhaps seek to influence the prevailing culture by asking for project work or producing a writing output to be part of your annual work appraisal.

Writing the project report

A very common writing activity attached to undertaking research or evaluation is the production of a project report. It is a relatively unthreatening kind of output, as it is primarily aimed at an internal audience rather than the wider world. The role of the research report is to ensure that the work increases the understanding of the LIS world and reduces uncertainty. The results are only part of the project report, which also needs to allow the reader to assess and then evaluate the reliability of the results. A typical format is:

- contents page
- introduction (including context, literature review, research rationale, relative importance)
- work carried out (including research design, methodology, analysis procedure)
- results (structure around research objectives)
- conclusion (must be supported by findings)
- recommendations
- appendices.

In many ways, the quality of the research will be judged by the research report. Readers' views will be influenced by the presentation and accuracy of the report as much as they will be by the validity and reliability of the study. The onus is therefore on you as the writer to make sure the research report is presented as professionally as possible, with accurate proof reading. It can be worth asking a colleague unconnected with the project to look at your report to ensure that your writing is transparent and the layout of your report consistent.

Options for disseminating writing

After undertaking an evaluation or research study and producing the report, you may have expended so much effort that the thought of wider dissemination will be daunting. At the outset you should consider you 'how, why, when and what' will disseminate over and above the research report itself. This planning approach will mean the writing is more likely to happen. The widespread impact of social networking tools has significantly increased opportunities for the LIS practitioner to write for a wider audience. Despite this prevalence, for many people, the preferred platform for their writing is the peer-reviewed academic journal. In a recent survey at Loughborough University, for 99% of respondents the academic journal was the most important for their writing (Ashby et al., 2011). For this reason, a significant part of this chapter will concentrate upon producing effective writing for the academic journal.

There are many other ways that the LIS practitioner can distribute their writing. Flatley and Weber (2004) provide an overview of writing options in the pre-social networking era, and the further opportunities available through social networking are covered by Kroski (2004). If you wish to gain experience before aiming for the academic journal, there are other less daunting avenues to head down. Editors are always looking for people who will review newly published books or e-resources. This can lead to you building up a portfolio that can be applied elsewhere. Equally, correspondence columns in professional journals provide the opportunity to have a well constructed and argued letter published. From here reputations and opportunities can spring where the writer is asked to contribute a chapter in an edited book.

Publishing in journals

The most effective way a writer can disseminate their research is through a journal article. There are various reasons why this is the case, including the fact that they have a well accepted value as a current source. The strong bibliographical control provided by indexes and abstracts are also significant. Journals (especially with the increase in e-journals) are widely accessed by an international readership. They also have a sense of permanence and value that social networking technologies will struggle to match.

When you are new to writing it can be difficult to know how to choose a journal in which to publish details of your project, so it's useful to know that there are broadly speaking two different types of journals – 'scholarly, academic journals' and 'professional journals' (Moore, 2000). Professional journals tend to focus on process and ideas so that others can learn from your experience; taking an idea from problem through to a workable solution. Scholarly, academic journals will also want their content to inform professional practice but are likely to place a greater emphasis on the methodological rigour of your project in reaching the conclusions you're presenting. Scholarly journals are also likely to be peer-reviewed, which means that others working in the same area will be invited to constructively comment on the writing before a decision is made about whether to publish it. This can sound daunting but if you think of it as receiving free advice to help make your paper the best you can, it can be a very positive experience.

Often journals seek to meet both scholarly and professional audiences, but as a writer, you need to be clear which type of journal – and its readership – is the most appropriate for your work. Being clear about the type of journal and its readership, ideally before you start writing, can help you focus your precious time by organizing your writing according to the journal's author guidelines regarding structure, length and referencing styles. Author guidelines can usually be found on the web page and the back cover of the journal, but which journal should you choose? It can be helpful to start by seeing where other people have published similar papers (and you'll have a ready-made list, having undertaken a literature review) and then looking at the aims and scope of those journals to see which is the best fit for your writing.

As mentioned above, journals have their own author guidelines but, generally speaking, they will expect an article about a project to be structured in the following way:

- **Abstract:** Outlined in more details below, your abstract should aim to provide a summary of your writing and include details of what stimulated you to write your paper (background), the methods you used (methods), a presentation of your findings (results), a discussion (of your findings) and a summing up (conclusion). Cruickshank, Hall and Taylor-Smith (2011) have reported that people want 'easily accessible research summaries' and most journals require structured abstracts with this in mind. Remember, the decision to read a full article is often based purely on the abstract, so this is your opportunity to really promote the message your writing makes.

- **Background:** Sometimes referred to as the introduction or literature review, the background sets out the context of why your project is important.
- **Methods:** What methods did you use when undertaking your project?
- **Results:** Your results arise from your data collection. As well as text you can use figures and tables to summarize your findings.
- **Discussion:** This section provides an opportunity to present an interpretation of your project findings, as given in the results section, in light of what is already known about the subject. This usually involves linking back to the literature review and explaining how the study moves the subject forward.
- **Conclusions:** Your conclusion should be based on everything that has previously been presented in your writing, including primary conclusions and their implications and suggestions areas for further investigation if appropriate. No new findings or literature should be introduced at this stage.

Knowing when your writing is ready for publication is difficult. Your aim should not be for a perfect piece of writing but, depending on the type of journal you are sending it to, ensuring that it is good enough to send for peer review. Setting yourself a deadline can help focus your energies. Then, having written your article, anticipated the likely questions a reader of your work might have and edited your writing accordingly, asked a colleague to comment on your work and edited your writing again, you're now ready to submit your article.

Each journal will have its own submission process, ranging from sending an e-mail attachment to the editorial team through to submitting via an online system; check the journal's web page or inside cover to know which one applies to your writing.

Responding to feedback

Having toiled over your writing, you may be disheartened when you receive a decision letter that indicates revisions are required, accompanied by several pages of referees' comments; after all, you probably only submitted it when you believed it was the best it could be. In truth, very few papers are accepted without revisions, and so the best way to view referee comments are as free support and advice given with the aim of helping you make your writing as good as it possibly can be. Having read the decision letter, put it aside for a week or so and then re-read it once your initial disappointment has dissipated; it's unlikely that the comments will be so fundamental that they are impossible to comply with through careful editing of your writing. Most journals will ask you to outline your changes either through tracked changes or providing a list of amendments; respond directly and positively to any feedback and, if you are genuinely unable to revise your writing, respond to the editor suggesting an alternative. Sometimes a resubmission is fine but, recognizing that a request for revisions is based on what the reviewer thinks of your work so far, a referee may request further work based on the revisions made thus far. Again, do your best to respond positively to their comments.

Your writing has been accepted!

Congratulations! Your writing has been accepted for publication! If you haven't already been asked, you'll probably be asked to sign a declaration confirming the authorship for the piece of writing, after which your writing will be sent for typesetting and will be reviewed by a copy editor, who will pick up grammatical errors and spelling mistakes and ensure consistency throughout the paper; you'll have an opportunity to respond when you receive the 'proof'. Rather than make extensive changes, the proof is your final opportunity to ensure that the format and content of the paper is correct before it is published. This is a time for checking for typographical errors and ensuring that things are accurately presented – e.g. that name and institution, figures and tables, and references are correct. The copy editor may also request clarification of some sections of your writing or query incomplete references.

Summary

This chapter has introduced you to the idea of writing in all its forms, ranging from social media through to project reports and peer-reviewed journal articles. We've considered motivation to write, outlined common barriers to writing activity and suggested some ways in which these can be mitigated. Finally we looked at the process of submitting your writing to a journal, responding to feedback and correcting proofs.

There are many rewards to engaging in writing as part of your professional practice but financial gains are rare. Nonetheless, writing is a great way to expand your networking opportunities, increase transferable skills, widen your influence and explore areas of interest in detail. The journey itself is a great experience and this chapter will help you along the way.

Points for reflection

- Are you starting a new project? How could you use social media to share your findings and elicit input from your peers as your project develops?
- Consider contacting journal editors to offer your services as a peer reviewer.
- Want to write a journal article? Do a quick literature review (see Chapter 6) to inform the context of your writing, then look at the references to see if one journal keeps coming up in your list. Look at the aim and scope of that journal and, if it looks potentially suitable, start structuring your paper in line with their author guidelines.
- Do you have a journal article that's been rejected? Take a second look at the decision letter and referees' feedback. Is there something you could do to further develop your paper before offering it to another journal?

References

Ashby, M., Ortoll Espinet, E., Fry, J., Lund, P., Stubbings, R. and Walton, G. (2011) *Scholarly Communication at Loughborough University: a study by Loughborough University Library*, Loughborough University Library, www.lboro.ac.uk/media/wwwlboroacuk/content/library/downloads/ surveyresults/scholarly-comm-lboro2011.pdf.

Belcher, W. L. (2009) *Writing Your Journal Article in Twelve Weeks: a guide to academic publishing success*, Sage Publications, London.

Bradley, F. (2008) Writing for the Profession: the experience of new professionals, *Library Management*, **29** (8/9), 729–45.

Clapton, J. (2010) Library and Information Science Practitioners Writing for Publication: motivations, barriers and support, *Library and Information Research*, **24** (106), 7–18.

Cruickshank, P., Hall, H. and Taylor-Smith, E. (2011) *Enhancing the Impact of LIS Research Projects*, RiLIES project report, www.researchinfonet.org/wp-content/uploads/2012/01/RiLIES_report_FINAL.pdf.

Day, A. (2007) *How to Get Research Published in Journals*, 2nd edn, Gower, Farnham.

Fallon, H. (2009) A Writing Support Programme for Irish Academic Librarians, *Library Review*, **58** (6), 414–22.

Fallon, H. (2010) *Academic Writing Librarians*, http://academicwritinglibrarian.blogspot.co.uk/p/my-writing-resources.html.

Flatley, R. K. and Weber, M. A. (2004) Professional Development Opportunities for New Academic Librarians, *Journal of Academic Librarianship*, **30** (6), 488–92.

Gordon, R. S. (2004) *The Librarian's Guide to Writing for Publications*, Scarecrow Press, Oxford.

Grant, M. J., Munro, W., McIsaac, J. and Hill, S. (2010) Cross-disciplinary Writers' Group Stimulates Fresh Approaches to Scholarly Communication: a reflective case study within a higher education institution in the north west of England, *New Review of Academic Librarianship*, **16** (S1), 44–64.

Kroski, E. (2004) *Web 2.0 for Librarians and Information Professionals*, Neal-Schuman Publishers, New York, NY.

Langley, A. and Wallace, J. D. (2010) *A Practical Writing Guide for Academic Librarians: keeping it short and sweet*, Chandos Publishing, Oxford.

MindTools (2012) *Writing Skills: getting your written message across clearly*, www.mindtools.com/CommSkll/WritingSkills.html.

Moore, N. (2000) *How to Do Research: the complete guide to designing and managing research projects*, Library Association Publishing, London.

Murray, R. (2005) *Writing for Academic Journals*, Open University Press, Maidenhead.

Murray, R. and Moore, S. (2006) *The Handbook of Academic Writing: a fresh approach*, Open University Press, Maidenhead.

Shenton, A. (2005) Publishing Research in LIS Journals, *Education in Information*, **23** (2), 141–63.

Shenton, A. (2008) The Frustrations of Writing Research Articles for Publication and What to do about Them, *Library and Information Research*, **32** (101), 7–18.

Silvia, P. J. (2007) *How to Write a Lot: a practical guide to productive academic writing*, APA Life Tools, Washington, DC.

SkillsYouNeed (2011) *Writing Skills*, www.skillsyouneed.com/writing-skills.html.

Sullivan, D. (2011) Publishing Anxiety: emotion and the stages of publishing in the library and information science literature, *Australian Library Journal*, **61** (2), 133–40.

Tysick, C. and Babb, N. (2006) Perspectives on Writing Support for Junior Faculty Librarians: a case study, *Journal of Academic Librarianship*, **32** (1), 94–100.

Recommended further reading

Blicq, R. S. and Moretto, L. A. (2001) *Writing Reports to Get Results*, 3rd edn, Wiley, New York, NY.

Bowden, J. (2004) *Writing a Report: how to prepare, write and present effective reports*, 7th edn, How To Books, Oxford.

12

Disseminating your project findings

Jane Shelling

'What exactly is dissemination?'

'My work is specific to my library; I doubt anyone else would be interested in it.'

'When should dissemination be planned?'

Introduction

Dissemination can be a confusing term and its definition can depend on context. As library and information practitioners, many of us are familiar with dissemination as it applies in the term 'selective dissemination of information' or SDI. Whilst this term is also open to interpretation, it usually means a current awareness service which involves screening documents to select information to meet the specific research needs of a user and delivering that information directly to them (Hossain and Shiful, 2008). Dissemination is one of as many as 29 terms identified and used to describe knowledge to action; others include knowledge translation, knowledge transfer, knowledge exchange, research utilization, implementation and diffusion (Graham et al., 2006).

In the context of this chapter dissemination is a term used to describe ways to alert interested parties to your research findings and encourage the uptake of that evidence into practice. No particular theory or model is being advocated; presented here are ideas and suggestions to establish or improve the dissemination of research.

Dissemination is an integral part of the research process and is often included as a requirement in a research-funding contract. Dissemination can become complex, because it involves a number of processes and different target groups, but it can and should be viewed as just another part of the wider research process. In addition to planned dissemination activities, approaches and opportunities to disseminate findings may present themselves during the research. As suggested in Chapter 11, if you are new to project work you may wish to consider approaching an experienced colleague or mentor in your workplace for their advice in developing your dissemination plan.

Plan and evaluate

A dissemination plan may contain five major elements (Carpenter et al., 2005):

1 What is going to be disseminated
2 Who are the end users
3 Dissemination partners
4 How to disseminate
5 Evaluation.

Other related aspects that can also be included are: 'Who is the messenger?' and 'What is the expected outcome?' (Reardon, Lavis and Gibson, 2007)

What is going to be disseminated? What is the message?

It is important to understand and be fully conversant with all aspects of your research, and in particular to know your key messages. Not all of your audience will be interested in all aspects of the research. For example, some may want to replicate the research method, in which case technical aspects will be of interest, but others may only be concerned with the bottom line. It is essential to keep your message easily understood by your potential audience, which may include those from other disciplines, hierarchy within your organization, librarians and non-librarians associated with libraries (Crumley and Koufogiannakis, 2004). One strategy is to write short, jargon-free papers that use case studies and relevant examples and highlight the key messages (Arney et al., 2009). When writing, consider a message that is driven by facts or data and that expresses an actionable idea or one that will provide discussion (Reardon, Lavis and Gibson, 2007).

The form of the message should suit the target audience and also help clarify who the target audience is. A research report may be suitable for one audience but another audience may be more easily reached through an article in a targeted, in-house newsletter. This could be an opportunity for you to write a short newsletter article about the research result or some aspect of the research. So think like a journalist: prepare a few key points (think about the key message); think of a 'hook' to engage the interest of your readership and tie yourself in with your audience; mention other related research or researchers and consider obtaining a quote from them to enhance credibility (Panos London, 2011).

Preparing messages for your different potential audiences in advance will ensure that you can quickly and easily meet individual information needs. The process will also deepen your understanding of how your research might meet the needs of different audiences.

Who are the end users? What are their needs? Who needs to know?

Librarians and those concerned with LIS are an obvious primary audience for LIS research. However, consider specific groups within this field, many of which have their own communication networks, as potential dissemination targets. This could include those working in different library types (special, academic, government); libraries within different disciplines (health or law librarians), specific tasks within a library (researcher, reference librarian or cataloguer) or special interests within LIS (evidence-based practice or information technology).

Moving away from the safety of our own discipline, 'out of sector' dissemination is a great way to raise the profile of librarianship and also an opportunity to gain a greater impact from the research. Ideas that may seem commonplace in our own discipline could be new and exciting when presented for the first time to those outside libraries (Shenton and Beautyman, 2009), particularly if the message is well formulated with the user in mind. Consider dissemination across the discipline that your research was conducted in.

Dissemination partners or collaborations and the messenger

Research project participants may have been involved in the project's first attempts at dissemination and this group forms a ready-made partnership. A relationship with these stakeholders can continue for further dissemination and feedback opportunities, such as sending a regular 'Here's where we are now' e-mail, which will keep people feeling involved and part of the process.

Just as it is important to involve research project participants in the dissemination process, other stakeholders such as administrators, decision makers and funders can also be kept informed through regular e-mails with summaries or links to findings. Knowledge brokering has long been seen as an effective means of transferring research evidence into policy and practice (Ward, House and Hamer, 2009). This role could be taken by someone who has a position that sits somewhere between the researcher and a decision maker. One possibility is an organization's communication officer or media officer. This person is skilled in communication and able to help with delivering key messages.

Make use of your relationships with practitioners, researchers and administrators to establish who might have an interest in your area of research and keep them informed of your progress. These contacts can help to disseminate your research through their networks. For example, if they are presenting a paper to a conference it may be appropriate for your research to be mentioned and you could repay the effort at your next conference presentation.

Often an organization has a person who is a talented networker and who enjoys being 'in the know'. Ensure that these people, with their numerous useful contacts, are included in your dissemination activities and acknowledge their efforts.

Dissemination can also be achieved through the use of information-sharing groups such as journal clubs, research groups within and external to your organization, and professional groups. The key to tapping into this dissemination opportunity is to ensure that the group sees that there is something in it for them. Perhaps your research leads in or is a continuation of something they are involved in; or your research involves a user group that is their primary client. A motivation to be involved is important to ensure buy-in.

How to disseminate

When choosing how to disseminate, bear in mind who you want to be affected by your research and what you want to achieve. The dissemination method should match your intended audience. Whilst LIS practitioners may be likely beneficiaries of your work, they may choose to access their information in different ways, necessitating a variety of dissemination practices, from informal interactions through to conference presentations. Academic papers should also be considered when developing your dissemination plan. Here are some suggested dissemination methods.

Talk

Conferences, workshops, meetings and seminars are all good places to present your research and disseminate your findings. At these gatherings you may present a paper or a poster or even take part in hosting a booth for your organization. All these methods offer an opportunity to disseminate face to face.

Preparing an abstract and then a paper to present at a conference needs adequate preparation time. If presenting using PowerPoint don't have too many slides – approximately 1 slide for every 2–3 minutes that you have available to speak (Kennan and Olsson, 2011) – and reveal salient points on slides one at a time. This enables the audience to digest information before you move onto your next point (Race, 2000). A good entrée into the art of presenting and disseminating your project findings is to start with a poster presentation. Designing a poster will help you to structure your key messages effectively. Many conference organizers are now recognizing the importance of poster presentations and offering new and innovative ways for presenters to reach their audiences. These include scheduling a specific time within the conference for posters to be viewed and also giving those presenting posters short time slots to address all conference participants.

Some organizations hold regular lunchtime professional development meetings and may welcome a discussion of your research. Meetings of this type are useful dissemination points but still require adequate preparation time and presentation skills to reach an audience effectively. It is also essential to match the information to the audience and the environment. Presentations give the opportunity to grab the attention of your audience; make good use of photos, graphs and video (Kennan and Olsson, 2011). If appropriate, training sessions can also be a good opportunity to connect with your target audience and disseminate research.

Bywood, Lunnay and Roche (2008) conducted a systematic review of 16 dissemination strategies and identified that the four most successful approaches in changing behaviour were interactive educational meetings, educational outreach visits, prompts and reminders, and audit and feedback. For your own dissemination activity, this could translate as organizing meetings and visits both within and outside your organization to facilitate a sharing of ideas and knowledge arising from your project work, and writing and sharing project updates through existing channels, for example e-mail, newsletters and notice boards (see Chapter 13).

Write

Submit an article to a journal carefully selected to take account of its major focus, style, treatment and readership (Shenton and Beautyman, 2009; see also Chapter 11). The style, focus and length of an article will depend on the type of journal you are submitting to; it may be a professional periodical or an academic journal. An article submitted to an academic journal may need to be peer-reviewed; this can mean that it takes longer for the article to appear in print but it can enhance your professional standing within your workplace. Write for relevant publications in the widest sense – journal articles for library and other related disciplines, grey literature, online blogs, web pages and small print-run newsletters (see Chapter 10). Also vary the content, tailoring different messages to meet the interests of different audiences (see Chapter 11).

Network

Use a wide range of contacts to disseminate to discussion groups (online and face to face), meetings, journal clubs and local library groups. Specific sector events, morning teas or celebrations are all opportunities to connect with audiences. Find ways to display and promote your whole organization's research activities (an organization's 'What's New' website section or newsletters) – and then ensure that library research projects are included too. This builds relationships with researchers and puts library researchers on an equal footing.

Online

E-mail publications are useful for dissemination because they are timely, inexpensive to produce, can include hyperlinks to full text and are more easily remembered than verbal communication, and read receipts can be used to track acceptance.

Web 2.0 applications are useful tools to disseminate your research; think blogs, microblogs (e.g. Twitter), Facebook and wikis. When deciding on how to disseminate research it is important to consider the use of technology and its ability to empower or exclude users through access. Related issues such as likely IT literacy or recipient age may also need to be considered (Adams and Blandford, 2005).

Find a champion

In an effort to bridge the gap between research and practice, the use of opinion leaders (alternatively known as champions, change agents, facilitators or knowledge brokers) in the workplace has become more common over a number of different disciplines (Bywood, Lunnay and Roche, 2009). In theory it would appear that opinion leaders play an important role but this area has not been well researched (Bywood, Lunnay and Roche, 2009; Green et al., 2009).

Broader community

Writing opinion pieces, internal memos or blogging within your workplace or professional organization can achieve a broader reach. When doing so, cite other internal work where relevant, as well as your own research.

By using different ways to disseminate research information, you encourage end users to access information both passively (material provided to them) and actively (material is available to them) (Arney et al., 2009). It is most likely that successful dissemination will occur using a number of different approaches (Freemantle and Watt, 1994).

Evaluation

It is useful to evaluate your dissemination in order to improve any future efforts. There are two aspects that can be examined; the first is how you conducted the dissemination process and the second is evaluating the success of the dissemination itself and determining impact.

As part of the dissemination plan, examine all of the methods that were used and gather evidence to evaluate how successful the dissemination has been. Identify the groups you intended to disseminate to and determine if those groups received your research message and if the message had any impact/effect on them over a particular timescale.

To measure receipt of the research message requires gathering feedback from those that you disseminated to. There are a number of ways to do this, including focus groups and surveys, but of course you would need to know who you disseminated to. If you are hosting your project findings on a website, using an URL shortening service such as 'bitly' when sharing the site details will also enable you to gather data on the number of times your site is accessed. Although this will not provide information about who accessed your site, nor indeed what they thought of your findings, it will give an indication of the level of interest it has attracted. If feedback was received it should be noted if the dissemination methods were changed as a result of that feedback (Carpenter et al., 2005). Some factors which could affect aspects of evaluation include costs of dissemination methods, adequate resources and staffing to make changes, barriers to change and whether individual or organizational level change was required (Bywood, Lunnay and Roche, 2008).

The evaluation process provides a good opportunity to think about the impact, if any, of the dissemination (see Chapter 13). Defining the expected impact in terms of likely outcomes will give you a measure for the success of your dissemination effort (Reardon, Lavis and Gibson, 2007).

Case study 12.1 The life cycle of a research project dissemination plan

---

Background
The National Drug Sector Information Service (NDSIS), Australia, wished to conduct a research project to measure the response from clients to an unsolicited but regularly e-mailed, relevant, current awareness product. The research question was: 'Does a librarian-initiated, tailored information product delivered electronically to clients have a positive effect as demonstrated by the fulfilment of the project aims?'

The dissemination plan
A dissemination plan was begun once the research project planning was underway, with a primary emphasis on disseminating the research to library and information practitioners through conference papers and a journal article.

As the project progressed the findings began to reveal information that would be of interest more broadly to the alcohol and other drugs (AOD) sector. The dissemination plan was therefore extended to include ways to disseminate to this wider audience.

What is going to be disseminated?
The key findings arising from the project were:

- AOD researchers and policy writers responded positively to targeted outreach.
- AOD workers did not respond at all to targeted outreach.

Who are the end users?

LIS and AOD sectors. Each group was assigned one of the three information messages.

- AOD sector
  — AOD researchers, AOD information agencies. *Interest: Full report research process, methodology and findings*
  — AOD policy writers, AOD workers. *Interest: Research findings*
  — AOD workforce development. *Interest: Research findings*
  — AOD funding bodies. *Interest: Full report research process, methodology and findings*
  — AOD agencies. *Interest: Research findings*
- LIS sector
  — Librarians and LIS researchers. *Interest: Research process, methodology, and findings*
  — Health Libraries and AOD Libraries. *Interest: Research process, methodology and findings*
- Broader sector
  — Government funding agencies. *Interest: Research process, methodology and findings.*

Dissemination partners

Research project participants, NIIS Advisory Committee and the greater Alcohol and other Drugs Organisation and Board were kept informed of the research project progress and received brief research findings reports through e-mail and regular reporting channels. The methods, messages and end users are summarized in Table 12.1 (see next page).

Evaluation

The study findings generated a high level of interest from those working in the AOD field including AOD workers, managers; researchers, policy writers and funders. The research findings of this project still provide interest to the library and information sector in particular health and special librarians who could find parallels in their user groups.

Table 12.1 *How to disseminate*

Dissemination method	Message	End users
Journal article – LIS journal Short article – LIS Newsletter	Research method and findings	Librarians and LIS researchers
Conference presentation Conference poster Conference presentation (2)	Research method and finding	AOD sector (includes all areas of AOD) LIS
Articles in local sector newsletter (3)	Research finding	AOD sector (includes all areas of AOD)
Entry in research index	Research method and finding	AOD sector (includes all areas of AOD)
Online sector bulletin board (Update) www.adca.org.au/ndsis/e_list.php	Brief research method and findings	AOD sector
Face-to-face in-house meetings	Brief research method and findings	AOD agencies
Champions enlisted	Research report	Parent organization Board members

In this case study the dissemination plan evolved as the project progressed, with the project findings generating interest beyond that originally envisaged. A variety of dissemination methods were used, key messages being tailored to the end users. The evaluation illustrated that while the research dissemination can lead to unexpected results, a well executed dissemination plan will successfully guide the process.

Summary

Disseminating research findings will enrich your research experience. It adds depth to your understanding of research and its uses, and gives real purpose to your work. On a wider scale, disseminating your research will progress the profession and improve practice and has the potential to impact on other disciplines, too, while the feedback you receive is not just about your research but is also an acknowledgement of you as a researcher and the library as a source of research.

Reflection and planning at all stages will lead to the best result in terms of research, dissemination and personal professional growth. When you do disseminate your own research be mindful of what your message is, who you are disseminating to and how you can best reach them. Constantly evaluating your practice will inevitably lead to continuous improvement and satisfaction.

Points for reflection

As a library and information practitioner you are accustomed to the principles of dissemination. In order to turn this appreciation into action and successfully apply it to your project work:

- Try and identify any disseminating activities that you are currently involved with in your practice. Do they work? How do you know? What else could you try?
- Develop a dissemination plan for a project you would like to undertake/are currently involved with/have recently completed and evaluate your progress.

References

Adams, A. and Blandford, A. (2005) Social Empowerment and Exclusion: a case study on digital libraries, *ACM Transactions on CHI*, **12** (2), 174–200.

Arney, F., Bromfield, L., Higgins, D. and Lewig, K. (2009) Integration Strategies for Delivering Evidence-informed Practice, *Evidence & Policy*, **5** (2), 179–91.

Bywood, P., Lunnay, B. and Roche, A. (2008) *Effective Dissemination: a systematic review of implementation strategies for the AOD field*, Adelaide, National Centre for Education and Training on Addiction, 157.

Bywood, P., Lunnay, B. and Roche, A. (2009) Effectiveness of Opinion Leaders for Getting Research into Practice in the Alcohol and Other Drug Field: results from a systematic literature review, *Drugs: Education, Prevention and Policy*, **16** (3), 205–16.

Carpenter, D., Nieva, V., Albaghal, T. and Sorra, J. (2005) Development of a Planning Tool to Guide Research Dissemination. In Henriksen, K., Battles, J. B., Marks, E. S. and Lewin D. I. (eds), *Advances in Patient Safety: from research to implementation*, Vol. 4, Agency for Healthcare Research and Quality, Rockville, MD, 83–91.

Crumley, E. and Koufogiannakis, D. (2004) Disseminating the Lessons of Evidence-based Practice. In Booth, A. and Brice, A., *Evidence-based Practice for Information Professionals: a handbook*, Facet Publishing, London, 138–43.

Freemantle, N. and Watt, I. (1994) Dissemination: implementing the findings of research, *Health Libraries Review*, **11**, 133–7.

Graham, I. D., Logan, J., Harrison, M. B., Straus, S. E., Tetroe, J., Caswell, W. and Robinson, N. (2006) Lost in Knowledge Translation: time for a map?, *Journal of Continuing Education in the Health Professions*, **26** (1), 13–24.

Green, L. W., Ottoson, J. M., García, C. and Hiatt, R. A. (2009) Diffusion Theory and Knowledge Dissemination, Utilization, and Integration in Public Health,

Annual Review of Public Health, **30**, 151–74.

Hossain, M. J. and Shiful, M. I. (2008) Selective Dissemination of Information (SDI) Service: a conceptual paradigm, *International Journal of Information Science and Technology*, **6** (1), 27–44.

Kennan, M. A. and Olsson, M. (2011) Writing It Up: getting your LIS research out there, *Australian Academic & Research Libraries*, **42** (1), 14–28.

Panos London (2011) *A Journalist's Guide to Reporting Research Findings*.

Race, P. (2000) *2000 Tips for Lecturers*, Kogan Page, London.

Reardon, R., Lavis, J. and Gibson, J. (2007) From Research to Practice: a knowledge transfer planning guide, *Insight and Action*, **1**, 1–2.

Shenton, A. and Beautyman, W. (2009) Getting Our Message Across to Other Disciplines, *Library & Information Update*, January, 60–1.

Ward, V., House, A. and Hamer, S. (2009) Knowledge Brokering: the missing link in the evidence to action chain, *Evidence & Policy*, **5** (3), 267–79.

Recommended further reading

Booth, A. (2004) Evaluating your Performance. In Booth, A. and Brice, A. (eds), *Evidence-based Practice for Information Professionals: a handbook*, Facet Publishing, London, 125–43.

Carpenter, D., Nieva, V., Albaghal, T. and Sorra, J. (2005) Development of a Planning Tool to Guide Research Dissemination. In Henriksen, K., Battles, J. B., Marks, E. S. and Lewin D. I. (eds), *Advances in Patient Safety: from research to implementation*, *Vol. 4*, Agency for Healthcare Research and Quality, Rockville, MD, 83–91.

13

What next? Applying your findings to practice

Robert Gent and Andrew Cox

'I don't understand some of the decisions that are made in this place.'

'How can I get the support I need to carry on my research?'

'How can I ensure my project has impact?'

This book is an introduction to research, evaluation and audit techniques for library and information service practitioners. You may well have an interest in pure research for its own sake but it is more likely that you are interested in using research to prompt a change in policy or to improve service delivery. The reality is that much research never does get into practice. If you do not want this neglect to befall your own work, this chapter will give you some pointers about how to design your project with impact in mind and how to plan to influence organizations and wider communities to make use of your project findings.

In most organizations research, evaluation or audit does not take place in a vacuum. This chapter explores the important question of how you can make your project findings count, to help bring about the changes that will make your organization stronger and more responsive. Equally you may want to influence a whole sector or community of organizations. The techniques explored in this chapter can be summarized under four headings:

1 Understanding the organization
2 Establishing your credibility
3 Designing projects to make change happen
4 Pilot projects.

Understanding your organization

Large organizations are complex entities and they have many different ways of making decisions. These are not always totally rational; you cannot assume that because your project has identified what you believe is the most appropriate course of action that this will be recognized immediately and the necessary changes made as a matter of course. Changing a service can take time, and may involve challenging long-held beliefs and assumptions. If you are not sensitive to your organization's values and culture, and fail to tailor your strategy accordingly, you are likely to be disappointed when others fail to share your enthusiasm. Change will always meet some resistance because it involves effort, and there will always be rival priorities and competition for resources. In some organizations, such as public service organizations, there will also be a political dimension to any major decision but, whichever sector you work in, you will need to be able to place your project findings within the overall direction of the organization.

Strategic and service plans can all help you gauge the potential reaction to your idea but printed sources can reveal only so much of the thinking which underpins organizational and service development; organizations are led by people. If your project findings indicate a fundamental shift in policy or a change in practice that carries significant financial implications, you will need to seek approval through a formal decision-making process. Such mechanisms may include committees, boards and senior management teams. These processes take time and will require you to have done a great deal of preparation and negotiation in advance of the final decision.

Other decision processes will be less formal; it may be merely a case of identifying the right person to champion and support your proposal. You may find that with the right support you can promote your project as the basis for a local, small-scale or time-limited pilot to test the viability of a change in policy or practice.

You will need to be more proactive in immersing yourself in the organization and its culture, discovering where are the levers of power, who are the people who can make things happen. They are the movers and shakers who will determine whether your work finds its way on to the 'to do' pile or the (much larger) 'for information' pile.

Aligning your research questions with issues raised by the overall service objectives and priorities and with an awareness of what current resourcing is available will ensure your research has impact. Research suggests that some organizations are more open to influence through research than others: particularly open to this influence are large organizations, with a degree of under-capacity and guided by professional values (Titler, 2008). A culture of learning also influences the 'absorptive capacity' of an organization, that is, its ability to successfully adopt new ideas.

Case study 13.1 Low achievers, lifelong learners

In 2005 Derbyshire County Council acted on the research findings of the 'Low Achievers, Lifelong Learners' report, initiating a three-year project to bring together the Derbyshire and Sheffield county council services, the public library service and the Derbyshire Adult and Community Education Service (DACES) with the aim of:

- improving the employment chances for local people in disadvantaged areas
- increasing the numbers of adults, particularly those from under-represented groups, participating in vocational training
- increasing the range of learning opportunities delivered in libraries, in association with libraries and on line.

Librarians directly involved in the original research were active in shaping the design of the DACES project proposal with a personal awareness of the research findings. In turn the published research gave substance to the original case for the project in the eyes of the funders.

Appropriate software was installed onto libraries' computers to assist with the delivery of DACES computer courses and to help engage with hard-to-reach learners. A series of joint training courses was arranged for tutors and library staff on the use and application of the Storybook Weaver software, a program used successfully to particularly engage harder-to-reach parents. A number of Children's Centre staff also attended this training. Taster courses were arranged in libraries across the county to encourage new learners to enrol onto vocational courses during 2007/08. Subjects ranged from 'Confidence' to 'Computers'. A total of 23 libraries were used as venues during the project.

In the final year of the project, the academic year 2007/08, there were a total of 2743 enrolments, 1070 unique learners, and a grand total of 1004 adults achieved qualifications at level 1 or level 2 as defined by QCA/BSA (Basic Skills Agency).

The project reinforced the findings of the 'Low Achievers, Lifelong Learners' research report and demonstrated how a public library service could both encourage increased take-up of learning opportunities in disadvantaged communities and improve the achievement of learners from traditionally under-represented groups.

The case study illustrates the value of collaboration, both within the research and in acting on the research findings. The involvement of librarians within the research project ensured that the research objectives aligned with institutional objectives, such as reaching disadvantaged communities. It was also the personal and active engagement of the librarians within the original research that gave impetus to exercise their political influence to develop a new service. They had effectively become champions for the research findings, and they used their networks in turn to diffuse the research impact through many services and to the users themselves.

Although the funding for the three-year project was on a one-off basis, the partnership that was created between libraries and adult and community education in Derbyshire continued to prosper at both operational and strategic level.

Establishing your credibility

We have already indicated that the decision-making processes in organizations are subject to many different influences. If you understand what these influences are and how they operate you will be in a position to make your ideas count. You will need support and possibly resources to enable you to carry out your project; you will certainly need managerial and maybe political support if your project findings are to be acted upon. The key to securing this support is personal credibility.

If your aim is to make change happen, it goes without saying that you need to position yourself where you can exercise the greatest influence. This will not happen overnight. The groundwork needs to have been done before you embark on your research. Through your performance, your integrity and your commitment to the goals of the organization, you will establish a reputation and a credibility that will enhance your chance of receiving a sympathetic hearing. However great your technical research competence, you will need to network to grow your influence at an organizational level.

Work at developing a network that is wider than the immediate team in which you work. This does not mean a sycophantic attachment to senior managers whom you think might be able to help you, but a way of behaving that demonstrates your ability to see the wider picture, to be constructively critical when necessary, and to step outside your specific job role when that is in the interests of the organization. There may be many opportunities to make a contribution at a strategic level, through active engagement in working groups, planning and development activities. You may need to take a risk, to commit yourself in areas where you lack confidence or experience; but you will learn and grow as a result. Over a number of years organizations have been moving away from reliance on functional specialisms to an emphasis on the competencies required of effective managers. Peter Drucker wrote:

> Core competencies are different for every organisation; they are, so to speak, part of an organisation's personality. But every organisation – not just businesses – needs one core competence: innovation.
>
> Drucker, 1999, reprinted 2007, 103

In this context your openness to new ways of doing things, your flexibility and your personal credibility will be rewarded with further opportunities.

Wherever you are in the organization, you can exercise leadership at some level. You want to be sure that your project findings are used to the benefit of your service and its users. To make that happen you will have devoted time and thought to developing a good understanding of your organization, establishing your personal credibility and securing the support of other key players.

Designing projects to make change happen

Countless books have been devoted to the subject of change management. Here we look specifically at the considerations you will need to bear in mind when using your research to bring about organizational change.

First, think about your audience. Has your work been prompted or sponsored by senior management, or are you self-directed? If the latter, you will need to do some preparatory work, some self-advocacy, to ensure that there is awareness of and support from managers, and that they are willing to consider the results. You could invite some senior figures or opinion leaders onto a steering group for the project. This will help align the research to organizational priorities and the needs of different stakeholder communities. It will almost certainly also mean that your findings achieve greater visibility in the organization. Your objective will ultimately be to see your research findings get into organizational policy statements.

If your work is designed to influence what your immediate team does, then you will need to engage them in the process from the start. Actively involving them in the research process, including the formulation of the research questions, will pay dividends later in terms of willingness to adopt the findings. It will certainly mean that the research identifies issues with direct practical implications and addresses practical needs. Because people are most likely to be influenced by other people, rather than written research findings, turning colleagues into change champions could be an effective way to achieve change. If you are working with other organizations, again the deeper their involvement in the project the more impact it will probably have.

Indeed, it makes sense to design the whole research project from the beginning with potential impact in mind. This could imply collecting the form of data you think will most likely persuade the organization to accept the findings (see Chapters 7, 8 and 9). Generally speaking, people tend to be impressed with statistics but, whichever approach you choose, ensuring that your project is conducted in a demonstrably valid way is essential to the project's impact. If you can build into your data collection information about how your organization performs against the rest of its sector, you may find this helpful in persuading the organization to change. Organizations do not want to feel they are falling behind peer organizations, so finding appropriate benchmarks is a priority.

Implementation issues are an important potential barrier to the adoption of project findings, more so even than dissemination of those findings (Best and Holmes, 2010). Building data collection about implementation issues into your project or pilot project (see below) can help your organization delineate appropriate paths of development, rather than needing a second project to explore these issues; your project findings may even form the basis of a training programme that will promote research findings through direct retraining. How to implement the findings is as much a part of the research process as asking more abstract questions.

Communicating your vision

If your project is designed to address a work or organizational issue, the way you present your investigation and its findings will be critical. Blaxter, Hughes and Tight (2006) draw a clear distinction between academic research and research that is work-related. The outputs from the two exercises will be very different. An academic paper is likely to include the results of an extensive literature survey, a full description of the methodology used, a lengthy description of the findings, discussion of the issues raised and a bibliography; a thorough yet often inaccessible style of writing. Practitioners' usual reasons for not adopting research results are lack of time to read research findings and a suspicion of anything too academic or theoretical in tone (Cruickshank, Hall and Taylor-Smith, 2011). Publication in a peer-reviewed journal may be one of your objectives, but you are likely to want to disseminate your findings through other channels to maximize your impact.

Kotter (1996) recommends not limiting yourself to a single mode of communication, but instead spreading the word through multiple channels. In Chapter 11 we saw how written communication such as reports and journal papers can be part of the dissemination strategy, while Cruickshank, Hall and Taylor-Smith (2011) highlight a preference within the library and information community for informal interactions such as meetings and conferences in learning about relevant research.

Case study 13.2 The eVALUEd project

---

eVALUEd, An evaluation toolkit for e-library development, www.evalued.bcu.ac.uk.

The purpose of the eVALUEd project was to create 'a transferable model for e-library evaluation in higher education'. The project involved a substantial body of sound research: a questionnaire surveying all UK HEIs about their e-resource evaluation practices, followed up with interviews with respondents and other experts in the field. Yet it is clear that the intention was explicitly to affect practice by offering a model toolkit.

Brief notices were published in a number of news services. As the project progressed, as well as peer-reviewed journal papers, freely available project reports were issued at regular intervals and accessible articles were put in the professional press, such as SCONUL News, the official publication of the Society of College, National and University Libraries, and Library and Information Update, a publication of the Chartered Institute of Library and Information Professionals (CILIP). The ultimate resource created is an open website with downloadable tools that library services can use directly as part of their day-to-day processes. In addition, training courses were run to support use of the toolkit, soon after it was released. ■

Dissemination was evidently central to the project plan, for the eVALUEd team used their knowledge of the sector to employ many channels to reach the community they were seeking to influence. The project team had a dissemination plan that was primarily concerned with keeping in touch with the community it sought to influence and was built around synthesizing best practice from across a library sector, taking into account differing needs, rather than a one size fits all model. Case studies were also provided to help libraries understand the resources needed to implement the tools.

Pilot projects

Adair (2008) lists three strategies that work in delivering projects:

1 Recruit a senior sponsor
2 Run a pilot project or experiment
3 Present innovation as a gradual/incremental development.

Even if you secure high-level support for your idea, the likelihood is that you will need to be realistic about its implementation and accept an incremental approach. Adair echoes the work of Drucker, who said:

> Neither studies nor market research nor computer modelling are a substitute for the test of reality. Everything improved or new needs therefore first to be tested on a small scale, that is, it needs to be PILOTED.
>
> Drucker, 1999, reprinted 2007, 75

The purpose of a pilot project is to test new ideas and new ways of doing things in a controlled environment that minimizes risk (and cost). It is easier in a pilot project to identify the relationship between cause and effect, which can be masked by the 'noise' of a large organization where there is a lot going on. If well conducted, a pilot project also has the benefit of winning the hearts and minds of a committed group of people who can help sell the idea to the rest of the organization, which may contain its fair share of sceptics.

Bourne and Bourne stress the value of this team approach:

> Collaboration occurs when members of a team work together through a change programme. Obviously not everyone in the team will have the same status or an equal say in what happens, but during collaboration the team work together to develop the plan and deliver the change.
>
> Collaboration has a number of advantages:
>
> • It creates an understanding of why change is needed.
> • It enables individuals with different experience and skills to become involved in key change decisions.

- It builds a commitment to implementing the change.
- It creates a critical mass of people to help push the change through.

Bourne and Bourne, 2012, 37

A pilot is by definition a test bed, a learning exercise that will establish whether the outcomes of your research are applicable and appropriate in a real-life environment. It may result in your original intention having to be modified or even abandoned. It might also result in the need to conduct further research before redesigning your project. You and your team must therefore guard against isolation and a siege mentality if things do not go according to plan. You and they will need to approach the pilot in the same open frame of mind that you brought to your original research.

Summary

This chapter has explored the challenges associated with translating evidence into practice, both within your own organization and ensuring it is accessible for those within the wider library and information community. It has considered the importance of understanding and being relevant to the needs of your stakeholders, establishing credibility to ensure your work is given the time and attention it deserves and communicating your vision in a way that is both meaningful and accessible to your audience. The value of pilot projects in establishing the applicability of your work in everyday practice was discussed.

Points for reflection

- Make some notes on how you think you could involve senior management perspectives in your project. Who needs to be involved and why? How could they be involved? Which institutional agendas and values do you think your research aligns with?
- Identify a piece of research that has been conducted in your organization or sector and influenced policy or practice. Make a study of how this change was achieved. Contact the researcher to talk about how they went about making change.
- Brainstorm a list of stakeholders in your research, then categorize your stakeholders using the 9 Cs framework (NHS Institute for Innovation and Improvement, 2008):
  — Commissioners: those that pay the organization to do things

— Customers: those that acquire and use the organization's products or services
— Collaborators: those with whom the organization works to develop and deliver services
— Contributors: those from whom the organization acquires content for products
— Channels: those who provide the organization with a route to a market or customer
— Commentators: those whose opinions of the organization are heard by customers and others
— Consumers: those who are served by our customers e.g. users
— Champions: those who believe in and will actively promote the project
— Competitors: those working in the same area who offer similar or alternative services.

Finally, map your stakeholders onto the grid shown in Figure 13.1:

High Power		
	To be satisfied	*To be closely managed*
Low Power		
	To be monitored	*To be informed*
	Little Impact	High Impact

Figure 13.1 *Stakeholder mapping grid*

References

Adair, J. (2008) *The Best of John Adair on Leadership and Management*, Thorogood, Abingdon.

Best, A. and Holmes, B. J. (2010) Systems Thinking, Knowledge and Action: towards better models and methods, *Evidence and Policy*, 6 (2), 145–9.

Blaxter, L., Hughes, C. and Tight M. (2006) *How to Research*, 3rd edn, Open University Press, Maidenhead.

Bourne, M. and Bourne, P. (2012) *Successful Change Management in a Week*, Hodder Education, London.

Cruickshank, P., Hall, H. and Taylor-Smith, E. (2011) *Enhancing the Impact of LIS Research Projects*, RiLIES *project report*, www.researchinfonet.org/wp-content/uploads/2012/01/RiLIES_report_FINAL.pdf.

Drucker, P. F. (1999, reprinted 2007) *Management Challenges for the 21st Century*, Butterworth-Heinemann, Oxford.

Kotter, J. P. (1996) *Leading Change*, Harvard Business School Press, Boston, MA.

NHS Institute for Innovation and Improvement (2008) *Stakeholder Analysis*, www.institute.nhs.uk/quality_and_service_improvement_tools/quality_and_service_improvement_tools/stakeholder_analysis.html.

Titler, M. (2008) The Evidence for Evidence-based Practice Implementation. In *Patient Safety and Quality: an evidence-based handbook for nurses*, Agency for Healthcare Research and Quality, www.ahrg.gov/professionals/clinicians-providers/resources/nursing/resources/nurseshdbk/TitlerM_EEBI.pdf.

Recommended further reading

JISC Sustaining and Embedding Innovations Good Practice Guide, https://sustainembed.pbworks.com/w/page/31632855/Welcome.

Kotter International, www.kotterinternational.com.

Closing remarks

Maria J. Grant, Barbara Sen and Hannah Spring

When we started this project we had a vision of what this book might look like: a practical introduction to research, evaluation and audit for those new to or wishing to refresh their project management skills set. What we've achieved has more than exceeded our expectations.

We've been fortunate enough to work with colleagues from across library and information sectors and geographic locations. The completed edited collection graphically realizes the fact that the issues we all face when getting started with projects – be they research, evaluation or audit – are universal and can be universally addressed. The book is a coherent set of discrete, yet complementary, chapters that truly lead you from initial general thoughts about a topic, through the planning process, the data collection and analysis, the writing up and dissemination activities, and beyond, ensuring that you are able to maximize the impact of your project wherever you are situated.

We hope you have found this book as enjoyable a read as we have in compiling it. We invite you to get in touch (@ResearchEvalAudit) to let us know what you think and also what else you would have liked to have seen represented. Who knows, perhaps your feedback could prove the inspiration for our next project.

Index